At the Margins

AT THE MARGINS

Presidential Leadership of Congress

George C. Edwards III

Yale University Press
New Haven and London

Designed by James J. Johnson and set in Caledonia types by
The Composing Room of Michigan, Inc., Grand Rapids,
Michigan
Printed in the United States of America by Vail-Ballou Press,
Binghamton, New York.

Library of Congress Cataloging-in-Publication Data

Edwards, George C.
   At the margins : presidential leadership of Congress / George
C. Edwards III.
      p.   cm.
   Bibliography: p.
   Includes index.
   ISBN 0-300-04404-6 (alk. paper)
   1. Presidents—United States.   2. United States Congress.
3. Political leadership—United States.   I. Title.
JK585.E32 1989
353.03'72—dc19   88-27526
                                                          CIP

The paper in this book meets the guidelines for permanence
and durability of the Committee on Production Guidelines for
Book Longevity of the Council on Library Resources.

10 9 8 7 6 5 4 3 2 1

To Carmella

Contents

Tables

Preface

This is a book about leadership, and specifically about the efforts of presidents to lead Congress. The analysis covers various avenues of presidential leadership and how and why they might succeed or fail. The implications of the study reach well beyond the boundaries of the relations between the president and Congress.

I rely in this study on a large empirical database, but I mix quantitative analysis with documentary and historical analysis to enrich each analytical method. I believe this integration of different approaches puts me in a good position to reach theoretically sound, significant conclusions.

This is not a quantitative study of presidential leadership but rather a study of presidential leadership that employs quantitative data. The use of data is straightforward, and the findings and analysis are accessible to virtually all readers. Yet I have not had to dilute the questions I pose or the conclusions I reach in the interests of clarity. Quantitative analysis is useful, but it is not an end in itself, and the data should not drive the analysis but support it. Although quantitative analysis helps us to determine with more rigor the existence and extent of relationships, it is no substitute for explaining them. It is understanding presidential leadership of Congress and the consequences of it in which I am most interested.

Marian Ash of Yale University Press has played a special role in developing this volume. Beginning with a serendipitous meeting at Princeton, she has provided patient encouragement and sound advice throughout the development of the research. Because the project has undergone a considerable transformation over several years, her role has been crucial.

Several scholars have read parts of the manuscript and offered constructive criticism, including Tom Cronin, Jeff Fishel, John Kessel, Gary King,
Bert Rockman, Lee Sigelman, Norman Thomas, and Stephen Wayne. To
them I am deeply indebted. I am also grateful to my talented research assistant, Carl Richard, for his invaluable aid. Fred Kameny did a superb job of
editing the manuscript.

As always, my greatest debt is to my wife, Carmella, for providing me
with the peace of mind to ponder politics and the freedom to write about it.
She has received the dedications of many books, and she deserves them all.

CHAPTER ONE

Studying Leadership

The government of the United States is not a fertile field for the exercise of presidential leadership, and nowhere is this clearer than in the president's dealings with Congress. Every president bears scars from his battles with the legislature. Many of the proposals of every president fail to pass Congress, while legislators champion initiatives to which the president is opposed. Yet these conflicts make presidential leadership all the more necessary.

The peculiar sharing of powers by the two institutions established by the Constitution prevents either from acting unilaterally on most important matters. Moreover, the differences in the constituencies, internal structures, time perspectives, and decision-making procedures of the two branches guarantee that they will often view issues and policy proposals differently.[1] As a result, our political system virtually compels the president to attempt to lead Congress.

Extraconstitutional processes, such as the preparation of an elaborate legislative program in the White House, have evolved in response to the system's need for centralization. Yet such changes only provide instruments for presidents to employ as they seek support from the legislature. They carry no guarantee of success and are no substitute for leadership.

As we would expect, relations between presidents and Congress have attracted considerable scholarly attention over the years, and the press has given the subject an enormous amount of coverage. Nevertheless, we have a long way to go before we can claim to understand presidential leadership of Congress.

1. See George C. Edwards III, *Presidential Influence in Congress* (San Francisco: W. H. Freeman, 1980), pp. 35–48.

Many of the scholarly writings on the relation of the president to Congress focus on such topics as the appropriate powers of each branch,[2] or describe and analyze the institutions and processes involved in their interactions.[3] These are unquestionably important subjects, but they do not go to the heart of the issue of leadership.

Although interest in leadership has increased in recent years, it remains an elusive phenomenon, and there is little consensus even on what leadership is. According to James MacGregor Burns, "Leadership is one of the most observed and least understood phenomena on earth."[4] Barbara Kellerman lists ten different definitions of political leadership.[5]

Our lack of understanding of presidential leadership is not without costs. The news media abound with inferences about the impact of presidential leadership and references to mandates, deals, threats, and the like—all based on little or no systematic evidence and seemingly little reflection. More than a few scholars have fallen into the same routine. As a result, discourse in both the press and the academy on relations between presidents and Congress is less illuminating than it might be. An aide to President Jimmy Carter expressed his frustration at the lack of public understanding when he compared the administrations of Carter and Ronald Reagan:

> I could not help but laugh when [President Reagan] got credited with great legislative victories, when he succeeded in getting a twenty-five percent reduction in taxes over a three-year period. Contrast that with what we had to do, with the windfall profits tax, the largest tax increase in the history of the republic . . . And we got it through. The public perception was that when we did it, it was because we did not screw up; when they did it, it was because of their legislative brilliance.[6]

Gerald Ford was recently asked what could be done to improve presidential-congressional relations. The response of the former president, who had served in Congress for a quarter of a century, longer than any other chief executive, is poignant testimony to the need to devote more attention to the

2. An excellent example is Louis Fisher, *Constitutional Conflicts Between Congress and the President* (Princeton: Princeton University Press, 1985).

3. See for example Stephen J. Wayne, *The Legislative Presidency* (New York: Harper and Row, 1978).

4. *Leadership* (New York: Harper and Row, 1978), p. 2.

5. "Leadership as a Political Act," in Barbara Kellerman, ed., *Leadership: Multidisciplinary Perspectives* (Englewood Cliffs, N.J.: Prentice-Hall, 1984), p. 70.

6. Quoted in Mark Peterson, "Domestic Policy and Legislative Decision Making" (paper presented at the annual meeting of the Midwest Political Science Association, Chicago, April 1985), p. 32.

question of presidential leadership of Congress. He simply replied, "I don't know."[7]

Our lack of understanding of executive-legislative relations also potentially distorts our expectations and evaluations of presidential leadership. The notion of the dominant president who moves the country and Congress through strong, effective leadership has deep roots in our political culture. Those chief executives whom Americans revere, such as Washington, Jefferson, Jackson, Lincoln, Wilson, and both Roosevelts, have taken on mythic proportions as leaders. Even though we are frequently disillusioned with the performance of presidents and recognize that stalemate is common in our political system, we eagerly accept what appears to be effective presidential leadership, as in the case of Ronald Reagan in 1981, as evidence on which to renew our faith in the potential of the presidency. After all, if presidential leadership works some of the time, why not all of the time?

This perception directly influences our expectations and evaluations of presidents. If it is reasonable to expect successful leadership from the White House, then failures of leadership must be personal deficiencies. If problems arise because the leader lacks the proper will, skills, or understanding, then the solution to our need for leadership is straightforward and simple: all we have to do is elect a president willing and able to lead. Because the system is responsive to appropriate leadership, it will function smoothly with the right leader in the Oval Office. We can indulge in high expectations of the president and freely criticize him if he fails to bring around Congress to his point of view. The blame lies clearly in the leader rather than the environment. We need not concern ourselves with broader forces in American society that may influence executive-legislative relations: because these conditions are complex and perhaps even intractable, to focus on the individual as leader simplifies our analysis and evaluation of the problems of governing.

On the other hand, what if presidential leadership is not preeminent in executive-legislative relations? What if presidential leadership has less potential than holders of the conventional wisdom believe and the president actually operates at the margins in obtaining support in Congress? What if our national preoccupation with the chief executive is misplaced and our belief in the impact of the individual leader largely a myth, a product of a search for simple solutions in an extremely complex, purposefully inefficient system in which the founding fathers' handiwork in decentralizing power defeats even the most capable leaders?

If this is the case, we should expect less of the president and be less disappointed when he is not successful in leading Congress. In addition, we

7. Remarks at U.S. Military Academy, West Point, N.Y., April 30, 1986.

should focus less exclusively on the president and devote more attention to the context in which the president seeks to lead Congress. We should recognize that major changes in public policy require more than just the "right" person in the job and do not necessarily turn on a president's leadership qualities. It does not, of course, follow that failures of presidential leadership may never be attributed to the White House or that the president has no control over the outcome of his relations with Congress. It does mean that we need a better understanding of presidential leadership of Congress to think sensibly about the role of the chief executive in our political system.

Analyzing Leadership

This book is subtitled *Presidential Leadership of Congress* because it focuses on just that—leadership. The exercise of influence is central to my conception of leadership, as it is for most political scientists. We want to know whether the president can influence the actions and attitudes of others and affect the output of Congress. If no change occurs at the individual or aggregate level, one cannot sensibly conclude that leadership has been exercised. Thus, one must distinguish between attempts to lead and leadership itself. Both are of primary interest to me in this book, and I devote much of my effort to exploring the relationships between the two.

Leadership has the potential to fail only if it has the potential to succeed: that is, if the leader can persuade others to behave in certain ways. Leadership without choice is an empty concept: if those whom the leader seeks to influence have no real options, one cannot discuss leadership.

Presidential leadership of Congress typically revolves around obtaining or maintaining support for the chief executive's legislative stances. Members of Congress are free to choose whether or not to follow the chief executive's lead; the president cannot force them to act. This therefore presents a classic case of the challenge of political leadership.

Director or Facilitator?

Although conceiving of leadership in terms of influence is useful for the study of presidential leadership of Congress, the concept remains somewhat nebulous. To guide our examination of presidential leadership in Congress, it is useful to refine the concept of leadership by contrasting two broad perspectives on the presidency. In the first the president is the director of change. Through his leadership he creates opportunities to move in new directions, leading others where they otherwise would not go. In the role of director he is out in front, establishing goals and encouraging others to follow.

A second perspective is less heroic but nonetheless important. Here the president is primarily a facilitator of change. He exploits opportunities to help others go where they want to go anyway. In the role of facilitator the president reflects and perhaps intensifies widely held views, using his resources to achieve his constituency's aspirations.

The director creates a constituency to follow his lead, whereas the facilitator endows his constituency's views with shape and purpose by interpreting them and translating them into legislation. The director restructures the contours of the political landscape to pave the way for change, whereas the facilitator exploits opportunities presented by a favorable configuration of political forces.

There is of course a third possibility: that of the president who is disposed not to lead. Although this description may accurately apply to some occupants of the Oval Office, it is not useful for our purposes. We may learn a great deal about leadership from those who do not succeed in their efforts, but we can learn little from those who do not even try.

The director moves mountains and influences many independent actors. He has the more formidable task because he establishes the legislative agenda and persuades a reluctant Congress to support his policies. By contrast, the facilitator works at the margins, influencing a few critical actors and taking advantage of the opportunities for change already present in his environment. In both cases the president exercises leadership, yet the scale of the leadership is clearly different. The range and scope of the director's influence are broad whereas those of the facilitator are more narrow.

The distinction between director and facilitator is not meant to represent a division in the literature. Instead, the two types of leader represent different emphases of writing on the presidency, sometimes explicit, but more often implicit. The two perspectives are not neat categories: my goal is neither to classify presidents nor resolve an academic dispute. Instead, I employ these types to increase understanding of leadership by exploring its possibilities. Once we understand the possibilities of leadership, we are in a better position to assess the performance of presidents.

It is useful to distinguish the leadership types I employ from the polar positions that characterize the debate over the "great man" interpretation of history. The two sides of this issue assumed their best-known forms in the nineteenth century. In *Heroes and Hero-Worship and the Heroic in History*, published in 1841, Thomas Carlyle argued that great men alone were responsible for the direction of history. The environment of the hero seems generally malleable and thus receptive to leadership. Viewing history from quite a different perspective, various schools of social determinists, including the

Spencerians, Hegelians, and Marxists, saw history as an inexorable march in one direction, with change occurring only when the culture was ripe for it. They concluded that great men could not have acted differently from the way they did. This view is advanced perhaps most memorably in Tolstoy's portrayal of Napoleon in *War and Peace*.

Most will agree that these perspectives are inadequate, and we have no need to become mired in this ancient debate. Our contrasting leadership types are much less extreme, and the issue is not whether leadership matters, but rather how much and under what conditions. It is not sufficient to conclude, however, that sometimes the environment is receptive to change and at other times it is not. This simply begs the question of whether leaders are able to influence the environment so as to create the opportunity for change. It is useful to recall Sidney Hook's contrast between the "eventful man," who influences developments noticeably, and the "event-making man," an eventful man whose actions are the consequences of outstanding capacities rather than accidents of position and who not only appears at but also helps define the forks in the road of history.[8]

Both director and facilitator fall within Richard Neustadt's concept of the persuasive presidency.[9] The goal of studying presidential-congressional relations is to achieve a richer understanding of how and under what conditions presidents persuade, what we can reasonably expect of them, and how we should evaluate their performance. Neustadt's outstanding contribution to the study of the presidency alerted us that the president was not in a position to command and that he had to make the right choices and use his resources wisely to achieve his goals. What has remained unresolved is just what the potential is of presidential leadership. Is it possible to be a director? Are presidents in control of their resources or highly dependent on their environment? Answers to these questions are fundamental to understanding presidential leadership of Congress and take on even greater significance in light of the extraordinarily high expectations Americans have of the chief executive.

Structure of the Analysis

Most of the remainder of the book is structured around potential sources of influence. Rather than approach them from the perspective of their direct impact on members of Congress, I view them as potential resources for the president in his efforts to obtain support in Congress. The use of resources is the realm of leadership, and understanding it is essential to understanding presidential-congressional relations. For each source of influence I begin by

8. *The Hero in History* (Boston: Beacon, 1943), chap. 9.
9. Richard E. Neustadt, *Presidential Power* (New York: John Wiley and Sons, 1980).

analyzing the president's strategic position. By this I mean the potential of each source as an instrument of leadership. The aim is to know whether members of Congress might be responsive to the source and in what degree and under what conditions they might be more responsive.

To investigate these questions I pose two fundamental questions in each discussion of strategic position: what explains the responsiveness of members of Congress to this source of influence, and what evidence is there of the impact of the source? Once we have answered these questions and understand the parameters of leadership, we can examine the president's employment of these sources of influence to lead Congress. One should not assume that a president skillful in employing resources will be successful in leading Congress. Such an assumption evades the theoretically crucial question of whether the resources are likely to be useful sources of influence.

There is surprisingly little systematic research on the presidents attempts to lead Congress; most relevant material is in the form of case studies on individual policies. My approach is to focus on the president's attempts to use each source of influence as an instrument of leadership. The analysis is guided by two basic questions: what do presidents do to try to lead Congress, and how reliably can they use each source of influence? Answering these questions leads us to consider both the employment of sources of influence and their dependability.

There must be a special concern for the interdependence of leaders and followers. We cannot assume Congress will respond to the president's efforts of leadership. Even if the president enjoys a favorable strategic position regarding a source of influence, it does not follow that he can call on the source at his discretion. Finally, outcomes in Congress favorable to the president do not necessarily result from responsiveness to the White House. We must thus examine presidential leadership with an open mind and a critical eye.

Sources of presidential influence in Congress are of three basic kinds: party, public support, and legislative skills, each of which has many components. There are many other possible influences on the decisions of members of Congress in addition to influences flowing from the president, including ideology, constituency, committee interactions, and the personal views of senators and representatives. A study of the relative impact of all these factors is well beyond the scope of this research. I focus on the presidency because of its special role as a driving force in American politics. Nevertheless, it is well to remember that the White House is constantly in competition with others for influence, and to remain sensitive to the broader environment of American politics in which presidential efforts at leadership occur.

I focus on party, public support, and legislative skills as sources of influence because they are centered on the presidency. The president is the leader of his party, even if he is inept at the task or out of step with his party cohorts. Similarly, whether he enjoys a high standing in the polls or suffers public disapproval, he is the center of political discourse and public evaluation in the United States. At least in theory, legislative skills directly reflect his personal abilities and choices. Further, each of these potential sources of influence varies both within and between administrations and is at least potentially manipulable by the president in ways that other influences on Congress are not.

Ideology, for example, is not centered on the presidency, for it is something that all politicians can share. Nor will it vary much within an administration. Most importantly, it is not a potential instrument of presidential influence. Members of Congress may well respond to the president's proposals based at least in part on their ideology, but the president is not able to change their ideological orientations and does not try to.

Some authors approach leadership as social exchange and place a strong emphasis on interpersonal bargaining.[10] Although bargaining can be an important technique of leadership, a view of presidential leadership based solely on it is too confining for our purposes. For example, the responsiveness of Congress to the perception of a mandate is not an exchange in any meaningful sense and requires no interpersonal actions on the president's part. Emphasis on interpersonal acts also ignores the creation or control of sources of influence. As we shall see, this undermines analysis of what attempts at leadership can accomplish.

In addition, it is not illuminating and is indeed virtually circular to argue that successful efforts at influence always meet a follower's needs. This is undoubtedly true, except for people acting irrationally (which has occurred more than once in politics), but by explaining literally everything, this approach does little to increase our understanding of leadership.

The Context of Presidential Leadership

Presidential efforts at leading Congress do not occur in a vacuum. To understand presidential leadership one must also understand the context in which it takes place. Such prominent features of our political system as the president's formal powers, the formal and informal constraints on his actions, and the nature of public opinion, organized interests, and political parties are all part of the environment of presidential leadership. They have deservedly received a great deal of attention in scholarly writings.

---

10. See for example Barbara Kellerman, *The Political Presidency* (New York: Oxford University Press, 1984), chap. 2. See also Burns, *Leadership*, on "transactional" leadership.

The environment of presidential leadership looms large in the chapters that follow, and it is best to integrate an examination of environmental matters with an analysis of leadership itself. At this point, however, it is well to take a step back from the presidency and other political actors and institutions and examine the cultural context of presidential leadership. The American political culture, at once less tangible and more pervasive than the environmental components mentioned above, establishes unique parameters for leadership within which every president must contend.

The cultural environment of presidential leadership is extraordinarily complex, and the public's expectations of the president extremely high.[11] Americans expect their chief executive to insure peace, prosperity, and security. As President Carter remarked, "The President is naturally held to be responsible for the state of the economy . . . [and] for the inconveniences, or disappointments, or the concerns of the American people."[12] We want the good life, and we look to the president to provide it. In addition to expecting successful policies from the White House, Americans expect their presidents to be extraordinary individuals. (This of course buttresses the public's policy expectations.) The public expects the president to be intelligent, cool in a crisis, competent, highly ethical, and in possession of a sense of humor. Many also want the president to have imagination and charisma.

The public has high expectations not only for the president's official performance, but also for his private behavior. A large percentage of the population strongly object if the president engages in questionable behavior, even if it is very common in American society. For example, when the Watergate tapes revealed that President Nixon frequently used profane and obscene language in his private conversations, many Americans were outraged, probably more by the president's language than by the substance of his statements. Citizens demand that the president's public and private life be exemplary.[13]

Interestingly, the public seems aware of both the increasing difficulty of being president and its own high expectations of his performance. The public overwhelmingly believes that the president's job is more difficult than in the past and that the president is likely to receive more criticism in the press. It also believes that expectations of the president are higher than in the past. Nevertheless, there is no statistically significant relationship between peo-

11. See George C. Edwards III, *The Public Presidency* (New York: St. Martin's, 1983), chap. 5.

12. Office of the White House Press Secretary, *Remarks of the President at a Meeting with Non-Washington Editors and Broadcasters*, September 21, 1979, p. 12.

13. See Roberta S. Sigel, "Image of the American Presidency: Part II of an Exploration into Popular Views of Presidential Power," *Midwest Journal of Political Science* 10 (February 1966): 131.

ple's perceptions of the difficulty of being president and their approval of his performance, when one controls for party. Those who feel the president's tasks are more challenging than in the past do not take this into consideration when they evaluate him.

Equally surprisingly, expectations of the president remain high despite the disappointment in their presidents many Americans have experienced over the last generation. The tenacity with which Americans maintain high expectations of the president may be due in large part to the encouragement they receive from presidential candidates to do so. The extremely lengthy process of selecting presidents lends itself to political hyperbole. For at least one year out of every four, voters are encouraged to expect more from a president than they are receiving. Evidently they take this rhetoric to heart and hold their presidents to ever higher standards, regardless of the unreasonableness of these expectations.

High expectations of presidents are also supported by political socialization: American history as it is taught in schools is often organized according to presidential eras. Implicit in much of this teaching is the view that great presidents were largely responsible for the freedom and prosperity Americans enjoy. From such lessons it is a short step to presuming that contemporary presidents can be wise and effective leaders and that citizens should expect them to be so.

Those most attentive to the presidency and politics are as susceptible as other citizens to the influence of a remembered past on their expectations. Neustadt's comments about reactions in Washington to Jimmy Carter are especially insightful on this point:

> Almost from the outset of his term, and savagely at intervals since his first summer, press commentators and congressional critics have deplored Carter's deficiencies in ways suggestive of a markedly higher standard, apparently compounded out of pieces of performance by the Presidents since Truman, as Washingtonians recall them . . .
>
> The standard raised by Carter's critics seems to me too high, higher than realism counsels or necessity compels.
>
> Too much is expected of a President in Carter's shoes . . . Washingtonians, like less attentive publics, tend to project on the Presidency expectations far exceeding anyone's assured capacity to carry through. Objectively, 1977 had little in common with 1965; still, as Carter started out the LBJ analogy filled many minds, some of them in his own entourage. Whatever were they thinking of? Ignorance is bliss.[14]

14. Neustadt, *Presidential Power*, pp. 210–212.

Yet another factor encouraging high expectations of the White House is the prominence of the president. He is the national spokesman, the person- ification of the nation—the closest thing Americans have to a royal sovereign. On his election he and his family dominate the news in the United States. The president's great visibility naturally induces people to focus their attention and thus their demands and expectations on him.

Related to the president's prominence is the tendency to personalize. Issues of public policy are often extremely complex, and to simplify them people tend to think of issues in terms of personalities, especially the presi- dent's. It is easier to blame a specific person for personal and societal problems than it is to analyze and comprehend the complicated mix of factors that really cause them. Similarly, it is easier to project one's frustrations onto a single individual than it is to deal with the contradictions and perhaps the selfishness in one's own policy demands. At the midpoint of his term in office President Carter reflected: "I can see why it is difficult for a President to serve two terms. You are the personification of problems and when you address a prob- lem even successfully you become identified with it."[15]

Part of the explanation for the public's high expectations of the president probably lies in its lack of understanding of the context in which the president functions. Although the president in our constitutional system is basically weak rather than strong, this is widely misperceived by the public. In 1979, for example, only 36 percent of the public felt the president had too little power, and 49 percent felt the amount of power he enjoyed was "just right."[16] Twenty years earlier, after five years of divided rule in which a Republican occupied the White House and Democrats dominated Congress, only 35 percent of the public felt it was disadvantageous for the presidency and Con- gress to be controlled by different political parties.[17]

Complicating the cultural context of leadership even further is the con- tradictory nature of the public's expectations of presidential leadership, hav- ing to do both with the content of policy and the style of performance. Ameri- cans' expectations of policy are confused and seemingly unlimited: they want taxes and the cost of government to decrease, yet do not want a decrease in public services; they desire plentiful gasoline, but not at a higher price; they wish inflation to be controlled, but not at the expense of higher unemploy-

15. "Carter Interview," *Congressional Quarterly Weekly Report*, November 25, 1978, p. 3354.

16. Gallup Poll, *Attitudes Toward the Presidency* (Princeton: 1980), p. 21. See also Jack Dennis, "Dimensions of Public Support for the Presidency" (paper presented at the annual meeting of the Midwest Political Science Association, Chicago, 1975), tables 3, 5.

17. George H. Gallup, *The Gallup Poll: Public Opinion, 1935–1971*, vol. 3 (New York: Random House, 1972): 1624–1625.

ment or interest rates; they yearn for a clean environment, yet are eager for economic growth.

It is of course true that the public is not entirely to blame for holding these contradictory expectations. Presidential candidates often encourage voters to believe that they can have their cake and eat it too. In the presidential campaign of 1980 Ronald Reagan promised among other things to slash government expenditures, substantially reduce taxes, increase military spending, balance the budget, and maintain government services. Because the public has little concern for the consistency of its views, any encouragement it receives to hold contradictory ones falls on receptive ears.

Expectations of the president's leadership style are also contradictory, and show that the public expects something of everything from the president. It wants the president to be a leader, an independent figure who speaks out and takes stands on the issues even if his views are unpopular.[18] It also expects the president to preempt problems by anticipating them before they arise. Similarly, the public counts on the president to provide novel solutions to the country's problems. To meet these expectations the president must be ahead of public opinion, acting on problems that may be obscure to the general populace and contributing ideas that are different from those currently in vogue in discussions of policy.

In sharp contrast to the public's desire for presidential leadership is that for the chief executive to be responsive to public opinion and constrained by majority rule as represented in Congress. We now have a substantial number of polls taken over more than four decades that show the public overwhelmingly desiring Congress to have final authority in policy disagreements with the president, and not wanting the president to be able to act against majority opinion.[19]

Even in the area of national security, the public is not necessarily deferential to the president. It had more confidence in the judgment of Congress than in that of the president on the question of entry into World War II and on the reorganization of the Defense Department in the 1950s, even when the president was the former general of the army, Dwight Eisenhower.[20]

18. See Sigel, "Image of the American Presidency," pp. 125, 130; Eric B. Herzik and Mary L. Dodson, "The President and Public Expectations," *Presidential Studies Quarterly* 12 (Spring 1982): 172.

19. Dennis, "Dimensions of Public Support," tables 4, 8; Hazel Erskine, "The Polls: Presidential Power," *Public Opinion Quarterly* 37 (Fall 1973): 492, 495; *CBS News/The New York Times Poll* (news release, September 14, 1987), table 12. An exception is Sigel, "Image of the American Presidency," p. 125, who found more people favoring the president leading Congress and the people rather than following what the people and Congress decided. Perhaps this is due to the survey having taken place in 1966 in Detroit, where the population was highly favorable toward the president.

20. Erskine, "The Polls," pp. 499–500.

In 1973, 80 percent of the people supported a requirement that the president obtain the approval of Congress before sending armed forces into action outside the United States.[21] That year Congress passed the War Powers Resolution over the president's veto. The purpose of this law was to limit substantially the president's use of armed forces in hostile actions without the approval of Congress.

The public expects presidents to be open-minded politicians in the American tradition and thus to exhibit flexibility and a willingness to compromise on policy. At the same time it expects the president to be decisive and to take firm, consistent stands on the issues. These expectations are clearly incompatible, and presidents can expect to be criticized for being rigid and inflexible when they are standing firm on an issue. Ronald Reagan suffered such a fate when he refused to yield on defense spending in the face of massive deficits. Presidents will also be disparaged, however, for being weak and indecisive when they do compromise.

The public wants the president to be a statesman and to place the country's interests ahead of politics, but the same public also wants its president to be a skilled politician, and a substantial minority expects the president to be loyal to his political party. If the president acts statesmanlike, he may be criticized for being too far above the political fray, for being an ineffective idealist insufficiently solicitous of his party supporters. Jimmy Carter began his term on such a note when he attempted to cut back on pork-barrel water projects. If he emphasizes a party program, however, the president may be criticized for being a crass politician, without concern for the broader national interest.

Americans like their presidents to run open administrations. They desire a free flow of ideas within the governing circles in Washington, and they want the workings of government to be visible to them and not sheltered behind closed doors. At the same time they want to feel that the president is in control of things and that the government is not sailing rudderless. If a president allows internal dissent in decision making in the White House and does not hide this dissent from the public, he will inevitably be reproached for not being in control of his own aides. But if he should attempt either to stifle dissent or to conceal it from the public, he will be accused of being isolated, undemocratic, and unable to accept criticism, and of attempting to muzzle opposition.

Finally, Americans want their presidents to relate to the average person so that the chief executives will inspire confidence in the White House and have compassion and concern for the typical citizen. Yet the public also ex-

21. George H. Gallup, *The Gallup Poll: Public Opinion, 1972–1977*, vol. 1 (Wilmington, Del.: Scholarly Resources, 1978), pp. 210–211.

pects the president to possess characteristics far different from its own and to act in ways that are beyond the capabilities of most people. To confuse the matter further, Americans also expect the president to act with a special dignity befitting the leader of their country and the free world, and to live and entertain in splendor; presidents are not supposed to resemble the common person at all.

If a president seems too common, he may be disparaged for being just that. One has only to think of the political cartoons of Harry Truman and Gerald Ford that suggested they were not up to the job of president. On the other hand, if a president seems too different, appears too cerebral, or engages in too much pomp, he will likely be denounced as snobbish, isolated from the people, and too regal for American tastes. Richard Nixon offers a recent example of a president subjected to such criticisms.

These high and contradictory expectations of American political culture place extreme demands on presidential leadership. In addition, the values that predominate in our political culture not only are less than conducive to leadership, but virtually stand as a barrier to it. According to Samuel Huntington, "The distinctive aspect of the American Creed is its antigovernment character. Opposition to power, and suspicion of government as the most dangerous embodiment of power, are the central themes of American political thought."[22]

Many have commented on the importance in our political culture of limited government, liberty, individualism, equality, and democracy.[23] These cultural values generate a distrust of strong leadership, authority, and the public sector in general. The loner is the archetypal American folk hero, not the leader who always depends on followers.

Americans are basically individualistic and skeptical of authority. They may admire its exercise, as long as it is over others. Although Americans are attracted to strong leaders, they do not seem to feel a corresponding obligation to follow their leadership. Although each of the strong presidents mentioned above had a loyal following during his tenure, each was also reviled by a large part of the populace. Only on their deaths did these presidents attain nearly universal adulation.

22. Samuel P. Huntington, *American Politics: The Promise of Disharmony* (Cambridge, Mass: Belknap, 1981), p. 33.

23. See Huntington, *American Politics*; Bert A. Rockman, *The Leadership Question* (New York: Praeger, 1984); Daniel Boorstin, *The Americans*, 3 vols. (New York: Random House, 1958, 1965, 1973); Louis Hartz, *The Liberal Tradition in America* (New York: Harcourt, Brace and World, 1955); Richard Hofstadter, *The American Political Tradition and the Men Who Made It* (New York: Vintage, 1957).

This is the cultural context within which the president attempts to lead Congress. It forces him into an active leadership role, and at the same time complicates his efforts by failing to provide reliable support and insisting that he be all things to all people. This is leadership with one hand tied behind the leader's back, and presidents inevitably find their cultural parameters frustrating. Nevertheless, this environment of presidential leadership colors in one way or another all that follows.

CHAPTER TWO

Measuring Presidential Success

There are numerous obstacles to studying presidential relations with Congress, including the difficulty of measuring independent variables that may explain them and of defining such core concepts as influence. An equally daunting problem facing scholars wishing to study presidential-congressional relations is the difficulty of measuring presidential success. How do we know it when we see it? The question is crucial because some notion of presidential success in the House and Senate is the dependent variable most studies of presidential relations with Congress try to explain.

Passage or Support?

The first and perhaps most important step in investigating presidential-congressional relations is to clarify just what we want to explain. Only then can we develop a dependent variable that is a valid measure. Although this may appear to be a straightforward or even pedestrian task, it is actually a stage at which researchers may easily stumble and undermine the remainder of their efforts.

    The fundamental question is whether we are interested in explaining the influence and leadership that presidents exercise to elicit congressional support for their proposals, or simply in explaining their success in obtaining passage of legislation. Although at first glance passage seems at least as important to investigate as support, there is less to it than meets the eye. Success in passing legislation is measured in the aggregate, and the results of an analysis focused on it cannot provide a solid basis for inferences about the causes of congressional behavior. Instead, we are left to conclude, for example, that

An early version of this chapter appeared in the *Journal of Politics*.

presidents have greater success in obtaining congressional passage of their programs when they have a cohesive majority in Congress. This is of course correct, but it is also virtually a truism and explains very little about congressional behavior. We can make few theoretical advances in pursuing such a course.

If the dependent variable is a yearly aggregate of presidential success in obtaining passage of legislation, it will mask variability in support for the president among individual members of Congress or groups of members. This level of aggregation makes very tenuous any inferences about the causes of behavior of individual members of Congress toward the president. Further, what theoretical sense does it make to combine aggregate figures for the House and the Senate? For most purposes, very little.

The figures in table 2.1 illustrate the problems of using aggregate measures of presidential success. They show the president's victories on votes on which he took a stand,[1] a seemingly straightforward and useful summary statistic for evaluating presidential performance. On examining the data, however, we find that we cannot tell whether Republicans and Democrats or Northerners and Southerners respond differently to various influences on their voting. Nor can we compare the House with the Senate. It is obvious that changes in the number of seats controlled by each party account for much of the variation in victories over time, but there is no straightforward way to control for their impact. Without knowing who the president's supporters are, it is difficult to understand why they are the president's supporters It is also possible for the president to obtain substantial support on votes requiring extraordinary majorities, such as those for ratifying treaties, suspending the rules, or bringing cloture to debate, and still end up with a loss. In addition, measures of success share all the problems of measures of support in general that I discuss below.[2]

Until 1975 Congressional Quarterly calculated a well-known box score of presidential success in Congress that had the same drawbacks as the measurement of victories on votes. Further, this box score counted a request as approved only if it passed in the same calendar year during which it was submitted (although most important legislation takes two years or more to pass after its introduction). It did not take into account that complex legislation

1. The basis of these calculations is the identification by Congressional Quarterly of votes on which the president took a stand. Because of occasional errors by CQ in computing the number of votes on which the president took a stand and the percentage of victories in each year, I have independently calculated the number of stands and the percentage of victories.

2. See George C. Edwards III, *Presidential Influence in Congress* (San Francisco: W. H. Freeman, 1980), pp. 14–15.

TABLE 2.1   Presidential Success on Votes in Congress

President	Year	Percentage of Victories
Eisenhower	1953	89
	1954	78
	1955	75
	1956	70
	1957	68
	1958	76
	1959	52
	1960	65
Kennedy	1961	81
	1962	85
	1963	87
Johnson	1964	92
	1965	93
	1966	78
	1967	79
	1968	75
Nixon	1969	75
	1970	77
	1971	75
	1972	66
	1973	51
	1974	60
Ford	1974	58
	1975	61
	1976	54
Carter	1977	76
	1978	78
	1979	77
	1980	75
Reagan	1981	82
	1982	72
	1983	67
	1984	66
	1985	60
	1986	57

was sent to Congress by some presidents as one bill and by others in several parts, or that some, anticipating congressional opposition, did not send some bills to Capitol Hill at all. As a result of these severe problems of validity, Congressional Quarterly stopped producing its box score.

A box score has another important limitation: it misses too much. In the words of one of President Reagan's top legislative aides, "A favorite word of the Congress in the last several years is 'conditionality.' For everything there are conditions now. What you read in the headlines is that Reagan 'won' on X vote. What you don't read in the headlines—or watch on network news—are the conditions that Congress incorporated in the Reagan win. . . . Congress likes to always have a little bit of a hedge, a little bit of a hook, to keep their jurisdiction."[3] Box scores do not reflect these important aspects of policy making: they simply report a presidential victory.

Aggregate data may be useful if one is concerned with comparing of political eras,[4] success rates of different presidents,[5] or the success of proposals introduced at various points in the electoral cycle.[6] But the more concerned we are with the rigorous investigation of theoretically significant questions of causation, the less likely it is that aggregate measures will suffice.

Because of the limitations of aggregate measures, it is usually better to calculate presidential support for each member of Congress. This makes it possible to disaggregate the analysis as much as theory and independent variables will allow, and to compute aggregate figures for groups of representatives and senators when it is appropriate to do so. On the other hand, beginning with one aggregate figure to represent behavior makes it impossible to disaggregate the figure to the individual level.

Measuring Support

The second crucial step in exploring presidential-congressional relations is to develop measures of presidential support. This is not an easy task, and efforts to measure support inevitably raise important theoretical issues.

One of these issues goes to the heart of attempts to understand presidential support in Congress. The essential question is what votes to include in a measure of support. This is of critical importance, because we want to know whether variables that may explain behavior, such as public approval and legislative skills, operate uniformly across all issues and all votes, or influence some issues and votes more than others. Measures of presidential support that are very broad may mask important relationships that are revealed by more exclusive measures. Conversely, relationships that appear to hold across a wide range of issues and votes may actually be weak or nonexistent on especially important matters.

3. Quoted in Murray Marder, "Congress' Drive for Strings in Reagan's Foreign Policies," *Washington Post Weekly Edition*, September 19, 1984, p. 120.

4. Jeffrey E. Cohen, "The Impact of the Modern Presidency on Presidential Success in the U.S. Congress," *Legislative Studies Quarterly* 7 (November 1982): 515–532.

5. Thomas H. Hammond and Jane M. Fraser, "Judging Presidential Performance on House and Senate Roll Calls," *Polity* 16 (Summer 1984): 624–646.

6. Paul Light, *The President's Agenda* (Baltimore: Johns Hopkins University Press, 1982).

There is considerable controversy and little consensus on what measure of presidential support is most appropriate. The most commonly employed measures of presidential support are the Presidential Support Scores of Congressional Quarterly, but scholars have often criticized these for weighing all issues equally and including lopsided votes and often several votes on the same issue.[7] Some scholars find them rather blunt measures that obscure as much as they reveal. On the other hand, Sigelman focused only on key votes,[8] and was criticized by Shull and LeLoup for doing so.[9]

Comparing Indexes of Support for the President

In this section I develop and compare four indexes of presidential support in the House and Senate for the years 1953–86. They range from the comprehensive to the very selective, and each is designed to capture a different aspect of support for the president. My goal is to obtain a clear understanding of the advantages and drawbacks of various ways of measuring this support and the implications of using them in research. I also want to see whether the indexes produce distinctive results. If they do not, one can reach the theoretically significant conclusion that there is stability in congressional voting on presidential requests. Conversely, if there are distinctive differences in the results, one will be in a better position to choose the measure or measures best suited to specific research questions.

Overall Support

The most inclusive index of presidential success in Congress is Overall Support, which includes all the votes on which the president has taken a stand. The basis for determining these issues is the yearly almanac of Congressional Quarterly (CQ). CQ analyzes all the public statements and messages of the president to determine what legislation he desires or does not desire. Only issues on which the president has taken a stand are included in the indexes, and CQ includes votes only if the legislation that the president origi-

7. See for example Edwards, *Presidential Influence in Congress*, pp. 50–53; Anthony King, "A Mile and a Half Is a Long Way," in Anthony King, ed., *Both Ends of the Avenue* (Washington: American Enterprise Institute, 1983), p. 253; John F. Manley, "White House Lobbying and the Problem of Presidential Power" (paper presented at the annual meeting of the American Political Science Association, Washington, September 1977), pp. 36–52; Stephen J. Wayne, *The Legislative Presidency* (New York: Harper and Row, 1978), pp. 168–172.

8. Lee Sigelman, "A Reassessment of the Two Presidencies Thesis," *Journal of Politics* 41 (November 1979): 1195–1205; "Response to Critics," *Journal of Politics* 43 (May 1981): 565.

9. Steven A. Shull and Lance T. LeLoup, "Reassessing the Reassessment: Comment on Sigelman's Note on the 'Two Presidencies' Thesis," *Journal of Politics* 43 (May 1981), pp. 563–564.

nally supported is voted on in a similar form: bills are excluded if they have been so extensively amended that a vote can no longer be characterized as reflecting support for the president or opposition to him. The position of the president at the time of the vote is the basis for measuring support or opposition in cases where his position has changed before or after the vote. Key votes to recommit, reconsider, or table legislation are included, but appropriations bills are included only if they deal with specific funds that the president requested be added or deleted. This last distinction helps keep the measure one of support for the president rather than for the institutionalized presidency.

Although I rely on the judgments of CQ in determining the issues on which the president has taken a stand, I have not simply adopted the Presidential Support Scores of CQ. The index of Overall Support was coded independently, owing partly to occasional errors in the calculations of CQ, partly due to the deletion by CQ of certain votes pertaining to the Civil Rights Act of 1964, and partly to my handling of paired votes (discussed below).

There are drawbacks as well as advantages to an index that measures the support of members of Congress on all the votes on which the president has taken a stand. Such an index may include lopsided votes and many votes on the same issue, and it weighs all issues equally. More restrictive indexes of presidential support do not have these limitations.

There is no evidence that presidents have varied in their use of posturing, that is, trying to inflate their degree of congressional support by proposing popular but frivolous legislation or by withholding unpopular legislation. Although some instances of each device have undoubtedly occurred, there seem to be no systematic differences in the degree to which presidents have employed them.

Nonunanimous Support

Because many of the issues on which the president takes a stand are not controversial and are decided by nearly unanimous votes, including them in a measure of support for the president can distort the results by inflating the measure. Further, the number of these votes varies over time, and including them in a measure of presidential support can therefore frustrate attempts to correlate the measure with possible explanatory variables. Comparisons between the House and Senate may also be distorted if these votes are included, because the Senate tends to have more unanimous votes, owing at least in part to its special responsibilities for confirming appointments and ratifying treaties, most of which are not controversial.

To avoid the problem of unanimous votes, I employ the measure Non-unanimous Support, an index of support for the president in votes on which the winning side numbered less than 80 percent of those who voted. Although this figure is somewhat arbitrary, it is a reasonable cutoff, beyond which presidential influence appears to be largely irrelevant. It is worthwhile to note that there are many instances of nearly unanimous votes that the president lost. Evidently the president felt it necessary in these cases to take a principled stand against hopeless odds. A drawback to the measure Non-unanimous Support is that the overwhelming consensus on an issue may be due to the president's influence. Thus when we omit unanimous and nearly unanimous votes from an index of presidential support, we may lose useful information.

Single-Vote Support

Very often there are many roll-call votes on the same issue. In some cases there are a dozen or more on one bill, as amendment after amendment is decided by roll-call vote. In the most extreme case, the Senate took 116 roll-call votes on the Civil Rights Act of 1964. When one issue provides a large percentage of the votes on which the president took a stand, the potential for distortion is obvious. The resulting index will be biased toward both the president's influence and the broader configuration of forces at work on the one issue.

The index Single-Vote Support avoids this problem. This is an index of support for the president on the most important nonunanimous vote on each bill. There is only one vote per bill in this index. If a key vote was designated for an issue, this is the vote used; if there were two key votes and one was on final passage, the index uses the latter; if there were two key votes and neither was on final passage, the one with the closest vote is used, on the theory that close votes are the best tests of the president's influence. Typically, no key vote is designated by Congressional Quarterly. In such cases the first choice is the vote on final passage of the bill. If this is not available, the most closely contested remaining vote is used.

There is no objective way to determine the most important vote on a bill. Although passage is often the crucial vote, at other times hotly contested amendments or even procedural votes may be more significant. By choosing among amendments on the basis of how closely contested they were, there is the possibility of choosing votes on which the president was less successful and excluding votes on which he was more so; one simply cannot tell. Finally, a few bills cover several disparate issues. For example, consideration of the continuing appropriations bill of fiscal 1983 in the Senate included votes on the MX missile, the Clinch River breeder reactor, licensing of professions by the Federal Trade Commission, public works jobs, social security benefits, abortion funding, and funds for Central American guerrillas. Excluding multiple votes on the same issue thus avoids and creates problems in measuring presidential support.

Key Votes

Each year Congressional Quarterly selects key votes that occurred in each house during the session. A key vote is one or more of the following: a matter of major controversy, a test of presidential or political power, and a decision of potentially great impact on the nation and on lives of Americans. A measure of presidential support relying on key votes is attractive because these votes represent only significant issues, and thus help to avoid distorting measurements of presidential success with less important ones. It is possible that a president's success on relatively inconsequential issues may mask his failure to obtain support on more important ones.

Nevertheless, there are several reasons to exercise caution in the use of key votes. First, the president does not take a stand on all of them. Over the thirty-four years covered here, the president took a stand on 72 percent of the key votes in the House and 66 percent in the Senate, and from 1969 only on 60 percent and 56 percent. Second, in 7 percent of the key votes in the House and 11 percent in the Senate the winning side included at least 80 percent of the legislators who voted, and these votes may therefore not be a useful test of presidential influence. Third, the number of key votes on which the president has taken a stand is very small: the yearly average is ten in the House and nine in the Senate. This is a very modest basis for generalizations about presidential leadership of Congress. Fourth, there is sometimes more than one key vote on a single issue (for example, four of ten key votes in the House in 1985 were on one issue).

Finally, although weighing votes equally may mask important information, it also has certain advantages. What appear to be the most significant votes are not necessarily the best tests of presidential influence or leadership. Even if we know the president's complete set of priorities (which we do not), and even if he has a comprehensive set of priorities (which he often does not), each member of Congress responds to presidential requests with his or her own set of priorities (to the degree that the member has one). One cannot assume that the issues the president cares about most and therefore fights for the hardest are those that members of Congress care about most, and for this reason we cannot assume that these issues are the best tests of presidential influence. The president's task in such cases is not necessarily especially difficult, as the occasional nearly unanimous results on key votes indicate.

Another reason why the varying degrees of presidential effort to influence Congress may not be a particularly serious problem is that the direct involvement of the president and his staff is only one of several potential sources of influence. A number of others, such as public approval and party affiliation, are not manipulable on a given issue but may be important influences on congressional voting. Further, legislative activities of the White House are frequently strategic rather than tactical, aimed at generating goodwill and not at gaining a particular person's vote on a particular issue. Thus it should not be assumed that a president's tactical efforts are dominant in determining congressional votes.

The Indexes in Perspective

Because of their individual limitations, one should be hesitant in selecting any one index as the only dependent variable for studying presidential leadership in Congress, but rather employ more than one. Using more than one measure provides a more complete picture of presidential support, increases the probability of our understanding presidential leadership, and allows us to identify the types of votes that correlate most highly with different independent variables.

In addition to their individual limitations, the indexes also have some problems in common. They are based solely on roll calls, yet many important decisions are made in committee and on other types of votes. Although there is evidence that roll calls reflect less visible decisions,[10] it is not certain that this is so. Nevertheless, roll calls typically occur on a wide range of significant issues and are worthy of study in and of themselves, and roll calls are the only systematic data available on the decisions of the individual members of Congress. The results of studying roll calls also guide us in evaluating presidential legislative strategies such as the setting of the agenda.

Another problem is nonvoting. Support scores are lowered by the absences of members of Congress, most of which are due to illness or official business, but some of which occur when members of Congress desire to support or oppose the president but not to express their positions publicly. Because there is no way to know how to interpret absences, we are forced to assume that the reasons for nonvoting balance out and are evenly distributed throughout each house. This assumption is probably safe, because members from each region have similar rates of voting participation on these sets of roll calls. Moreover, those unable to vote because of prolonged illness, death, or resignation were eliminated from the analysis. Anyone taking part in fewer than 50 percent of the votes in the Overall Support Index was deleted. Unlike *Congressional Quarterly*, I counted announced pairs in the same way as votes,

10. See Aage Clausen, *How Congressmen Decide* (New York: St. Martin's, 1973), pp. 19–20; Joseph K. Unekis, "From Committee to the Floor: Consistency in Congressional Voting," *Journal of Politics* 40 (August 1978): 761–769.

because they have the same effect. This also gives a more accurate view of presidential support.

Each of the four indexes produces a score for each member of Congress in each year rather than a yearly aggregate for each house or the entire Congress. The indexes make it possible to measure the level of support for a president's program provided by each representative and senator or by any group of them.

Computation

Calculating each of the four measures involved a massive gathering of data. I first examined each of the several thousand roll calls taken in the House and Senate during the period 1953–86 to identify those on which the president had taken a stand, those on which 80 percent or more of the voting members were on one side, those that were on the same issue, and those that were key votes.

The next step was to calculate the percentage of support each member of Congress gave the president on the votes represented in each measure in each year. To arrive at these percentages I divided the number of times a member of Congress voted or announced a pair for the president's position by the number of stands the president took. These calculations produced over seventy-two thousand index scores.

Relationships among the Indexes

Once the indexes for every member of Congress have been calculated, they must be compared to show whether they measure presidential support in distinctive ways. Tables 2.2 and 2.3 show the averages for the entire House and Senate for each of the four indexes of presidential support over the period 1953–86. They help give an overview of the relationships among the measures.

Overall Support is often not much higher than Nonunanimous Support. The difference depends on the number of lopsided votes in the session (there were forty-nine in the House in 1967 and ninety-five in the Senate in 1973) and the percentage of them that go in the same direction. Nearly unanimous votes are not always in the president's favor. In 1981, for example, there were twenty such votes in the House, but 40 percent of them went against the president. In 1984 the president lost twenty of thirty-seven nearly unanimous votes in the House.

There are generally very small differences between Nonunanimous Support and Single-Vote Support. Evidently, including more than one vote per issue in an index of presidential support has little impact on the index.

TABLE 2.2   Presidential Support in the House (in Percent)

Year	Overall Support	Nonunanimous Support	Single-Vote Support	Key Votes
1953	63	58	58	55
1954	61	55	55	52
1955	58	47	47	44
1956	63	54	55	57
1957	53	50	49	59
1958	59	53	54	52
1959	52	47	49	48
1960	51	52	48	48
1961	59	54	55	49
1962	62	55	53	50
1963	59	53	52	54
1964	61	56	57	54
1965	50	59	59	59
1966	59	52	52	54
1967	60	51	52	51
1968	61	51	53	48
1969	53	52	52	51
1970	61	49	49	45
1971	58	53	51	53
1972	56	55	55	43
1973	48	46	46	47
1974	51	47	47	52
1975	43	47	47	44
1976	44	43	42	44
1977	57	51	54	50
1978	56	55	51	50
1979	54	50	49	49
1980	55	51	51	43
1981	54	54	50	50
1982	51	44	40	45
1983	44	45	39	45
1984	45	45	39	51
1985	46	45	42	49
1986	42	43	40	47

Support for the president on Key Votes is usually very similar to Single-Vote Support in the House, but there are differences of more than 5 percentage points in eight of the years studied (1957, 1961, 1972, 1980, and 1983–1986). Even in these years, however, one should not conclude that the index Key Votes has tapped a special aspect of presidential support. In 1957, for example, there were only five key votes in the House on which President Eisenhower took a stand. One of these was a nearly unanimous vote on Eisenhower's Middleast Doctrine, and three of the remaining four were disproportionately likely to elicit support from the Democratic majority (two were on the Civil Rights Act of 1957 and one was on Mutual Security, or foreign aid, appropriations). Because the number of key votes in a session of Congress is always small, one or two nearly unanimous or deviant votes loom large in relative terms. The number of votes in each index for each chamber in each year is shown in tables 2.4 and 2.5.

Differences between the indexes Single-Vote Support and Key Votes are typically greater in the Senate than in the House. In fifteen of the thirty-four

TABLE 2.3   Presidential Support in the Senate (in Percent)

Year	Overall Support	Nonunanimous Support	Single-Vote Support	Key Votes
1953	58	54	55	59
1954	58	56	55	52
1955	66	53	51	52
1956	58	52	52	52
1957	64	56	52	59
1958	58	51	51	50
1959	52	44	42	47
1960	53	50	54	48
1961	58	55	54	54
1962	58	53	51	47
1963	60	54	53	61
1964	62	61	53	57
1965	61	57	53	64
1966	55	47	50	58
1967	60	51	51	64
1968	50	44	47	55
1969	56	51	54	45
1970	56	47	44	50
1971	53	47	48	52
1972	56	49	48	62
1973	49	41	38	43
1974	48	40	44	50
1975	56	48	47	39
1976	50	42	40	39
1977	63	53	55	50
1978	57	53	51	58
1979	62	55	60	50
1980	56	51	51	48
1981	66	58	60	62
1982	60	55	49	48
1983	60	58	53	52
1984	61	54	54	62
1985	56	53	52	55
1986	58	54	52	51

TABLE 2.4   Number of Votes in Indexes of House Presidential Support

Year	Overall Support	Nonunanimous Support	Single-Vote Support	Key Votes
1953	32	26	19	7
1954	38	20	14	8
1955	41	24	10	5
1956	34	20	15	8
1957	60	44	19	5
1958	50	37	24	9
1959	54	43	29	11
1960	43	36	19	8
1961	65	48	34	12
1962	60	43	26	12
1963	72	53	32	11
1964	52	37	25	9
1965	112	73	36	17
1966	104	67	39	12
1967	127	78	44	11
1968	103	59	40	11
1969	47	28	20	8
1970	65	36	31	9
1971	57	45	18	7
1972	37	27	21	6
1973	125	96	48	9
1974	107	65	38	8
1975	89	74	52	12
1976	51	43	33	7
1977	79	52	26	6
1978	113	91	48	12
1979	145	113	41	12
1980	117	81	40	10
1981	76	56	23	12
1982	77	53	36	9
1983	82	79	46	11
1984	113	76	41	11
1985	80	66	36	10
1986	90	71	42	10

years the difference is more than five percentage points, although in only ten years does it exceed seven percentage points. As in the House, the inclusion of nearly unanimous votes and the small number of votes included in the index Key Votes magnifies any real differences between the indexes.

When the index Key Votes deviates from the index Single-Vote Support in either house, there is little consistency in the direction. This does not allow one to conclude that presidents typically do better or worse on those votes they presumably care about most.

A second way of comparing the different measures of presidential support is to examine them in a more aggregate form that smooths out some of the inevitable yearly distortions in the measurements. Table 2.6 displays a variety of aggregate percentages for each index for both the House and Senate. Because of the strong influence of party affiliation on presidential support, I include controls for the party of both the president and the members of Congress.

TABLE 2.5   Number of Votes in Indexes of Senate Presidential Support

Year	Overall Support	Nonunanimous Support	Single-Vote Support	Key Votes
1953	49	38	15	6
1954	77	63	30	7
1955	52	23	13	8
1956	65	54	19	6
1957	57	39	19	4
1958	98	73	29	10
1959	121	87	36	13
1960	86	63	25	9
1961	124	102	35	9
1962	125	91	30	11
1963	116	80	32	8
1964	203	163	21	10
1965	162	120	37	16
1966	125	87	29	8
1967	167	104	32	7
1968	164	124	34	11
1969	72	47	22	10
1970	91	52	30	6
1971	82	61	19	12
1972	46	31	18	8
1973	185	90	40	9
1974	151	108	46	9
1975	95	57	29	6
1976	53	32	25	7
1977	89	60	28	6
1978	151	122	40	8
1979	161	117	46	9
1980	116	85	37	11
1981	128	78	28	11
1982	119	88	24	8
1983	85	72	29	6
1984	77	57	25	10
1985	102	80	34	9
1986	84	62	22	11

TABLE 2.6   Aggregate Presidential Support (in Percent)

House

President's Party	Members' Party	Overall Support	Nonunanimous Support	Single-Vote Support	Key Votes
All	All	54	51	50	50
All	D	52	49	47	47
All	R	56	52	52	53
R	R	65	65	64	68
R	D	43	38	36	36
R	All	53	49	48	49
D	R	40	28	29	26
D	D	69	69	68	66
D	All	58	53	53	51

Senate

President's Party	Members' Party	Overall Support	Nonunanimous Support	Single-Vote Support	Key Votes
All	All	57	51	51	53
All	D	52	44	43	45
All	R	63	58	57	59
R	R	70	69	68	69
R	D	46	34	34	35
R	All	57	51	50	51
D	R	48	39	37	40
D	D	64	61	61	65
D	All	59	53	52	56

D = Democrat
R = Republican

The results are striking. Despite the substantial differences in how the indexes are measured and the number of votes included in each year, the aggregate results reveal a strong consistency among the indexes, especially among the three more exclusive ones. In no instance in the entire table does the difference between the lowest of these three indexes and the highest exceed three percentage points.

A third method of evaluating the relationships between measures of presidential support is to correlate them with each other. To do so one must use a dummy variable to control for the party of the president, because much of the variance in the indexes, especially for party groups, may be the result of the party occupying the White House changing in 1961, 1969, 1977, and 1981.

The results of these computations for the entire House and Senate and for party groups are shown in tables 2.7 and 2.8. The correlations are typically quite high, although there are a few exceptions, and the Senate figures are as a whole a bit lower than those for the House. The index Nonunanimous Support seems the most representative of the four. It has the strongest correlations with the others: very high ones with Single-Vote Support and generally strong ones with Overall Support and Key Votes.

White House Measures of Presidential Support

From 1961 to 1967 the administrations of John Kennedy and Lyndon Johnson compiled their own indexes of presidential support for each member of Congress. Although at first glance using these measures seems appealing, they have several drawbacks for our use, in addition to their existing only for seven of the thirty-four years being studied.

The White House voting scores were compiled over the years by different people using vague criteria. This raises substantial questions of validity and reliability. If we look at 1965, for example, we find that from mid-October to mid-November the White House developed at least seven different lists of the major items in the president's legislative program. This should give us little confidence in the selection of votes for the support scores.

TABLE 2.7   Correlations (r) among Indexes of House Presidential Support

	Nonunanimous Support	Single-Vote Support	Key Votes
Overall Support			
All Representatives	.63	.70	.31
Democrats	.76	.77	.59
Republicans	.77	.69	.36
Northern Democrats	.89	.86	.79
Southern Democrats	.67	.65	.53
Nonunanimous Support			
All Representatives		.90	.53
Democrats		.88	.71
Republicans		.87	.53
Northern Democrats		.90	.86
Southern Democrats		.85	.80
Single-Vote Support			
All Representatives			.48
Democrats			.62
Republicans			.52
Northern Democrats			.78
Southern Democrats			.62

TABLE 2.8 Correlations (r) among Indexes of Senate Presidential Support

	Nonunanimous Support	Single-Vote Support	Key Votes
Overall Support			
All Senators	.84	.76	.45
Democrats	.82	.65	.44
Republicans	.91	.70	.45
Northern Democrats	.87	.69	.56
Southern Democrats	.89	.67	.52
Nonunanimous Support			
All Senators		.83	.46
Democrats		.82	.51
Republicans		.71	.50
Northern Democrats		.80	.61
Southern Democrats		.81	.63
Single-Vote Support			
All Senators			.44
Democrats			.57
Republicans			.65
Northern Democrats			.55
Southern Democrats			.66

There is also a question of accuracy. In the study of the Senate for 1965 the presidential support percentages shown for each senator are impossible to obtain from the data provided in the study. Either the percentages were simply calculated incorrectly, or there was some additional step in the calculations that the Office of Congressional Relations failed to report. At any rate, this inspires little confidence in its figures.

The possibility should also not be overlooked that the studies of voting support done in the White House were in part self-serving. For example, absences did not count against support scores, inflating almost everyone's level of support. In 1965 Sen. Eugene McCarthy had the second highest presidential support rating (98 percent) although he was absent from 35 percent of the votes.

The strongest objection of the Office of Congressional Relations to the use of Congressional Quarterly's support scores was the inclusion of non-controversial votes. Because these votes are excluded from the index Non-unanimous Support, the index is in effect one like that which the White House desired—but compiled more systematically.[11]

11. Letter from Judge Barefoot Sanders to author, May 28, 1987. I am indebted to Judge Sanders, legislative counsel to President Johnson, for his explanation of the Office of Congressional Relations support scores.

It is important to be clear about what one wants to research. To investigate most theoretically significant questions about presidential success in Congress, it is best to begin with data at the individual level. These are more suited to explanation than aggregate measures.

The question of which votes to include in an index of presidential support is also theoretically important. The results of the analysis of the four measures of presidential support in Congress have been very revealing. No matter how one compares the indexes, it is clear that they have a great deal in common. Although this is especially true of the indexes Nonunanimous Support and Single-Vote Support, the differences among all four of the indexes are typically small. Presidential support seems to be due to factors that operate with a large degree of similarity across a wide range of roll calls. This stability in congressional responsiveness to presidential proposals is theoretically quite significant and should make us skeptical that idiosyncratic or personal factors are fundamental explanations for presidential success in Congress.

Yet there are some differences in the computation and the results of the indexes that are important to consider. For example, Overall Support appears to inflate support levels artificially whereas Key Votes tend to be somewhat idiosyncratic. The careful researcher will want to employ more than one measure of presidential support when studying the impact of independent variables, such as the level of the public's approval of the president, or the president's legislative skill at obtaining support for his programs in Congress.

The best approach is probably to use the indexes Nonunanimous Support and Key Votes in conjunction with each other when analyzing presidential success in Congress. Nonunanimous Support is a comprehensive index subject to few distortions, and Key Votes, if used with caution, may reveal relationships that a broader measure masks. Single-Vote Support is not distinctive from Nonunanimous Support and is less inclusive, whereas Overall Support is too prone to distortion to be of much use for most purposes. As long as the inevitable limitations of any measures are kept in mind, the measures should lead to an increased understanding of presidential leadership in Congress.

CHAPTER THREE

Strategic Position as Party Leader

Decentralization characterizes the American political system, creating centrifugal forces that afflict the relationship between the president and Congress. The White House requires means of countering the natural tendencies toward conflict of the executive and legislative branches. The only institution with the potential to foster cooperation systematically between the institutions at either end of Pennsylvania Avenue is the political party.

Leadership of his party in Congress is one of the most important but most overlooked tasks of the chief executive. No matter what other resources a president may have at his disposal, he remains highly dependent upon his party to move his legislative program. Representatives and senators of the president's party almost always form the nucleus of coalitions supporting his proposals. As an aide to President Nixon put it, "You turn to your party members first. If we couldn't move our own people, we felt the opportunities [of passage] were pretty slim."[1]

If the president is to be a director of change, his party leadership is likely to occupy a prominent place in his overall strategy. There must be a firm basis for his leadership, and senators and representatives must respond reliably to his calls for support. If party leadership is less dependable, if his fellow partisans in Congress are less amenable to his leadership, then the chief executive is more likely to be restricted to the more modest role of facilitator.

Despite the significance of presidential party leadership in Congress, scholars have devoted surprisingly little attention to it. Too often they appear

1. Quoted in Paul C. Light, *The President's Agenda: Domestic Policy Choice from Kennedy to Carter* (Baltimore: Johns Hopkins University Press, 1982), p. 135.

either to take party leadership for granted or to dismiss it as irrelevant in an age of party decline. In this chapter and the one that follows I examine the president's strategic position as party leader by exploring the potential for influence that party leadership provides the White House in its relationship with Congress, the levels of party support the president receives, and the obstacles he must attempt to overcome. The goal is to understand the basis for party leadership and the nature of the task the president faces as party leader. In Chapter 5 I focus on presidents as they attempt to lead their parties.

The Ties That Bind

Shared party affiliation is more than a superficial characteristic that the president and some members of Congress hold in common. For most senators and representatives belonging to the president's party creates a psychological bond that generates a proclivity for supporting the White House. Equally important, this attitude strongly influences the context within which the president's attempts to lead his party occur.

The president comes to his position as party leader with a clear advantage. Members of his party are open to his influence, much more so than are members of the opposition party. When John Kingdon asked members of the House in early 1969 who played a role in their decision making, 42 percent of Republicans spontaneously mentioned the administration of Richard Nixon, a high figure for unprompted mentions. Only 14 percent of the Northern Democrats and 12 percent of the Southern Democrats gave a similar response. One-third of the Republicans replied that the administration played a major or determining role in their decisions, about five times the figure for Democrats.[2]

Members of the president's party typically have personal loyalties or emotional commitments to their party and their party leader, which the president can often translate into votes when necessary. These members give the president the benefit of the doubt, especially if they are unsure about their own opinion on an issue.[3] As Speaker of the House "Tip" O'Neill said in 1977, "We loved to send Jerry Ford's vetoes back to him. But we have a Democratic President now, and who needs that?"[4] One presidential aide described as

2. John W. Kingdon, *Congressmen's Voting Decisions* (New York: Harper and Row, 1973), pp. 175–176.

3. Ibid., pp. 172, 175, 178, 180. See also Donald R. Matthews, *U.S. Senators and Their World* (New York: W. W. Norton, 1973), p. 140.

4. Quoted in "Shadowboxing," *Newsweek*, June 6, 1977, p. 15.

"just amazing" how often members voted for the administration's proposals not on substance but on loyalty and a desire to be helpful.[5]

These sentiments helped President Reagan, even with those Republicans most disturbed by his policies. According to one close observer, they "did not drive as hard a bargain as their number would have allowed, for they were uneasy about abandoning the President. They could not play hardball with their own leader and they settled for less than they could have gotten."[6] As one Senate Republican put it, "I had to subordinate my own feelings. I figured, Ronald Reagan was elected the Republican President. That was always in the back of my mind. I'm not here to pick a fight with a brand new president."[7]

This predisposition to supporting the president complements related attitudes that enhance the effectiveness of the president's party leadership. Members of the president's party want to avoid embarrassing "their" administration. They have a highly utilitarian motive for this attitude in addition to their emotional stakes in the White House. Members of the president's party have an incentive to make him look good, because his standing in the public may influence their own chances for reelection.[8]

Ronald Reagan's White House was quick to point out to congressional Republicans this relationship. As one presidential aide commented, "We'll never ask a member to vote against his own political interest, but we sure will . . . try to show them why it may be in their interest to support the President, whose strength and popularity will be a factor in their own election."[9] The Republican congressional leaders were also persuasive in making this argument to their party colleagues.[10]

The reluctance of the president's party to embarrass him can be seen from an examination of votes to override presidential vetoes. In most cases many members of the president's party who voted for a bill when it was originally passed vote against the bill after their party leader has vetoed it. For

5. Quoted in Stephen J. Wayne, *The Legislative Presidency* (New York: Harper and Row, 1978), p. 151. See also Lawrence F. O'Brien, "Larry O'Brien Discusses White House Contacts on Capitol Hill," in Aaron Wildavsky, ed., *The Presidency* (Boston: Little, Brown, 1969), p. 482.

6. Allen Schick, "How the Budget Was Won and Lost," in Norman J. Ornstein, ed., *President and Congress: Assessing Reagan's First Year* (Washington: American Enterprise Institute, 1982), p. 21.

7. Quoted in Steven R. Weisman, "Reaganomics and the President's Men," *New York Times Magazine*, October 24, 1982, p. 89.

8. On this point see chapter 5.

9. Quoted in Dick Kirschten, "Reagan's Political Chief Rollins: 'We Will Help Our Friends First,'" *National Journal*, June 12, 1982, p. 1057.

10. Hedrick Smith, "Coping with Congress," *New York Times Magazine*, August 9, 1981, p. 20.

example, in June 1982 President Reagan vetoed a supplemental appropriations bill. After the veto forty-eight House Republicans changed their votes to bring them in line with the president's position. This was a change on the part of more than half the Republicans who had opposed the president originally. Only one Republican changed to vote against the president. The Democrats were quite a different story: only nine changed their votes to support the president and seven went in the opposite direction, from support for the president to voting to override his veto.

A basic distrust of the opposition party further strengthens the inclination of members of the president's party to support him. There is a natural tendency to view the opposition party as eager to undercut the White House,[11] and this perception induces the president's party to rise to his defense.

A president may find it easiest to unify the party behind his program if his party regains control of one or both houses of Congress at the time of his election. Many new members may feel a sense of gratification for what they perceive as the president's coattails.[12] The prospect of exercising the power to govern may also provide a catalyst for party loyalty, whereas the loss of power may temporarily demoralize the opposition party. According to a leading student of Congress: "Had the Republicans moved into majority status in Congress two or four years before Reagan's election, or had majority status been less novel to them, they probably would have displayed less party unity on key votes in 1981."[13] But power was new to Republicans in 1981, who had not had a majority in either house since 1953–54. No Republican senator had ever served in a Republican Senate majority. Even before Reagan took office the renewed party spirit of the Republicans was a source of comment by Washington insiders. Many freshman and sophomore members of Congress were eager to make their mark on policy. They were also aware that there was a power in unity; many felt Reagan's policy success was the key to holding the Senate. This enthusiasm was infectious and spread to their more senior Republican colleagues.[14]

Yet sharing the burdens of governing is not a long-term adhesive. By 1983 Republican senators were calling their nearly unanimous support for President Reagan's taxing and spending proposals an aberration and unlikely to be repeated during the remainder of his tenure in office. Sen. Slade Gorton

11. Kingdon, *Congressmen's Voting Decisions*, pp. 172–173.

12. See for example Smith, "Coping with Congress," p. 20.

13. Norman J. Ornstein, "Assessing Reagan's First Year," in Ornstein, ed., *President and Congress*, p. 92.

14. Schick, "How the Budget Was Won and Lost," p. 16; Smith, "Coping with Congress," p. 20; "Numerous Factors Favoring Good Relationships Between Reagan and New Congress," *Congressional Quarterly Weekly Report*, January 24, 1981, p. 172.

described the high levels of support as resulting from unique circumstances: a "new President with a big victory and strong views, a large number of new senators and a Republican majority for the first time since 1954." Sen. Rudy Boschwitz added, "In the first two years, there was a great sense we had to govern. Now we've started to go beyond that."[15] At the end of 1984 the chairman of the Senate Finance Committee, Robert Dole, contrasted the beginning and end of Reagan's first term: "The President was fresh. The Republican Senate was fresh. We were all finally committee chairmen and subcommittee chairmen. We knew we had to stick together. Now the bloom is gone."[16]

Reinforcing the pull of party ties and easing the burden of party leadership is another important component of the president's strategic position as party leader: that of policy agreement. Members of the same party typically share many policy preferences, and often have similar electoral coalitions supporting them and their views. For example, much of the support that a liberal Democratic president receives from Northern Democrats in Congress for liberal policies results as much from agreement on policy as from party loyalty or presidential party leadership. In such a case there is not much need for conversion, at least on fundamentals. The president has simply taken stands that are in accord with the normal policy positions of this group of fellow party members. He can thus focus on leading on the particulars of policies rather than their principles.

In 1981 President Reagan won several crucial votes in Congress on his taxing and spending proposals. He was immediately credited with extraordinary party leadership because nearly all the Republicans in Congress supported his programs. If one examines voting on budget resolutions under the Democrat Jimmy Carter, however, one finds nearly the same degree of Republican party unity in the House.[17] Thus we should not necessarily ascribe Reagan's success to party leadership. Republican members of the House had been voting a conservative line well before Ronald Reagan came to Washington. As the *New York Times* reported, the most fundamental reason for the president's success was that he had chosen tax reduction as his first priority, on which there was already a strong consensus.[18] Tax reform, however, which was the president's first priority in 1985, was not a primary interest of congres-

---

15. Quoted in Richard E. Cohen, "Senate Republicans' Control May Be Put to Test by Tough Issues This Fall," *National Journal*, September 10, 1983, pp. 1824–1827.

16. "Senate Republicans See Obstacles for Reagan," *New York Times*, November 28, 1984, sec. A, p. 11.

17. See Lance LeLoup, "After the Blitz: Reagan and the U.S. Congressional Budget Process," *Legislative Studies Quarterly* 7 (August 1982): 321–340.

18. Smith, "Coping with Congress," p. 17.

sional Republicans. The president found the going much tougher, especially in the House.

The remarkable productivity of the Eighty-ninth Congress (1965–66) is an example of the same phenomenon. According to Carl Albert, then the House majority leader, Congress was not rubber-stamping the president's proposals but doing what it wanted to do. "We had the right majority," he recalled.[19] In other words, as President Johnson's domestic policy adviser Joseph Califano argued, the House had a liberal majority that was very receptive to the president's proposals.[20]

Lyndon Johnson was very much aware of the importance of shared outlooks in the passage of legislation. After the results of the liberal Democratic landslide in 1964 were in, he called his chief lobbyist, Lawrence O'Brien, and told him, "We can wrap up the New Frontier program now, Larry. . . . We can pass it now."[21] He even kept Congress in session until just seventeen days before the election of 1966 to exploit his sympathetic majority to the fullest, in the process limiting the opportunities for incumbent Democrats to campaign for reelection.[22]

Party Support for the President

Not only does shared party affiliation create a tendency among members of the president's party in Congress to be responsive to his party leadership, but this inclination is often reinforced by shared policy preferences. As a result one would expect to find that members of the president's party accord him substantially more support than do members of the opposition party.

Table 3.1 shows the average annual support given to the president on nonunanimous votes by members of each party in the House and Senate from 1953 through 1986, table 3.2 provides the same information for key votes, and tables 3.3 and 3.4 show summary measures of partisan presidential support for 1953–86 and for individual presidents.

Several important points emerge from an examination of these tables. First, there is a great deal of slippage of party loyalty in the president's party.

19. Carl B. Albert, interview by Dorothy Pierce McSweeny, August 13, 1969, interview 4, transcript, pp. 23–24, Lyndon Baines Johnson Library, Austin, Tex.

20. Joseph A. Califano, Jr., *A Presidential Nation* (New York: W. W. Norton, 1975), p. 155.

21. Quoted in Lawrence F. O'Brien, *No Final Victories* (New York: Ballantine, 1975), p. 180. See also p. 181.

22. Russell D. Renka, "Comparing Presidents Kennedy and Johnson as Legislative Leaders" (paper prepared for presentation at the Annual Meeting of the Southern Political Science Association, Savannah, Ga., November 1984), p. 21. See also Richard Bolling, *Power in the House: A History of the Leadership of the House of Representatives* (New York: Capricorn, 1974), p. 232.

TABLE 3.1   Presidential Support by Party on Nonunanimous Votes
            (in Percent)

Year	President's Party	House		Senate	
		Democrats	Republicans	Democrats	Republicans
1953	R	45	70	42	66
1954	R	34	74	36	74
1955	R	42	52	37	70
1956	R	38	72	35	69
1957	R	48	52	44	69
1958	R	52	55	37	66
1959	R	34	72	28	73
1960	R	46	64	41	66
1961	D	73	26	68	31
1962	D	72	30	64	31
1963	D	75	21	63	37
1964	D	78	26	63	56
1965	D	75	24	64	44
1966	D	67	20	53	35
1967	D	70	28	56	42
1968	D	63	36	46	41
1969	R	48	57	42	65
1970	R	41	60	35	63
1971	R	41	71	33	65
1972	R	46	68	34	66
1973	R	31	65	24	64
1974	R	38	59	31	53
1975	R	37	68	36	67
1976	R	32	67	29	62
1977	D	61	32	62	39
1978	D	65	34	64	36
1979	D	64	26	67	39
1980	D	63	31	60	38
1981	R	39	72	33	81
1982	R	30	61	35	72
1983	R	28	71	39	73
1984	R	32	66	31	74
1985	R	28	68	27	76
1986	R	23	72	26	80

R = Republican
D = Democrat

Table 3.3 reveals that presidents can count on their own party members for support no more than two-thirds of the time, even on key votes. Thus there are obvious limitations to the support the president can obtain through party leadership.

Equally important is the substantial difference between the level of support enjoyed by the president in his own party and in the opposition party.

This partisan gap ranges from 22 to 41 percentage points. The tables cover the administrations of four Republican presidents and three Democrats who varied widely in their policies, personalities, and political environments, but invariably their fellow partisans in Congress gave them considerably more support than they gave presidents of the opposition party.

TABLE 3.2   Presidential Support by Party on Key Votes
(in Percent)

Year	President's Party	House		Senate	
		Democrats	Republicans	Democrats	Republicans
1953	R	41	69	42	76
1954	R	42	60	38	65
1955	R	40	50	27	76
1956	R	48	68	31	72
1957	R	52	66	46	74
1958	R	43	62	36	65
1959	R	32	77	33	74
1960	R	37	70	40	64
1961	D	72	16	67	31
1962	D	73	17	58	26
1963	D	78	19	71	40
1964	D	74	25	64	43
1965	D	75	28	71	50
1966	D	68	26	66	41
1967	D	69	28	68	57
1968	D	54	40	54	56
1969	R	43	62	41	51
1970	R	32	62	39	66
1971	R	43	66	33	77
1972	R	30	60	52	73
1973	R	31	68	23	68
1974	R	45	61	42	60
1975	R	34	64	26	59
1976	R	29	76	27	58
1977	D	61	29	70	19
1978	D	62	28	66	46
1979	D	61	28	61	34
1980	D	50	31	60	32
1981	R	32	73	41	80
1982	R	24	70	30	64
1983	R	26	75	34	67
1984	R	34	79	35	83
1985	R	34	71	27	80
1986	R	26	77	26	73

R = Republican
D = Democrat

TABLE 3.3　Aggregate Partisan Support for Presidents (in Percent)

Nonunanimous Support

President's Party	House			Senate		
	Democrats	*Republicans*	*Difference*[a]	*Democrats*	*Republicans*	*Difference*
Democratic	69	28	41	61	39	22
Republican	38	65	27	35	68	33

Key Votes

President's Party	House			Senate		
	Democrats	*Republicans*	*Difference*[a]	*Democrats*	*Republicans*	*Difference*
Democratic	66	26	40	65	40	25
Republican	36	68	32	35	69	34

[a]Differences expressed in percentage points

TABLE 3.4 Partisan Support for Individual Presidents (in Percent)

Nonunanimous Support

President	House			Senate		
	Democrats	Republicans	Difference[a]	Democrats	Republicans	Difference
Eisenhower	42	65	23	38	69	31
Kennedy	73	26	47	65	33	32
Johnson	71	27	44	56	44	12
Nixon[b]	41	64	23	34	65	31
Ford[c]	35	68	33	33	65	32
Carter	63	31	32	63	38	25
Reagan[d]	30	68	38	32	76	44

Key Votes

President	House			Senate		
	Democrats	Republicans	Difference[a]	Democrats	Republicans	Difference
Eisenhower	42	65	23	37	71	34
Kennedy	74	17	57	65	32	33
Johnson	68	29	39	65	49	16
Nixon[b]	36	64	28	38	67	29
Ford[c]	32	70	38	27	59	32
Carter	59	29	30	64	33	31
Reagan[d]	29	74	45	32	75	43

[a]Differences expressed in percentage points
[b]1969–73
[c]1975–76
[d]1981–86

Table 3.3 shows that the differences in party support for presidents of the two parties vary between the House and the Senate. House Democrats award Democratic presidents the strongest support they receive, whereas House Republicans are unusually unsupportive of Democratic presidents. On the other hand, House Democrats are more generous with support of presidents from the opposition party than are House Republicans, who support presidents of their own party to much the same degree as their Democratic colleagues support Democratic presidents. Democratic presidents clearly suffer under the burden of strong Republican partisanship in the House.

Things are different in the Senate. There senators of each party, especially Republicans, give presidents from the opposition party moderate support. Similarly, senators of each party (again, especially Republicans) are quite supportive of presidents from their own parties.

Just why partisanship is stronger in the House than in the Senate under Democratic presidents is not entirely clear. The answer may be that because of their larger, more diverse constituencies, Republican senators are more moderate than Republican members of the House.

The difference between support on nonunanimous votes and support on key votes is very small. This shows that presidents have not been able to elicit more support from either their fellow partisans or the opposition on particularly important votes. Again this shows the limitations of party as a leadership resource for the president.

When the data are disaggregated further, to the level of individual presidencies, there is a substantial variation in the level of partisan support from one president to another (table 3.4). In the House there has been a steady increase in the partisan gap for Republican presidents. (This is especially clear for key votes.) Much of this increase took place between the administrations of Richard Nixon and Gerald Ford, after the Watergate scandal, and partisan differences seem to have been further exacerbated by Ronald Reagan's sharp turn away from the policies of the New Deal and the Great Society.

Democratic presidents, on the other hand, have seen a substantial decline in the partisan gap. Although the gap was quite wide under John Kennedy and Lyndon Johnson, it narrowed considerably on both sides under Jimmy Carter: he obtained less Democratic support than Kennedy, but more Republican support. This may have been due to increased Republican acceptance over time of Democratic programs, Carter's relatively moderate policies, or both.

Patterns are more difficult to identify in the Senate. The partisan gap is basically stable for both indexes of presidential support. The biggest exception is the remarkable performance of Lyndon Johnson in obtaining Republican support. In addition, there was a reasonably small gap under Jimmy Carter on nonunanimous votes, whereas Ronald Reagan faced the widest gap, produced by his very strong Republican support rather than by weak Democratic support.

Another means of examining the influence of the president's party affiliation on Congress is to examine differences in congressional voting behavior under presidents of different parties. Some scholars have analyzed changes in congressional voting on policy scales that are independent of the occupant of the White House: they select issues for study on which they expect the policy stands of Democratic and Republican presidents to be the same, and can therefore attribute to shared party affiliation changes in the voting of members of Congress. [23]

These studies reveal that Republicans tend to be more supportive of internationalist foreign policies when a Republican is president. They are also more likely to accept governmental economic activity under a Republican president. Democrats, on the other hand, have a tendency to move in the opposite directions in foreign and economic policy when there is a Republican in the White House.

The events of 1981 parallel these findings. With a conservative Republican in the White House, many Republicans in Congress shifted to support foreign aid and increasing the ceiling on the national debt. Supporting these policies had been anathema to Republicans under the Democratic administration of Jimmy Carter.

In general, the largest shifts in congressional voting in response to presidential party affiliation occur in foreign policy. This is not surprising, because most members of Congress have more freedom from the pressures of their constituencies and interest groups in foreign policy, and are therefore less inhibited in following a president of their own party. Also, because the president has a greater personal responsibility for foreign affairs than for domestic affairs, his prestige is more involved in votes on foreign policy. His fellow

23. Mark Kesselman, "Presidential Leadership in Foreign Policy," *Midwest Journal of Political Science* 5 (August 1961): 284–289; idem, "Presidential Leadership in Congress on Foreign Policy: A Replication of a Hypothesis," *Midwest Journal of Political Science* 9 (November 1965): 401–406; Charles M. Tidmarch and Charles M. Sabatt, "Presidential Leadership Change and Foreign Policy Roll-Call Voting in the U.S. Senate," *Western Political Quarterly* 25 (December 1972): 613–625; Aage R. Clausen, *How Congressmen Decide: A Policy Focus* (New York: St. Martin's, 1973), chap. 8; Aage R. Clausen and Carl E. VanHorn, "The Congressional Response to a Decade of Change: 1963–1972," *Journal of Politics* 39 (August 1977): 632, 635, 653; Herbert B. Asher and Herbert F. Weisberg, "Voting Change in Congress: Some Dynamic Perspectives on an Evolutionary Process," *American Journal of Political Science* 22 (May 1978): 409–416; Malcolm E. Jewell, *Senatorial Politics and Foreign Policy* (Lexington: University of Kentucky Press, 1962), pp. 31–33, 41–46. See also Barbara Sinclair, *Congressional Realignment, 1925–1978* (Austin: University of Texas Press, 1982), pp. 84–85, 108–110, 120–121, 164–165, 174; Kingdon, *Congressmen's Voting Decisions*, pp. 173–175, 178.

party members in Congress have more reason to support him in these matters to save him from embarrassment.

In domestic policy two factors depress the influence of the president's party leadership. One is constituency: the constituents of a member of Congress are more likely to have opinions on domestic issues than on foreign policies. When the opinions of a constituency and the president's proposals conflict, as they often have, for example, for Southern Democrats on matters concerning civil rights, members of Congress are more likely to vote with their constituencies, to whom they must return for reelection.[24]

The second important factor is of course the policy agreement between the president and the members of his party in Congress. As long as the new president sends proposals to Capitol Hill that are consistent with the policy stands taken by most of the members of his party under the previous president, these members can support him without shifting their votes. If the president's party has been divided, then there will be more need and more potential for party leadership to play a prominent role. In general, the reason why party leadership is found to have had the greater impact in foreign policy is that this is where presidents have asked their party legions to shift the most.

Despite the many variations in party support for the president over the decades covered in this study, one finding is clear. Year in and year out members of the president's party provide him with considerably more support than do members of the opposition party. Although shared party affiliation and shared policy preferences interact and reinforce each other, making it difficult to isolate their separate influences on presidential support, we can have confidence that the party tie is a significant influence on presidential support in Congress. The president's strategic position as a party leader is favorable. Those whom he tries to lead are potentially quite responsive to his programs. Yet there is typically a substantial deviation from party unity among members of the president's party. Obviously, other factors such as public opinion, constituency interests, and individual evaluations of policies mediate the impact of party affiliation. The challenge to party leadership of reaping the potential rewards of party support is among the greatest faced by any president.

Obstacles to Party Unity

The strategic position of the president as party leader makes members of his party biased in his direction and leads them to form the core of nearly every winning coalition in support of his policies. One might therefore conclude that

24. See Kingdon, *Congressmen's Voting Decisions*, p. 112.

the president's primary task as party leader was to exploit his potential support by mobilizing those in his party inclined to support him for partisan or ideological reasons, that mobilization rather than conversion was the president's principal strategic objective.

If the president had only to ensure that his fellow partisans showed up to vote in support of his policies, his role as party leader would be relatively straightforward and much less burdensome than it actually is; it would also have a considerably greater payoff. In reality there are obstacles to unity within the president's party in Congress that compete with the bonds of party and shared policy preferences. These obstacles also compose part of the president's strategic position as party leader. They force him to adopt an activist orientation toward party leadership and to devote his efforts to converting members of his party as much as to mobilizing them.

All presidents experience slippage in party cohesion in Congress. Members of the president's party often oppose him, even on foreign policy. Jimmy Carter put this dramatically when he recalled, "I learned the hard way that there was no party loyalty or discipline when a complicated or controversial issue was at stake—none."[25] A generation earlier, an aide in the office of legislative liaison in President Kennedy's White House made a detailed study of the prospects for the newly elected president's programs in the House. He concluded that they were "very bleak," despite the clear Democratic majority there.[26]

The primary obstacle to party cohesion in support of the president is the lack of consensus among his party's members on policies, especially if the president is a Democrat. This diversity of views often reflects the diversity of constituencies represented by party members. The frequent defection from support of Democratic presidents by the Southern Democrats, or "boll weevils," is one of the most prominent features of American politics. Tables 3.5 and 3.6 show the average annual support given to Democratic presidents by Northern and Southern Democrats in the House and Senate on nonunanimous and key votes. Tables 3.7 and 3.8 give summary measures of Northern and Southern Democratic support for Democratic presidents.

There are clear differences between the two wings of the Democratic party (table 3.7). Under Democratic presidents the intraparty differences actually exceed the interparty differences in the Senate and are only somewhat less than the partisan gap in the House (see table 3.3). The findings are similar for nonunanimous and key votes. Democratic presidents face a substantial challenge in obtaining support from Southern Democrats.

25. Jimmy Carter, *Keeping Faith: Memoirs of a President* (New York: Bantam, 1982), p. 80.
26. Quoted in Wayne, *The Legislative Presidency*, p. 174 n. 170.

TABLE 3.5   Northern and Southern Democratic Support for Democratic Presidents on Nonunanimous Votes (in Percent)

	House		Senate	
Year	Northern Democrats	Southern Democrats	Northern Democrats	Southern Democrats
1961	85	52	78	46
1962	83	53	73	46
1963	86	56	73	41
1964	89	58	81	25
1965	87	47	72	44
1966	78	41	60	36
1967	82	46	60	46
1968	74	42	53	31
1977	66	48	65	53
1978	71	50	68	50
1979	69	51	70	58
1980	66	54	62	56

Jimmy Carter experienced the smallest differences in intraparty support. In the House this was the result of his lower support from Northern Democrats, whereas in the Senate his smaller differences can be traced to his having the highest support among Southern Democrats of the three Democratic presidents. Because Carter was more moderate than Kennedy and Johnson, these findings are not surprising.

TABLE 3.6   Northern and Southern Democratic Support for Democratic Presidents on Key Votes (in Percent)

	House		Senate	
Year	Northern Democrats	Southern Democrats	Northern Democrats	Southern Democrats
1961	89	44	80	41
1962	89	47	74	25
1963	92	55	83	47
1964	90	46	80	30
1965	90	39	82	45
1966	79	40	77	39
1967	83	40	71	60
1968	64	33	64	31
1977	67	44	77	50
1978	67	46	71	52
1979	68	44	67	44
1980	52	46	63	52

TABLE 3.7 Aggregate Northern and Southern Democratic Support for Democratic Presidents (in Percent)

	House			Senate		
	Northern Democrats	*Southern Democrats*	*Difference*[a]	*Northern Democrats*	*Southern Democrats*	*Difference*
Nonunanimous Support	78	50	28	68	44	24
Key Votes	78	44	34	74	43	31

[a]Differences expressed in percentage points

TABLE 3.8 Northern and Southern Democratic Support for Individual Democratic Presidents (in Percent)

Nonunanimous Support

President	House			Senate		
	Northern Democrats	Southern Democrats	Difference[a]	Northern Democrats	Southern Democrats	Difference
Kennedy	85	54	31	75	44	31
Johnson	82	47	35	65	36	29
Carter	68	51	17	66	54	12

Key Votes

President	House			Senate		
	Northern Democrats	Southern Democrats	Difference[a]	Northern Democrats	Southern Democrats	Difference
Kennedy	90	49	41	79	38	41
Johnson	81	40	41	75	41	34
Carter	64	45	19	70	50	20

[a]Differences expressed in percentage points

Although Democratic chief executives are plagued with party divisions, Republican presidents often lack stable coalitions as well. As we noted earlier, Ronald Reagan received nearly unanimous support from his party in Congress on his proposals to reduce taxes and domestic policy expenditures in 1981. The next year, when he proposed legislation to increase taxes, restrict abortions and busing for integration, and allow school prayer, some Republicans were in the forefront of the opposition.

Thus the nature of the president's proposals influences the cohesion the president can expect from his party, regardless of differences among constituencies. The issues of the 1970s and 1980s, such as energy, welfare reform, financing of social security, deregulation, containment of medical costs, and the social issues mentioned above lack sizable constituencies, common underlying principles, or both. Yet these are a necessary basis for consensus among party members.[27]

The nature of issues helps explain Carter's difficulties with Congress. As a moderate Democratic president with Democratic majorities dominated by moderates in each house, one might have expected him to have a relatively easy time obtaining support for his policies. The disagreements among Democratic legislators were not based on traditional differences between liberals and conservatives, however. New policy proposals raised new questions and with them new cleavages within the party. As Jeff Fishel argues, Carter failed where the Democratic party failed to develop a coherent political vision and obtain the party's consensus around its central elements.[28]

A shift in the status of party members may present another obstacle to party unity. Just as regaining power may encourage party unity, having to share it may strain intraparty relations. When a party that has had a majority in Congress regains the White House, committee and floor leaders of that party typically will be less influential, because they will be expected to take their lead on major issues from the president. This may cause tensions within the party and make party discipline more difficult.[29] As one senior White House aide put it during Carter's tenure, "There is a lack of cohesion among Democrats in Congress which can be traced to the Nixon-Ford years, when they made their own decisions and had their own agenda. Those habits have become ingrained. Some members look upon themselves as chiefs of state or

27. See Carter, *Keeping Faith*, pp. 68–69.
28. Jeff Fishel, *Presidents and Promises* (Washington: Congressional Quarterly Press, 1985), pp. 197–200. See also Nigel Bowles, *The White House and Capitol Hill* (New York: Oxford University Press, 1987), pp. 198–199.
29. See Carter, *Keeping Faith*, p. 71.

Secretaries of the Treasury or Secretaries of State or Secretaries of Agriculture."[30]

Additional obstacles may confront a president trying to mobilize his party in Congress. If the president's party has just regained the presidency but remains a minority in Congress, its members need to adjust from their past stance as the opposition minority to one of a "governing" minority. This is not always easily done, as Richard Nixon found when he sought Republican votes for budget deficits.[31]

A different problem may result when members of the president's party desire to avoid identifying too closely with the White House. According to Ronald Reagan's chief of legislative liaison, Max Friedersdorf, "It's a fact of life, a lot of Senators and Congressmen who may have come in on the President's coattails realize that the best politics for them is to show a little daylight. A Congressman or Senator doesn't want to be seen as a rubber stamp."[32]

Further difficulties may result when the winning presidential candidate is not the natural leader of his party. Some presidents, such as Jimmy Carter, may have campaigned against the party establishment and not identified with whatever party program existed.[33] Such a new president may arrive in Washington amid an atmosphere of hostility and suspicion that is not conducive to intraparty harmony. Appeals for party loyalty under such conditions may fall on less than receptive ears.

The problem may run deeper than mere campaign strategy. Carter was burdened with having to move against the tide of his party and its historic practices, rhetoric, and ideology. He was forced to plead for budgetary restraint and choose among programs. The latter is always difficult for a Democratic chief executive, but especially so for Carter, who had to hold down domestic spending so he could increase defense spending. As one of his aides later wrote, "Jimmy Carter had the enormous misfortune to be a Democratic president who was required to acknowledge the existence of budgetary limits and to try to alter strong-running budgetary currents."[34]

30. Quoted in Dom Bonafede, "The Strained Relationship," *National Journal*, May 19, 1979, p. 830.

31. William Safire, *Before the Fall: An Inside View of the Pre-Watergate White House* (New York: Doubleday, 1975), p. 176. See also Joseph Martin, *My First Fifty Years in Politics* (New York: McGraw-Hill, 1960), p. 229.

32. Quoted in Bernard Weinraub, "Back in the Legislative Strategist's Saddle Again," *New York Times*, May 28, 1985, p. 10.

33. See Light, *The President's Agenda*, p. 51.

34. W. Bowman Cutter, "The Presidency and Economic Policy: A Tale of Two Budgets," in Michael Nelson, ed., *The Presidency and the Political System* (Washington: Congressional Quarterly Press, 1984), p. 479.

Although his Democratic predecessors Kennedy and Johnson could propose legislation that ran with the tide of their party's thinking, Carter had to fight that same tide. The differences in political environments were made poignantly clear in Carter's remarks at the dedication of the John F. Kennedy Library in Boston in 1979: "The world of 1980 is as different from what it was in 1960 as the world of 1960 was from that of 1940. . . . We have a keener appreciation of limits now; the limits of government, limits on the use of military power abroad; the limits on manipulating without harm to ourselves a delicate and a balanced natural environment. We are struggling with a profound transition from a time of abundance to a time of growing scarcity."[35]

In addition, Carter had to contend with a challenge from the leader of the Democratic left, Ted Kennedy.[36] This exacerbated intraparty tensions and greatly increased the president's difficulties in forging a coalition around moderate policy proposals. Ultimately, it may have cost him reelection. It is interesting that in 1984, when budgetary limitations were clear, the leading candidates for the Democratic nomination did not campaign on a platform reminiscent of Kennedy's. Unfortunately for Carter, his party lagged behind him in recognizing the new trends in American politics.

Both the psychological bond of shared party affiliation and the reinforcement of shared policy preferences increase the probability that members of the president's party in Congress will respond positively to his party leadership. Yet party ties are not determinative, and all presidents experience substantial slippage in party cohesion in Congress. Finally, a number of obstacles inhibit party unity behind a president's programs. A numerical majority is not the same as a philosophical majority.

This is the strategic position of the president as party leader. Presidential party leadership requires converting party members as well as mobilizing them, and the role of director is difficult to play.[37] In addition, a recurrent theme in presidential leadership is the chief executive attempting to reach out to members of the opposition party without alienating his own.

35. Quoted in James MacGregor Burns, *The Power to Lead: The Crisis of the American Presidency* (New York: Simon and Schuster, 1984), pp. 23–24.

36. See for example Joseph A. Califano, Jr., *Governing America* (New York: Simon and Schuster, 1981), chap. 3.

37. For a discussion of the importance of mobilization see Cary R. Covington, "Mobilizing Congressional Support for the President: Insights from the 1960s," *Legislative Studies Quarterly* 12 (February 1987): 77–95.

CHAPTER FOUR

The Two Presidencies

The potential impact of presidential party leadership is greatest in the realm of foreign policy. Yet one must be cautious in drawing inferences from this conclusion. Can one infer that members of Congress provide a president of their party with more support on foreign policy than on domestic policy? To examine this fundamental question, one must dig more deeply and address the venerable issue of the "two presidencies."

The thesis of the two presidencies is a staple of the literature on executive-legislative relations. In its original formulation in 1966, Aaron Wildavsky argued that since World War II presidential-congressional relations had been characterized by "two presidencies": one for domestic policy and the other for defense and foreign policy. In the latter areas presidents had much more success in dealing with Congress. Foreign and defense policies, because they were perceived as important and irreversible, generally received higher priority from presidents, who thus devoted more effort to obtaining approval for them. In addition, the secret nature of these issues limited opposition, as did the general lack of interest, weakness, division, and deference to the president of those who might oppose them.[1]

This perspective did not go unchallenged. By 1975 things looked different. Donald Peppers argued that less secrecy surrounded defense and foreign policy decisions, members of Congress were less deferential toward the president, and more persons outside the executive branch were willing and able to challenge him. The Vietnam War made Americans sensitive to defense and foreign policy and more reluctant to view the country's involvement in world affairs as urgent or irreversible. At the same time, it had shattered whatever

1. Aaron Wildavsky, "The Two Presidencies," *Trans-Action* 4 (December 1966): 7–14.

consensus might have existed within the United States on defense and foreign policy. Defense and foreign policy issues were also increasingly evaluated in terms of their domestic implications: the relations of the United States with oil-producing nations could affect the price Americans paid for petroleum, and the sale of wheat to the Soviet Union could raise the cost of many food products at home. International trade and even foreign aid often had important impacts on domestic policy. Similarly, energy, monetary, and environmental policies could have important consequences for other countries. The United States belonged to an increasingly interdependent world, and the distinction between policy areas was becoming blurred.[2]

Lance LeLoup and Steven Shull compared Wildavsky's data (covering 1948 to 1964) with similar data for the years 1965 to 1975. They found that the difference between the approval rates for domestic policy and foreign and defense policy had narrowed considerably. Although the approval rates were 70 percent on defense and foreign policy and 40 percent on domestic policy in the earlier period, the comparable figures later were 55 percent and 46 percent. On domestic policy, 50 percent of the social welfare proposals and 49 percent of the agricultural proposals were passed by Congress between 1953 and 1975, figures almost equal to the 55 percent for foreign and defense policy over the same time period.[3]

Later in the same year Lee Sigelman contributed to the literature on the two presidencies. He began by criticizing the general box scores that Wildavsky and LeLoup and Shull had employed to measure the passage of legislation, and suggested that scholars focus instead on the most significant votes. He examined the Key Votes identified by Congressional Quarterly on which the president took a stand and found little difference between the percentage of victories for domestic issues and that for foreign and defense issues over the period 1957–78.[4]

There matters have stood. Still unresolved are several basic questions: Are there two presidencies, or were there? Has the phenomenon varied over time? Equally important, what is (or was) the locus of any additional support for foreign and defense policy? Was it members of the president's party, the opposition party, or both? Finally, if there are or were two presidencies, what

2. Donald A. Peppers, " 'The Two Presidencies': Eight Years Later," in Aaron Wildavsky, ed., *Perspectives on the Presidency* (Boston: Little, Brown, 1975).

3. Lance T. LeLoup and Steven A. Shull, "Congress Versus the Executive: The 'Two Presidencies' Reconsidered," *Social Science Quarterly* 59 (March 1979): 704–719.

4. Lee Sigelman, "A Reassessment of the Two Presidencies Thesis," *Journal of Politics* 41 (November 1979): 1195–1205. See also the exchange between Shull and LeLoup, and Sigelman: Steven A. Shull and Lance T. LeLoup, "Reassessing the Reassessment: Comment on Sigelman's Note on the 'Two Presidencies' Thesis," *Journal of Politics* 43 (May 1981): 563–546; Lee Sigelman, "Response to Critics," *Journal of Politics* 43 (May 1981): 565.

is their source? What gave foreign policy an advantage? One must answer these questions to understand the two presidencies and presidential party leadership in foreign affairs.

Measuring Presidential Success

Previous efforts at investigating the thesis of the two presidencies have been hindered by the use of aggregate measures of presidential success in Congress. If a yearly aggregate of presidential success in obtaining passage of legislation is employed, it will mask variability in support for the president among individual members of Congress or groups of members. This level of aggregation makes very tenuous inferences about the sources of support for the president. To search adequately for the sources of the two presidencies, one must therefore disaggregate presidential support.

In addition, one must discriminate between domestic policy issues and foreign and defense policy issues. This matter has received very little attention in the literature. Wildavsky, for example, simply asserts that Congress treats immigration and refugee matters primarily as domestic concerns.[5] Perhaps this is true on most such issues, but not all. This is not a trivial matter, because immigration and refugee proposals had the lowest probability of passage of any of Wildavsky's policy categories, and their inclusion under foreign policy would have notably altered his results.

To explore the area further, a colleague and I employed the original coding rules for each of the four indexes to code independently each vote on which the president took a stand from 1953 to 1986. Each vote was defined as involving primarily domestic policy or primarily foreign policy (which includes defense). We resolved our few differences in discussions. The range of issues is large, but most matters fall clearly into one category or the other. We decided that the space program, veterans benefits, and civil defense were domestic policy issues. In the end we had four foreign policy scores and four domestic policy scores for each member of Congress for each year in the period 1953–1986, a total of more than over 145,000 indexes.

Table 4.1 compares domestic and foreign policy support for the president among various groups in the House and the Senate, as measured by each of the four indexes. The figures for each group of members of Congress within each column show that no matter how one compares the indexes, they clearly have a great deal in common. Although this is especially true of the indexes Nonunanimous Support and Single-Vote Support, the differences among all four of the indexes are typically small. Presidential support seems to be due to factors that operate with a large degree of similarity across a wide range of roll

5. Wildavsky, "The Two Presidencies," p. 7.

TABLE 4.1   Presidential Domestic and Foreign Policy Support (in Percent)

Members of Congress	Support	House		Senate	
		Domestic	Foreign	Domestic	Foreign
All	Overall	53	58	55	63
	Nonunanimous	49	53	50	54
	Single-Vote	49	53	50	52
	Key Votes	49	52	52	55
Democrats	Overall	51	57	48	58
	Nonunanimous	47	53	42	48
	Single-Vote	46	52	41	46
	Key Votes	48	50	43	48
Republicans	Overall	56	59	60	67
	Nonunanimous	51	53	58	59
	Single-Vote	51	53	57	57
	Key Votes	51	55	59	61
Northern Democrats	Overall	54	59	49	58
	Nonunanimous	50	57	42	48
	Single-Vote	49	56	41	47
	Key Votes	52	54	43	48
Southern Democrats	Overall	48	55	48	59
	Nonunanimous	42	48	43	49
	Single-Vote	41	47	42	48
	Key Votes	42	45	43	51

calls. In the interests of economy and clarity, the best approach is again to use the indexes Nonunanimous Support and Key Votes in conjunction with each other.

Describing the Two Presidencies

There is good reason to hypothesize that the concept of the two presidencies is time-bound, characterizing only most of the 1950s and the early 1960s. Many authors have discussed the assertiveness of Congress in foreign affairs since the mid-1960s.[6] Yet these authors have not made systematic comparisons between support for foreign policy and support for domestic policy, so the

6. See for example Ronald C. Moe and Steven C. Teel, "Congress as Policy-Maker: A Necessary Reappraisal," in Ronald C. Moe, ed., *Congress and the President* (Pacific Palisades, Calif.: Goodyear, 1971); John F. Manley, "The Rise of Congress's Foreign Policy-Making," *Annals of the American Academy of Political and Social Science* 337 (1971): 60–70; Edward A. Kolodziej, "Congress and Foreign Policy: The Nixon Years," in Harvey C. Mansfield, Sr., ed., *Congress against the President* (New York: Praeger, 1975); I. M. Destler, "Executive-Congressional Conflict in Foreign Policy: Explaining It, Coping with It," in Lawrence C. Dodd and Bruce I. Oppenheimer, eds., *Congress Reconsidered?* 3d ed. (Washington: Congressional Quarterly Press, 1985); Thomas M. Franck and Edward Weisband, *Foreign Policy by Congress* (New York: Oxford University Press, 1979).

thesis of the two presidencies persists in the literature, in obvious opposition to arguments of a less deferential Congress than in the administrations of Eisenhower and Kennedy.

In addition, those who have studied the two presidencies have been unable because of their use of aggregate measures of support to investigate where any additional support lies for the president on foreign policy. The thesis of the two presidencies draws no distinction between members of the opposition and members of the presidential party, and thus implies that all members of Congress are more supportive of the White House on foreign policy than on domestic policy. At the same time, scholars have commented often on bipartisanship in foreign policy, especially before the Vietnam War.[7] It is possible that any increase in support for the president's foreign policy comes from the opposition party. If this is the case, it is an important refinement to the argument of the two presidencies and limits the scope of its impact.

Conversely, several studies have found that the greatest potential for the president as a party leader lies in the area of foreign policy. Because most members of Congress have more freedom from the pressures of constituency and interest groups in foreign policy than in domestic policy, they are less inhibited in following a president of their own party. Also, because the president has a greater personal responsibility for foreign affairs than domestic affairs, his prestige is more involved in votes on foreign policy. His fellow party members in Congress have more reason to support him in these matters to save him from embarrassment. This reasoning implies that we may expect additional support for the president from his own party on foreign policy.

In this section I analyze the four measures of presidential support to resolve these questions. The goal is to determine whether presidents actually receive more support in Congress on foreign policy than on domestic policy, what the locus is of any additional support, and whether this support has varied over time. The findings will have direct implications for understanding the source of the two presidencies.

To examine the question of the two presidencies one must disaggregate congressional support for the president's proposals. Tables 4.2–4.6 compare the success of administrations since that of Eisenhower in obtaining domestic and foreign policy support from each chamber in Congress and from various party groups within the House and the Senate.

During Eisenhower's administration (table 4.2), support for foreign policy exceeded that for domestic policy, owing entirely to Democrats in each

7. See for example Samuel P. Huntington, *The Common Defense* (New York: Columbia University Press, 1961); Julius Turner and Edward V. Schneier, Jr., *Party and Constituency: Pressures on Congress*, rev. ed. (Baltimore: Johns Hopkins University Press, 1970).

TABLE 4.2 Presidential Domestic and Foreign Policy Support in the Eisenhower Administration (in Percent)

Members of Congress	Support	House			Senate		
		Domestic	Foreign	Difference[a]	Domestic	Foreign	Difference
All	Nonunanimous	50	56	6	50	56	6
	Key Votes	49	58	9	49	59	10
Democrats	Nonunanimous	39	56	17	32	50	18
	Key Votes	41	55	14	27	53	26
Republicans	Nonunanimous	66	57	−9	70	64	−6
	Key Votes	63	61	−2	74	65	−9
Northern Democrats	Nonunanimous	44	69	15	29	56	27
	Key Votes	50	68	18	23	59	36
Southern Democrats	Nonunanimous	31	37	6	36	40	4
	Key Votes	28	35	7	33	44	11

[a]Foreign policy support minus domestic policy support

TABLE 4.3 Presidential Domestic and Foreign Policy Support in the Kennedy and Johnson Administrations (in Percent)

Members of Congress	Support	House			Senate		
		Domestic	Foreign	Difference[a]	Domestic	Foreign	Difference
All	Nonunanimous	54	55	1	53	52	−1
	Key Votes	51	58	7	58	57	−1
Democrats	Nonunanimous	72	71	−1	61	56	−5
	Key Votes	70	72	2	66	60	−6
Republicans	Nonunanimous	24	32	8	37	44	7
	Key Votes	22	36	14	41	51	10
Northern Democrats	Nonunanimous	83	84	1	70	64	−6
	Key Votes	84	87	3	79	70	−9
Southern Democrats	Nonunanimous	51	46	−5	40	40	0
	Key Votes	43	43	0	39	41	2

[a]Foreign policy support minus domestic policy support

TABLE 4.4   Presidential Domestic and Foreign Policy Support in the Nixon and Ford Administrations (in Percent)

Members of Congress	Support	House			Senate		
		Domestic	Foreign	Difference[a]	Domestic	Foreign	Difference
All	Nonunanimous	48	52	4	43	51	8
	Key Votes	47	48	1	44	51	7
Democrats	Nonunanimous	38	45	7	31	40	9
	Key Votes	35	38	3	31	41	10
Republicans	Nonunanimous	65	62	-3	61	68	7
	Key Votes	65	63	-2	63	66	3
Northern Democrats	Nonunanimous	34	43	9	25	31	6
	Key Votes	31	31	0	23	32	9
Southern Democrats	Nonunanimous	45	51	6	46	62	16
	Key Votes	48	54	6	53	63	10

[a]Foreign policy support minus domestic policy support

TABLE 4.5 Presidential Domestic and Foreign Policy Support in the Carter Administration (in Percent)

Members of Congress	Support	House			Senate		
		Domestic	Foreign	Difference[a]	Domestic	Foreign	Difference
All	Nonunanimous	51	50	−1	52	54	2
	Key Votes	49	48	−1	52	53	1
Democrats	Nonunanimous	63	61	−2	62	66	4
	Key Votes	61	55	−6	66	64	−2
Republicans	Nonunanimous	29	32	−3	39	37	−2
	Key Votes	26	35	9	32	37	5
Northern Democrats	Nonunanimous	68	66	−2	65	70	5
	Key Votes	68	59	−9	72	67	−5
Southern Democrats	Nonunanimous	52	47	−5	54	56	2
	Key Votes	43	45	2	48	56	6

[a]Foreign policy support minus domestic policy support

TABLE 4.6 Presidential Domestic and Foreign Policy Support in the Reagan Administration, 1981–86 (in Percent)

Members of Congress	Support	House			Senate		
		Domestic	Foreign	Difference[a]	Domestic	Foreign	Difference
All	Nonunanimous	42	52	10	56	56	0
	Key Votes	51	46	-5	57	53	-4
Democrats	Nonunanimous	27	33	6	34	32	-2
	Key Votes	36	25	-11	33	25	-8
Republicans	Nonunanimous	63	77	14	75	76	1
	Key Votes	70	75	5	77	77	0
Northern Democrats	Nonunanimous	24	23	-1	30	26	-4
	Key Votes	31	14	-17	29	16	-13
Southern Democrats	Nonunanimous	35	58	23	44	50	6
	Key Votes	49	51	2	46	52	16

[a]Foreign policy support minus domestic policy support

house, especially Northern Democrats. In three of four cases, Republicans gave the president notably less support for foreign policy than for domestic policy.

The administrations of Kennedy and Johnson displayed the mirror image of this pattern (table 4.3): it was the Republicans who gave the president increased support on foreign policy. The overall impact of the support of the opposition party was less than under Eisenhower, because Republicans were a distinct minority in each chamber throughout the eight years under Democratic presidents. The advantage for foreign policy was also much less in the Democratic administrations of the 1960s than in the Republican administrations the 1950s.

The administrations of Nixon and Ford were a period of transition for the two presidencies. The extra support for foreign policy proposals that Eisenhower enjoyed from Northern Democrats was now greatly diminished and of modest proportions (table 4.4). Southern Democrats and Republicans once again provided modest or no additional support for foreign policy, with the exception of Southern Democrats in the Senate on issues of Nonunanimous Support.

TABLE 4.7   Summary of Differences between Foreign and Domestic
            Policy Presidential Support (in Percent)

	Nonunanimous Support House		Senate	
Administration	President's Party	Opposition Party	President's Party	Opposition Party
Eisenhower	−9	17	−6	18
Kennedy and Johnson	−1	8	−5	7
Nixon and Ford	−3	7	7	9
Carter	−2	3	4	−2
Reagan (1981–86)	14	6	1	−2

	Key Votes House		Senate	
Administration	President's Party	Opposition Party	President's Party	Opposition Party
Eisenhower	−2	14	−9	26
Kennedy and Johnson	2	14	−6	10
Nixon and Ford	−2	3	3	10
Carter	−6	9	−2	5
Reagan (1981–86)	5	−11	0	−8

Jimmy Carter did not enjoy much in the way of benefits from the two presidencies (table 4.5). He often received less support on foreign policy than on domestic policy, and we find the advantage Republicans awarded Kennedy and Johnson slipping to typically modest levels. Democrats did not pick up the slack.

Ronald Reagan's tenure as president did not witness a significant revival of the two presidencies. In both houses the balance of support between domestic policy and foreign policy was mixed (table 4.6) and the differences were in both directions. Only Southern Democrats provided the president with consistently more support on foreign policy than on domestic policy, and Southern Democrats are of course the smallest of the three partisan groups.

Table 4.7 summarizes findings regarding the relative strength of domestic and foreign policy support over the last three decades. The president's party has never been a reliable resource of extra support for his foreign policies, in most instances providing less than for his domestic policies. On the other hand, the opposition party has been the locus of additional support for the White House's foreign policies. Yet this additional support has diminished substantially in both quantity and reliability since its peak in the 1950s.

Explaining the Two Presidencies

Specifying the locus and variance of the two presidencies is essential if one is to explain the occurrence and decline of the two presidencies, but it does not in itself constitute an explanation. To understand further the two presidencies one must focus on alternative explanations for the data displayed in tables 4.2–4.7.

Two questions that require attention are first, what accounts for the considerable additional support that Eisenhower received in foreign policy, and second, why have Eisenhower's successors not enjoyed this same advantage?

Where Did the Two Presidencies Come From?

There are three potential explanations for the flourishing of the two presidencies during Eisenhower's administration. One line of reasoning is that the 1950s were an era of bipartisanship and deference toward the president in foreign policy. Eisenhower's role as a leading figure on the world stage before he entered the White House and the consensus generated by the Cold War simply encouraged partisan differences in Congress to be set aside when foreign policy matters were considered. If this reasoning is correct, we should find similar levels of support for the president's foreign policy from members of both parties, and from Northern and Southern Democrats.

Nevertheless, there are clear differences between Democratic foreign policy support and Republican foreign policy support in the Senate, and very substantial differences between Southern Democrats and Republicans, and Southern Democrats and Northern Democrats, in each chamber. Although Northern Democrats and Republicans gave similar levels of support, one should not assume that this is a result of bipartisanship. In addition, the theory of bipartisanship and deference does not explain why Northern Democratic support exceeds that for Republicans in the House.

A second explanation emphasizes the relative advantage of the president in his efforts to obtain passage of his policies. It is essentially the argument of Wildavsky that a president devoting his full efforts to foreign policy issues, which are of a high priority, is too much for weak, meek, poorly informed potential congressional opponents to withstand.[8] If this hypothesis is correct, then there should not have been a decline of the two presidencies until the conditions underlying the president's advantages changed.

Yet the two presidencies declined while the president's relative advantages remained. One can hardly argue that foreign policy was less salient in the 1960s than in the previous decade. Nor could one maintain that Lyndon Johnson was less skilled in dealing with Congress than Dwight Eisenhower. Further, the reforms in Congress that complicated the president's task of persuasion and increased the information resources of Congress occurred in the decade following the 1960s. Nevertheless, the two presidencies did diminish notably after Eisenhower's tenure in office, and thus the thesis of relative advantage does not provide a compelling explanation for the thriving of the two presidencies in the 1950s.

A third explanation for the two presidencies in the 1950s focuses on the substance of the president's policies. Perhaps Eisenhower received additional support from Democrats on foreign policy simply because they agreed with his policies. Ideally, one would test this hypothesis by assessing the ideological character of Eisenhower's foreign policies and the ideological leanings of each member of Congress, and then determining whether a president's policies were congruent with the views of representatives and senators. It is very difficult, however, to place precisely on an ideological scale complex sets of foreign policies and views on them, and doing so is well beyond the scope of this study.

It is nonetheless reasonable to accept the widely shared view of Eisenhower's foreign policy as internationalist and, in the terms of the times, liberal. If the hypothesis of policy substance is correct, we should find that liberals in Congress gave the Republican president unusually strong support, while

8. Wildavsky, "The Two Presidencies."

conservatives (especially conservative Democrats), voting without the pull of party, gave him unusually weak support. This is exactly what happened. Table 4.2 shows that Northern Democrats, almost all of whom were liberal, gave the president impressive levels of foreign policy support considering that they were members of the opposition party, whereas Southern Democrats, almost all of whom were conservative, awarded him considerably less support, less than for any future Republican president. Republicans, torn between their generally conservative views and the policies of their party leader, accorded the president less support than members of their party gave to later Republican presidents. In the House they actually gave Eisenhower less support than did the Northern Democrats.

Although the question cannot be resolved definitively, the evidence supports the argument that the two presidencies of the 1950s were a product of the substance of President Eisenhower's foreign policies. It does not support the hypotheses emphasizing bipartisanship and deference or the relative advantages of the chief executive. As the discussion of our third hypothesis demonstrates, similar levels of support do not necessarily indicate bipartisanship.

The weakness of the hypothesis of bipartisanship and deference should not come as a surprise. In their work on the uses of history, Neustadt and May term the often cited bipartisan foreign policy consensus of the administrations of Truman and Eisenhower "almost pure fantasy." Instead, they were characterized by "bitter, partisan, and utterly consensus-free debate."[9]

Why Did the Two Presidencies Diminish?

Probably the most common explanation of why the two presidencies diminished focuses on the war in Vietnam. According to this well-known argument, the war shattered a bipartisan consensus on foreign policy, energized congressional opposition to the chief executive and skepticism of him, and encouraged the development of staff resources in the legislature. Under these conditions one would expect a broad decrease in support for the president's foreign policy.

Nevertheless, the two presidencies were never based on bipartisanship, deference, or relative advantage, and general support for presidential foreign policy did not fall after Vietnam. The level of foreign policy support for the president is striking (table 4.8). Despite all the differences among the presidents and the composition of Congress and the extraordinary events through which the country passed, support for the president's foreign policies has

9. Richard E. Neustadt and Ernest R. May, *Thinking in Time: The Uses of History for Decision Makers* (New York: Free Press, 1986), pp. 258–259.

TABLE 4.8   Presidential Foreign Policy Support by Administration
             (in Percent)

Administration	House Nonunanimous Support	House Key Votes	Senate Nonunanimous Support	Senate Key Votes
Eisenhower	56	58	56	59
Kennedy and Johnson	55	58	52	57
Nixon and Ford	52	48	51	51
Carter	50	48	54	53
Reagan (1981–86)	52	46	56	53

remained remarkably stable (with the partial exception of Nonunanimous Support in the House).

There is no question that the Vietnam War was traumatic for the nation. Certainly it was a catalyst for more extensive and intensive debate over foreign policy, and for the potential of greater restraints on the president. Yet it does not follow that in the end the president received less support from Congress, any more than the increased use of the legislative veto in foreign policy matters led to an increase in actual constraints on the White House.

To explain the decline in the two presidencies following the Eisenhower administration, one must focus on the conditions that underlay it in the 1950s. The phenomenon of two presidencies was confined to the opposition party. Eisenhower's combination of conservative domestic policies and internationalist foreign policies elicited support from liberal Democrats for the latter, creating the gap between domestic policy support and foreign policy support on which the two presidencies depend.

Later Republican presidents continued to offer conservative domestic policies, but their hawkish foreign policies no longer appealed to Northern Democrats. As tables 4.4 and 4.6 illustrate, Nixon, Ford, and Reagan did obtain relatively strong support from Southern Democrats (typically they received more support than Kennedy or Johnson). Thus there are some signs of the two presidencies. Yet the consistent responses of conservative Southern Democrats to conservative Republican presidents inhibited the development of systematic differences between foreign policy support and domestic policy support.

Democratic presidents simply received low support on both foreign and domestic policy from Republicans, who remained overwhelmingly conservative. Kennedy, Johnson, and Carter all failed to offer to the opposition foreign policies that it found congenial. This undermined the basis for the two presidencies.

Employing new measures of presidential support and disaggregating congressional behavior substantially increases one's understanding of the two presidencies. On the descriptive level, the two presidencies did flourish under President Eisenhower, but the additional support for foreign policy that characterizes the two presidencies has been modest since the 1960s and no longer reliably appears. Moreover, the locus of additional support for foreign policy has always been the opposition party. The president's party in Congress has never provided him with an additional increment of support for his foreign policy proposals, and the phenomenon of the two presidencies therefore does not improve his strategic position as party leader.

Equally important are alternative explanations for the two presidencies and their decline. Contrary to the conventional wisdom, the source of the two presidencies is not congressional bipartisanship or deference in foreign affairs, nor the relative advantages of the president in foreign policy making. Instead, the two presidencies appear to be a natural outgrowth of a president proposing foreign policies, but not domestic policies, that appeal to a substantial segment of the opposition party. Similarly, the decline of the two presidencies cannot be attributed to the trauma of Vietnam. Simply stated, when the appeal of a president's foreign policies to the opposition diminishes, so do the two presidencies.

There is less to the two presidencies than meets the eye. As a description of an important characteristic in national policy making, it was largely a short-term phenomenon. As an explanation for the gap between foreign policy support and domestic policy support, it confused the forest with the trees. Presidents have enjoyed no free ride in the foreign policy realm. They have generally obtained support the old-fashioned way: by appealing to independent power holders with the substance of their policies.

CHAPTER FIVE

Leading the Party

The president's strategic position as a party leader is reasonably favorable. His party cohorts typically want to support his policies and despite obstacles usually do. Yet Richard Neustadt reminds us that "What the Constitution separates our political parties do not combine."[1] Presidents cannot simply assume support from members of their party in Congress: the White House must lead them. The challenge of presidential party leadership remains just as great and important today as it was three decades ago, when Neustadt wrote his treatise on presidential power.

An examination of the president's leadership of his party in Congress must focus on means of leadership and explore the use and effectiveness of personal appeals to partisans, working with congressional party leaders, providing favors, and levying sanctions. It must also address the role of bipartisanship in partisan leadership. Because presidents cannot rely completely on support from their party members in Congress, they typically solicit votes from the opposition party. Such a strategy is not without its costs, and provides additional challenges for party leadership.

Appeals to Partisans

The inclination of members of Congress to support a president of their party certainly eases the path of presidential party leadership. It provides an open door for presidential persuasion. To exploit partisan sympathies, presidents sometimes make personal appeals for support to individuals or small groups in Congress who share their party affiliation.

1. Richard E. Neustadt, *Presidential Power: The Politics of Leadership from FDR to Carter* (New York: John Wiley and Sons, 1980), p. 26.

According to Neustadt, "when the chips are down, there is no substitute for the President's own footwork, his personal negotiation, his direct appeal, his voice and no other's on the telephone."[2] Members of Congress are typically impressed when the president calls them or invites them for a personal discussion at the White House. This is a rare occurrence for most of them, and a request for support from the chief executive naturally increases their sense of self-esteem.[3] They are after all dealing directly with the president and the leader of their party.

Despite their potential utility, personal appeals from the president for support are not common. A legislative aide to Lyndon Johnson commented, "it was a very rare thing that he called a member of the House respecting a vote."[4] Because this picture is quite different from that portrayed by the conventional wisdom, it bears an explanation.

Some presidents, Richard Nixon being the most notable, have found it difficult to press legislators individually for their votes, and others, such as Eisenhower, Kennedy, and Carter, were less likely to engage in personal appeals for votes than were Johnson, Ford, and Reagan.[5]

Even if the president is enthusiastic about calling for support, his aides must be concerned about conserving the uniqueness of a presidential appeal.

2. Richard E. Neustadt, "Presidency and Legislation: Planning the President's Program," in Aaron Wildavsky, ed., *The Presidency* (Boston: Little, Brown, 1969), 596.

3. See Lawrence F. O'Brien, *No Final Victories* (New York: Ballantine, 1975), p. 111; Jack Valenti, *A Very Human President* (New York: W. W. Norton, 1975), p. 178; Jack Bell, *The Johnson Treatment* (New York: Dell, 1965), p. 37; Eric F. Goldman, *The Tragedy of Lyndon Johnson* (New York: Dell, 1974), p. 71; "Turning Screws: Winning Votes in Congress," *Congressional Quarterly Weekly Report*, April 24, 1976, p. 954.

4. Henry Hall Wilson, interview by Joe B. Frantz, April 11, 1973, transcript, p. 9, Lyndon Baines Johnson Library, Austin, Tex. See also Harold Barefoot Sanders, interview by Joe B. Frantz, March 24, 1969, tape 2, transcript, pp. 5, 8, Lyndon Baines Johnson Library, Austin, Tex.

5. See George C. Edwards III, *Presidential Influence in Congress* (San Francisco: W. H. Freeman, 1980), pp. 124–127, 178 and sources cited therein; Harold Barefoot Sanders, interview by Joe B. Frantz, November 3, 1969, tape 3, transcript, pp. 13–14, Lyndon Baines Johnson Library, Austin, Tex; Carl B. Albert, interview by Dorothy Pierce McSweeny, August 13, 1969, interview 4, transcript, p. 22, Lyndon Baines Johnson Library, Austin, Tex.; Carl B. Albert, interview by Dorothy Pierce McSweeny, June 10, 1969, interview 2, transcript, pp. 11–12, Lyndon Baines Johnson Library, Austin, Tex.; Hale Boggs, interview by Charles T. Morrissey, May 10, 1964, transcript, p. 26, John F. Kennedy Library, Boston; Mike Mansfield, interview by Seth P. Tillman, June 23, 1964, transcript, p. 28, John F. Kennedy Library, Boston; Jack Valenti, interview by Joe B. Frantz, March 3, 1971, interview 4, transcript, p. 28, Lyndon Baines Johnson Library, Austin, Tex.; Norman J. Ornstein, "The Open Congress Meets the President," in Anthony King, ed., *Both Ends of the Avenue: The Presidency, the Executive Branch, and Congress in the 1980s* (Washington: American Enterprise Institute, 1983), pp. 208–209; "White House's Lobbying Apparatus . . . Produces Impressive Tax Vote Victory," *Congressional Quarterly Weekly Report*, August 1, 1981, pp. 1372–1373; "House Ratifies Savings Plan in Stunning Reagan Victory," *Congressional Quarterly Weekly Report*, June 27, 1981, p. 1127.

Calls from the president must be relatively rare to maintain their usefulness. If the president calls too often, his calls will have less impact. In addition, members may begin to expect calls, for which the president has limited time. As one former legislative aide at the White House remarked, if a president calls a member of the House regarding a vote, 434 members cry out, "Why didn't he call me?"[6]

An aide to President Carter made the same point: "You see, you have to be careful when you use the president. A visit with the president or a call from the president has to be an event in the life of a senator or representative, or it loses its magic. Or they say, 'Why should I give you a commitment? I want to talk to the President. John has talked to the President. And George has talked to the President. Are you taking us for granted?' You've got to be sure that you don't squander him."[7]

Ronald Reagan was the most active president in terms of appealing for support to individual members of Congress, especially in 1981. He may have been too zealous, however. Pamela J. Turner, the White House's chief lobbyist in the Senate, explained, "People now have the idea that if the president doesn't call them personally or see them, the White House doesn't care. Maybe we did our job too well in that first year."[8]

There are other potential costs to presidential appeals. Some members of Congress may resent high-level pressure being applied to them. On the other hand, they may exploit a call to extract a favor from the president and say they are uncertain about an issue. President Nixon was reacting against this form of bargaining during the battle over the confirmation of G. Harrold Carswell as a justice on the Supreme Court when he exclaimed, "The President is not going to lobby each of these Senators for this nomination. I'm not going to have Richard Schweiker in here, for God's sake. Marlow Cook has a fellow he wants to be a judge; he'll end up trading me that man for Carswell. Prouty has one too. Tell them they get no judge if they don't vote for Carswell."[9]

In addition, the president does not want to commit his prestige to a bill by personally lobbying and then lose. In 1987 President Reagan went to Capitol Hill to plead with thirteen Republican senators not to vote to override his veto of a highway bill. When not one of the thirteen supported him in the final

6. Wilson, interview by Frantz, transcript, pp. 8–9.

7. Quoted in Mark A. Peterson, "Congressional Responses to Presidential Proposals: Impact, Effort, and Politics" (paper presented at the Annual Meeting of the Midwest Political Science Association, Chicago, April 1986), p. 20.

8. Quoted in "White House Lobbyists Find Congress Less Supportive," *Congressional Quarterly Weekly Report*, June 16, 1984, p. 1433.

9. Quoted in John Ehrlichman, *Witness to Power* (New York: Simon and Schuster, 1982), p. 126.

showdown, the resulting stories of the president's failure did him little good.

Also, the credibility of the president's staff in speaking for him will decrease the more the president speaks for himself.[10] As President Carter explained, "I would try not to get involved in that process unless the legislation was important enough to warrant my direct consideration."[11] Thus most direct White House lobbying is done by presidential aides, not the president himself.

Presidents typically make personal appeals to individual legislators only after the long process of lining up votes is almost done and a last few votes are needed to win on an important issue.[12] These situations usually arise only a few times a year. When they do call, presidents focus on uncommitted or weakly committed members of Congress or, to make the most of their efforts, on key members who provide cues for others.[13]

Given the separation of powers, presidents are not in a position to issue orders to their congressional troops. Rather, they rely on the soft sell, as President Reagan did when calling members of Congress on the eve of a budget vote in 1981: "Gee, I know it's late back there and I'm sorry to bother you. I hear you're still on the fence. If I could answer any questions, I'd be happy to. I know you've been under a lot of pressure. But I hope you can find your way clear to supporting us tomorrow."[14]

When presidents do make personal appeals for support, they may very well receive it. President Reagan, for example, appeared to have great success with his appeals on his budget and taxing proposals and the sale of AWACS

10. Stephen J. Wayne, *The Legislative Presidency* (New York: Harper and Row, 1978), p. 151; John W. Kingdon, *Congressmen's Voting Decisions* (New York: Harper and Row, 1973), pp. 184, 187; Malcolm E. Jewell, *Senatorial Politics and Foreign Policy* (Lexington: University of Kentucky Press, 1962), pp. 160–161; Harry McPherson, *A Political Education* (Boston: Little, Brown, 1972), p. 192; Abraham Holtzman, *Legislative Liaison: Executive Leadership in Congress* (Chicago: Rand McNally, 1970), p. 247.

11. Quoted in Peterson, "Congressional Response to Presidential Proposals," p. 20.

12. See for example Doris Kearns, *Lyndon Johnson and the American Dream* (New York: Harper and Row, 1976), p. 235; William Chapman, "LBJ's Way: Tears, Not Arm-Twists," *Washington Post*, October 17, 1965, sec. E, p. 1; Dom Bonafede, "Ford's Lobbyists Expect Democrats to Revise Tactics," *National Journal*, June 21, 1975, p. 926; Merlo J. Pusey, *Eisenhower the President* (New York: Macmillan, 1956), p. 212; Stephen Horn, *Unused Power: The Work of the Senate Committee on Appropriations* (Washington: Brookings Institution, 1970), p. 195; Peterson, "Congressional Response to Presidential Proposals," pp. 18, 20.

13. Albert, interview by McSweeny, interview 4, transcript, p. 23; Kearns, *Lyndon Johnson*, pp. 234–236; Wayne, *The Legislative Presidency*, p. 151; Bonafede, "Ford's Lobbyists," p. 926; Lyndon B. Johnson, *The Vantage Point: Perspectives on the Presidency, 1963–1969* (New York: Popular Library, 1971), p. 459; Wilson, interview by Frantz, transcript, pp. 11–13.

14. Quoted in Hedrick Smith, "Coping with Congress," *New York Times Magazine*, August 9, 1981, p. 16.

(Advanced Warning and Control System) planes to Saudi Arabia in 1981.[15] Yet there are also many failures.[16] Sometimes members of Congress will not even listen to their party leader. In 1984 a freshman representative, Nancy Johnson, refused to attend a private meeting with Ronald Reagan about the MX missile.[17] In one instance the chairman of the House Appropriations Committee refused even to take a call from President Johnson.[18] Another time, the Senate majority leader, Mike Mansfield, asked Johnson to talk directly to the president's old friend, Sen. Richard Russell. Johnson complained to a White House legislative aide, "Well, goddamit . . . I couldn't get Dick Russell to vote with me when I was majority leader. What makes Mike think he's going to vote with me now?"[19]

Another limitation on the effectiveness of appeals is the resistance of representatives and senators to acting as rubber stamps. According to the chairman of the House Republican Policy Committee, Richard Cheney, "You can lean on the guys only so many times a month. . . . Every once in a while the troops have to rear up and establish their independence."[20]

Despite the prestige of their office, their position as party leader, their personal persuasiveness, and their strong personalities, presidents often meet resistance to their appeals for support. Personal appeals by themselves are useful but unreliable instruments for passing legislation. Later I will show that the context in which appeals are made is important, and the political environment of the president's efforts to persuade has a significant influence on both their use and their success.

15. See for example Ornstein, "The Open Congress Meets the President," p. 206 and sources cited therein; Anthony King, "A Mile and a Half Is a Long Way," in King, ed., *Both Ends of the Avenue* (Washington, American Enterprise Institute, 1983), pp. 264–265; "White House Lobbying Apparatus . . . Produces Impressive Tax Vote Victory," *Congressional Quarterly Weekly Report*, August 1, 1981, p. 1372. On the success of appeals of other presidents see McPherson, *A Political Education*, p. 192; Neil MacNeil, *Forge of Democracy* (New York: David McKay, 1963), p. 265; Horn, *Unused Power*, p. 195; Everett M. Dirksen, interview by Joe B. Frantz, July 30, 1969, tape 2, transcript, p. 7, Lyndon Baines Johnson Library, Austin, Tex.

16. See for example Edwards, *Presidential Influence in Congress*, p. 128 and sources cited therein; "Winning One for the Gipper," *Newsweek*, August 30, 1982, p. 25; James A. Miller, *Running in Place* (New York: Simon and Schuster, 1981), pp. 45–46; Stephen E. Ambrose, *Eisenhower the President* (New York: Simon and Schuster, 1984), p. 116.

17. "How Two GOP Freshmen in the House . . . Rate the White House Lobbying Effort," *Congressional Quarterly Weekly Report*, June 16, 1984, p. 1431.

18. Albert, interview by McSweeny, interview 2, transcript, pp. 11–12.

19. Mike Manatos, interview by Joe B. Frantz, August 25, 1969, transcript, p. 18, Lyndon Baines Johnson Library, Austin, Tex.

20. Quoted in "Reagan's First Defeat," *Newsweek*, September 20, 1982, p. 26. See also Wilson, interview by Frantz, transcript, p. 11.

Working with Congressional Leaders

Each party has floor and committee leaders in the House and Senate, and in theory those from the president's party should be a valuable resource for their party's leader in the White House.[21] Because of their perceptions of their roles, because they are susceptible to the same sentiments and pressures toward loyalty as are other members of Congress, and because their reputations for passing legislation give them a clear stake in the president's success, floor leaders of the president's party in Congress are usually very supportive of the White House. In the month before Ronald Reagan's inauguration, for example, the new Senate majority leader, Howard Baker, declared, "I intend to try to help Ronald Reagan [carry out] the commitments he made during the campaign."[22]

In speaking of President Kennedy, Senate Majority Leader Mike Mansfield reflected that he could not remember a single issue on which he had disagreed with the White House: "Not one. I was with him all the way."[23] Similarly, Carl Albert, the House majority leader, recalls, "From the day the leadership first met with President Kennedy, he had the complete support, unswerving support, of the entire Democratic leadership in both branches of Congress. . . . I did everything I knew how to do to help make his program a success."[24]

Table 5.1 shows the average support for the president of the floor leader and whip of his party in each house and compares it with the support from his party as a whole (the Speaker of the House is not included here because he

21. For one attempt to examine this question see Stephen L. Hayes et al., "Presidential Support among Senatorial Leaders and Followers," *American Politics Quarterly* 12 (April 1984): 195–209.

22. Quoted in James L. Sundquist, *The Decline and Resurgence of Congress* (Washington: Brookings Institution, 1981), p. 402. See also Allen Schick, "How the Budget Was Won and Lost," in Norman J. Ornstein, ed., *President and Congress: Assessing Reagan's First Year* (Washington: American Enterprise Institute, 1982), p. 18; I. M. Destler, "Reagan, Congress, and Foreign Policy in 1981," in Ornstein, ed., *President and Congress*, p. 76; Stephen J. Wayne, "Congressional Liaison in the Reagan White House: A Preliminary Assessment of the First Year," in Ornstein, ed., *President and Congress*, pp. 57, 63–64.

23. Mansfield, interview by Tillman, transcript, pp. 36–37.

24. Carl B. Albert, interview by Charles T. Morrissey, May 7, 1965, transcript, p. 21, John F. Kennedy Library, Boston; see also p. 20. Albert, interview by McSweeny, interview 2, transcript, pp. 6–7. On other presidents see Sinclair, *Majority Leadership in the U.S. House* (Baltimore: Johns Hopkins University Press, 1983), pp. 119–120; Gerald R. Ford, *A Time to Heal* (New York: Harper and Row, 1979), p. 89; Carl B. Albert, interview by Dorothy Pierce McSweeny, July 9, 1969, interview 3, transcript, pp. 6–7, Lyndon Baines Johnson Library, Austin, Tex.; Carl B. Albert, interview by Dorothy Pierce McSweeny, April 28, 1969, interview 1, transcript, p. 24, Lyndon Baines Johnson Library, Austin, Tex.

TABLE 5.1   Party and Party Leader Support for the President (in Percent)

		House Nonunanimous Support			Key Votes		
President	Party	Party Leaders	Party	Difference[a]	Party Leaders	Party	Difference
Eisenhower	R	76	65	11	78	65	13
Kennedy	D	90	73	17	96	74	22
Johnson	D	90	71	19	89	68	21
Nixon[b]	R	85	64	21	85	64	21
Ford[c]	R	88	68	20	96	70	26
Carter	D	79	63	16	79	59	20
Reagan[d]	R	83	68	15	91	74	17

		Senate Nonunanimous Support			Key Votes		
President	Party	Party Leaders	Party	Difference	Party Leaders	Party	Difference
Eisenhower	R	88	69	19	88	71	17
Kennedy	D	89	65	24	95	65	30
Johnson	D	71	56	15	77	65	12
Nixon[b]	R	78	65	13	82	67	15
Ford[c]	R	71	65	6	63	59	4
Carter	D	74	63	11	81	64	17
Reagan[d]	R	86	76	10	85	75	10

[a]Differences expressed in percentage points
[b]1969–73
[c]1975–76
[d]1981–86
R = Republican
D = Democrat

rarely votes).[25] In every instance the support of party leaders exceeds that of the party, often by sizable margins. Aside from being larger on the average in the House than in the Senate, there is little in the way of patterns in these margins. They do not favor systematically Republican or Democratic presidents or any individual president. For example, Eisenhower has the smallest margins in the House but the second largest in the Senate. Ford, on the other hand, has large margins in the House and very small ones in the Senate. Differences between presidents undoubtedly reflect both the nature of the

25. Senator Robert Taft, Senate majority leader in 1953, is excluded because his absences from votes distorted his support figures.

party cohorts with which they worked and the idiosyncrasies of the party leaders who served during their tenures.

Yet party floor leaders are not always dependable supporters. They certainly are not simple extensions of the White House. As one presidential aide said of Senate Majority Leader Robert Byrd in 1977, "God, is he independent. He ain't our man—he's the Senate's man."[26] President Eisenhower was opposed by many Republican congressional party leaders on some of his more significant domestic and foreign policies, such as aid to education, foreign trade, and budgetary matters, and he was unable to influence Joseph Martin (Speaker of the House and later minority leader) to involve more Republicans in party strategy and decision making.[27] Senate Majority Leader Mike Mansfield broke with President Johnson over the war in Vietnam and sustained his opposition for the rest of Johnson's term of office. Most of the House Republican leadership resisted President Reagan's pleas to support the tax reform bill in 1985, although it was the cornerstone of the president's second term in domestic policy.

Although sharing a party tie, a president and his party's leaders in Congress may be marching to different drummers. The process of winning a party's nomination for the presidency and the election itself does not require that a presidential candidate work with congressional party leaders, much less agree with them. Thus the new chief executive may well enter the White House without the leaders being committed to his policies.

The utility of congressional party leaders to the president may also be limited by the characteristics of the persons who occupy the positions. For example, Lyndon Johnson saw Senate Majority Leader Mike Mansfield as a weak leader who would not press the party's position on other Democratic senators, Speaker John McCormack as old and out of date, and House Majority Whip Hale Boggs as a poor vote counter.[28]

There is little the White House can do in such a situation. Presidents do not lobby for candidates for congressional party leadership positions and virtually always remain neutral during the selection process. Although they may occasionally express a preference for one of the candidates, they are reluctant

26. Quoted in "Jimmy's Oracle," *Newsweek*, October 3, 1977, p. 27. See also Jimmy Carter, *Keeping Faith: Memoirs of a President* (New York: Bantam, 1982), p. 69; and Howard Baker's statement in Martin Tolchin, "Howard Baker: Trying to Tame an Unruly Senate," *New York Times Magazine*, March 28, 1982, p. 19.

27. See Edwards, *Presidential Influence in Congress*, p. 80. But see also Charles Halleck, interview by Thomas Soapes, April 26, 1977, transcript, pp. 12–13, 20, 28, Eisenhower Library, Abilene, Kans.

28. Manatos, interview by Frantz, transcript, p. 27; Sanders, interview by Frantz, tape 3, transcript, pp. 10–11. See also Richard Bolling, *Power in the House* (New York: Capricorn, 1974), p. 232.

to do more.[29] They have no desire to alienate important members of Congress whose support they will need.

Similarly, committee chairmen and ranking minority members are usually determined by seniority, and the chairman always comes from the majority party in the chamber, which often is not the president's. The few exceptions to the seniority rule in recent years were not in any way inspired by the White House (which was controlled by Republicans while both houses of Congress were controlled by Democrats). For all practical purposes, the president plays no role in determining the holders of these important positions. Further, the pressure to support a president of one's party is weaker for committee leaders than for floor leaders.

One of President Carter's first proposals to Congress was a bill giving the president authority to reorganize the executive branch. Congressman Jack Brooks, chairman of the House Government Operations Committee, opposed the bill, and the president could not persuade any Democrat even to introduce it until the Republicans volunteered to do it themselves.[30]

Presidents and their staff typically work closely with their party's legislative leaders, meeting regularly for breakfast when Congress is in session. (On infrequent occasions these meetings include the leaders of the opposition party as well.) These gatherings provide opportunities for an exchange of views and for the president to keep communication channels open and maintain morale. The significance of these efforts has varied, however. At one extreme, President Nixon's meetings were often pro forma, more a ritual than a mechanism for leadership. On the other, Johnson used his meetings as strategy sessions, integrating congressional leaders into the White House's legislative liaison operation.[31]

29. See for example Dwight D. Eisenhower, *Mandate for Change, 1953–1956* (New York: Signet, 1963), pp. 274, 363, 530; Dwight D. Eisenhower, *Waging Peace, 1956–1961* (Garden City, N.Y.: Doubleday, 1965), p. 384; Robert Donovan, *Eisenhower: The Inside Story* (New York: Harper and Row, 1956), p. 112; Emmet John Hughes, *The Ordeal of Power* (New York: Atheneum, 1975), pp. 128–129; Dan Rather and Gary P. Gates, *The Palace Guard* (New York: Harper and Row, 1974), p. 303; Halleck, interview by Soapes, transcript, p. 18. For an exception see Hubert H. Humphrey, *The Education of a Public Man: My Life and Politics* (Garden City, N.Y.: Doubleday, 1976), p. 242.

30. Carter, *Keeping Faith*, p. 71.

31. See Edwards, *Presidential Influence in Congress*, pp. 122–123 and sources cited therein; Ford, *A Time to Heal*, p. 89; Sinclair, *Majority Leadership*, pp. 115–117, 155; Mansfield, interview by Tillman, transcript, pp. 4–5; Boggs, interview by Morrissey, transcript, pp. 14, 18; Ehrlichman, *Witness to Power*, pp. 203–204; Albert, interview by McSweeny, interview 4, transcript, p. 25; John McCormack, interview by Harrison T. Baker, September 23, 1968, transcript, pp. 39–40, Lyndon Baines Johnson Library, Austin, Tex.; Halleck, interview by Soapes, transcript, pp. 2–3, 5; Ambrose, *Eisenhower the President*, pp. 345, 509.

The White House also often relies on congressional party leaders for advice, works with the leaders on head counts, and even uses leaders' offices as bases of operation on Capitol Hill.[32] This close relationship can have considerable payoffs. For example, in 1981 it was the Senate Republican leaders who conceived the successful strategy of using the budget reconciliation procedure to cut expenditures.[33] As a practical matter, the president needs the congressional leaders' resources in his lobbying efforts because his own are so limited. Whether it be personnel, office space, or intangibles such as well-established personal relationships with members, the White House usually needs the leaders' aid. Naturally, most presidents go out of their way to curry favor with the leaders.[34]

Although these activities may be useful for coordinating and enhancing the White House's legislative efforts, they take place within the context of an independent congressional leadership. The Senate Democratic leader Robert Byrd described leadership meetings in President Carter's White House: "[The president] urges certain actions and says he hopes he'll have our support. But he can't force it. The president is expected to make proposals, and we have a responsibility to him and the country to weigh them and act on them only if, in the judgment of the Senate, we should."[35]

One reason why a president may not receive the support he desires from congressional party leaders is that he and his aides lack an understanding of the role of these leaders. This seems to have been especially a problem in Richard Nixon's administration. John Ehrlichman, Nixon's chief domestic adviser, complains in his memoirs of the president's troubles with "*his* own leaders" in Congress. Ehrlichman was also upset and surprised that Gerald Ford, then the Republican leader in the House, did not work for the White House's programs when he disagreed with them, and he termed Hugh Scott, the Senate Republican leader, a "hack."[36]

After his presidency had ended, Ford wrote that a president should have an open door for congressional leaders and involve them in his policy deci-

32. See for example Sinclair, *Majority Leadership*, pp. 115–117; Edwards, *Presidential Influence in Congress*, pp. 122–123 and sources cited therein; Mansfield, interview by Tillman, transcript, pp. 2–4, 40–41; Manatos, interview by Frantz, transcript, pp. 15, 29.

33. Roger H. Davidson, "The Presidency and Congress," in Michael Nelson, ed., *The Presidency and the Political System* (Washington: Congressional Quarterly Press, 1984), p. 387.

34. See for example Boggs, interview by Morrissey, transcript, pp. 10–11; Mansfield, interview by Tillman, transcript, pp. 15–17, 46; McCormack, interview by Baker, transcript, pp. 17, 21, 37; Albert, interview by Morrissey, transcript, pp. 16, 35–37; Fred I. Greenstein, *The Hidden-Hand Presidency: Eisenhower as Leader* (New York: Basic Books, 1982), p. 78.

35. "House, Senate Chiefs Attempt to Lead a Changed Congress," *Congressional Quarterly Weekly Report*, September 13, 1980, p. 2700.

36. Ehrlichman, *Witness to Power*, pp. 196–199.

sions; this makes it easier to ask for help.[37] Yet as the House Republican leader Ford was not consulted by the White House on legislative matters. In 1973 he went to the White House to discuss with President Nixon Vice President Agnew's problems with the law. He later recalled that "It was one of the few times while he was president that the two of us just sat and talked by ourselves." Nixon and his aides also preferred to work through individuals in Congress rather than the party leaders, which irritated the leaders and undercut their authority.[38]

Thus the president's relationship with his party's leaders in Congress is delicate. On the one hand, the leaders are predisposed to work for his policies, and they typically work closely with the White House. On the other, the leaders are free to oppose his policies or lend only symbolic support. The president's task in exploiting the potential of congressional party leaders, who possess independent power and varying levels of competence, is by no means easy.

The congressional party leaders' relations with their party colleagues in Congress are as important as their relations with the president. Major changes have occurred in the last 15 years that have weakened the ability of party leaders to produce votes for the president. Gerald Ford writes:

> Today a President really does not have the kind of clout with the Congress that he had 30 years ago, even in matters that affect national security. There is not the kind of teamwork that existed in the '50s, even if the President and a majority of the Congress belong to the same party.
>
> The main reason for this change is the erosion of the leadership in the Congress. Party leaders have lost the power to tell their troops that something is really significant and to get them to respond accordingly. The days of Sam Rayburn, Lyndon Johnson and Everett Dirksen are gone. That has adversely affected the Congress's ability to do things even in very difficult circumstances involving the national interest.[39]

One reason why party leaders have lost much of their power over their followers is the increased dispersion of power in Congress, especially in the

37. Gerald R. Ford, "Imperiled, Not Imperial," *Time*, November 10, 1980, p. 31.

38. Quoted in Ford, *A Time to Heal*, pp. 89, 140. See also Emmet John Hughes, *The Living Presidency* (Baltimore: Penguin, 1974), p. 258; William Safire, *Before the Fall: An Inside View of the Pre-Watergate White House* (New York: Doubleday, 1975), pp. 172–173, 375–376, 422, 676.

39. Ford, "Imperiled, Not Imperial," p. 30. See also Ford's comments quoted in Paul C. Light, *The President's Agenda: Domestic Policy Choice from Kennedy to Carter* (Baltimore: Johns Hopkins University Press, 1982), p. 212; and Jimmy Carter's similar views in Carter, *Keeping Faith*, p. 80.

House.[40] The face of Congress has changed over the last two decades. Seniority is no longer an automatic path to committee or subcommittee chairs, and the heads of committees must be more responsive to the desires of committee members. In the words of Representative Thomas Foley, "If I as Agriculture Committee chairman say to a member, 'I don't like your bill and I'm not going to schedule it,' I'll walk into the committee room and find a meeting going on without me."[41]

There are also more subcommittees and more heads of subcommittees now, and these subcommittees have a more important role in handling legislation.[42] This has greatly complicated the task of leadership, as was noted by Jim Wright, then House Majority Leader:

> The leadership's task must have been infinitely less complicated in the days of Mr. Rayburn and Mr. McCormack. In Mr. Rayburn's day, about all a majority leader or Speaker needed to do in order to get his program adopted was to deal effectively with perhaps 12 very senior committee chairmen. They, in turn, could be expected to influence their committees and their subcommittee chairmen whom they, in those days, appointed. . . . Well, now that situation is quite considerably different. There are, I think, 153 subcommittees. The full committee chairmen are not inviolable in their own precincts. They are not the great powers that they once were. They are dependent upon their own members for election and for the support of their subcommittees for the program. And so, the leadership sometimes has to go beyond the committee chairmen. . . . [Therefore] we have to deal with a great many more people than was the case in Mr. Rayburn's day or Mr. McCormack's day.[43]

Members of both parties also have larger personal, committee, and subcommittee staffs at their disposal, as well as new service adjuncts such as the Congressional Budget Office. These additional resources, combined with more opportunities to amend legislation, make it easier for members of Congress to challenge the White House and the congressional leadership and provide alternatives to the president's policies.

---

40. For useful discussions of the dispersion of power see Thomas E. Cavanagh, "The Dispersion of Authority in the House of Representatives," *Political Science Quarterly* 97 (Winter 1982–83): 623–637; and Eric L. Davis, "Legislative Reform and the Decline of Presidential Influence on Capitol Hill," *British Journal of Political Science* 9 (October 1979): 465–479.

41. Quoted in "Single-Issue Politics," *Newsweek*, November 16, 1978, p. 58.

42. See for example Steven H. Haeberle, "The Institutionalization of the Subcommittee in the United States House of Representatives," *Journal of Politics* 40 (November 1978): 1054–1065.

43. Quoted in Sinclair, *Majority Leadership*, pp. 19–20.

Other reforms have increased the burden of leaders. In 1970 the House
ended unrecorded teller votes (in which only the number of votes on each side
is reported), and in 1973 it began electronic voting. Both changes led to an
increase in the number of roll calls and thus an increase in the visibility of
representatives' voting behavior. (There were 33 percent more nonunanimous roll calls on which the president took a stand per year under Jimmy
Carter than under Lyndon Johnson.) This change in the rules has stimulated
the opposition to offer amendments on the floor and generated more pressure
on House members to abandon their party, making it more difficult for the
president to gain passage of legislation. Reforms that have opened committee
and subcommittee hearings to the public have had the same effect.

There has also been a heavy turnover in Congress in recent years, and
new members have brought with them new approaches to legislating. They
are less likely to adopt the norms of apprenticeship, reciprocity, and specialization than were their predecessors in their first terms. Instead, they have
eagerly taken an active role in all legislation.[44] They place a heavy emphasis on
individualism and much less on party regularity.[45] Substantial turnover in
membership also makes it more difficult for leaders to develop personal relationships with members, relationships on which persuasive efforts might be
based.

Congressional party leaders now have more decision makers to influence. They can no longer rely on dealing with the congressional aristocracy
and expect the rest of the members to follow. According to a lobbyist for the
Department of Transportation, "Ten years ago, if you wanted a highway bill,
you went to see [former House Public Works Committee chairman John]
Blatnik, the Speaker, and the chairman of the Rules Committee. There would
be a small collegial discussion—and all the political decisions would be made.
Now there's no one person to see . . . You have to deal with everybody."
Andrew Manatos, who worked in congressional liaison for the Commerce
Department, and his father, Mike, a congressional liaison aide in Lyndon
Johnson's White House, wrote a report in which they conclude that the
Ninety-fifth Congress (1977–78) was different from the Democratic con-

44. See for example Ornstein, "The Open Congress Meets the President," pp. 197–199;
Norman J. Ornstein, Robert L. Peabody, and David W. Rohde, "The Contemporary Senate: Into
the 1980s," in Larry C. Dodd and Bruce I. Oppenheimer, eds., *Congress Reconsidered*, 2d ed.
(Washington: Congressional Quarterly Press, 1981), pp. 16–19; Michael Foley, *The New Senate:
Liberal Influence on a Conservative Institution, 1959–1972* (New Haven and London: Yale
University Press, 1980), chap. 4.
45. See Sundquist, *The Decline and Resurgence of Congress*, chap. 13; "In the Senate of the
'80s, Team Spirit Has Given Way to the Rule of Individuals," *Congressional Quarterly Weekly
Report*, September 4, 1982, p. 2175.

gresses that President Johnson faced. "In the early 1960s, the 'Club' still controlled the congressional levers of power."[46] Now leaders must persuade more people.

Tip O'Neill is just one of many who wistfully recall the times when the party leadership could negotiate with a few other leaders who would deliver the promised votes. Today things are different: "You don't have the discipline out there."[47] According to one assistant to Johnson, "In 1965, there were maybe ten or twelve people who you needed to corral in the House and Senate. . . . Now, I'd put that figure upwards of one hundred. Believe it, there are so many people who have a shot at derailing a bill that the President has to double his effort for even routine decisions."[48]

The party leadership at least in theory possesses sanctions that it can exercise to enforce party discipline. These include discretion in making committee assignments, patronage, campaign funds, trips abroad, and aid with members' pet bills. The House Democratic party leadership theoretically has control over the Rules Committee, committee assignments, and the referral of proposals, in addition to less weighty matters. Yet in reality the leadership's discretion exists primarily on paper. Party leaders have not exploited their power to compel a common party stand. Most rewards are considered a matter of right, and it is the leadership's job to see that they are distributed equitably.[49] Party leaders do not dare withhold benefits, because they fear being overturned by the rank and file.[50] As one senior Republican put it, "The elected leaders of a modern Congress have very little to give and therefore very little to withhold in the exercise of discipline within the group that elects them."[51]

46. Quoted in Shirley Elder, "The Cabinet's Ambassadors to Capitol Hill," *National Journal*, July 29, 1978, p. 1196. See also William J. Lanouette, "Who's Setting Foreign Policy: Carter or Congress?" *National Journal*, July 15, 1978, p. 1119; "Organized Labor Found 1978 a Frustrating Year, Had Few Victories in Congress," *Congressional Quarterly Weekly Report*, December 30, 1978, p. 3539.

47. Quoted in "House, Senate Chiefs Attempt to Lead a Changed Congress," *Congressional Quarterly Weekly Report*, September 23, 1980, p. 2696. See also Light, *The President's Agenda*, p. 212; Davidson, "The Presidency and Congress," p. 376.

48. Quoted in Light, *The President's Agenda*, p. 211. See also Edwards, *Presidential Influence in Congress*, pp. 194–195.

49. See for example Loren Waldman, "Majority Leadership in the House," *Political Science Quarterly* 95 (Fall 1980): 373–394; Charles S. Bullock III, "U.S. Senate Committee Assignments: Preferences, Motivations, and Success," *American Journal of Political Science* 29 (November 1985): 789–808.

50. See for example Sundquist, *The Decline and Resurgence of Congress*, pp. 398–401.

51. Quoted in Paul Light, *Artful Work: The Politics of Social Security Reform* (New York: Random House, 1985), p. 17.

Threats of sanctions in such a situation are unconvincing and thus rarely occur. Senate Majority Leader Robert Dole sometimes termed his position that of "majority pleader."[52] As the House Majority Whip John Brademas commented in 1979, "When we say, 'vote with the party or else,' we don't have much on the 'or else' side of the equation." Jim Wright, then the House majority leader, agreed when he stated, "You have a hunting license to persuade—that's about all."[53] The next year Ted Stevens, the Senate Republican whip added: "I've never even once threatened to punish a member. We probably don't even have the power to do so if we wanted to." Even Tip O'Neill publicly admitted that defectors from the party line had little to fear.[54]

Incentives

The members of the president's party receive more attention from the White House than do the members of the opposition party. When a president seeks to build his winning coalition, he typically writes off a large part of the opposition party and can generally depend upon a core of supporters from his own. To obtain the additional votes he needs, a president usually begins with members of his party who are undecided or movable.

The Carrot

Because a member of Congress who is indebted to the president is easier to approach and ask for a vote, the White House provides many services and amenities for representatives and senators.[55] Although these favors may be bestowed on any member of Congress, they actually go disproportionately to members of the president's party. Personal amenities used to create goodwill include social contact with the president, flattery, rides on Air Force One, visits to Camp David, birthday greetings, theater tickets for the presidential box, invitations to bill-signing ceremonies, pictures with the president, briefings, and a plethora of others, the number and variety of which are limited only by the imagination of the president and his staff.

Also, the White House often helps members of Congress with their constituents. A wide range of services is offered, including greetings to elderly and other worthy constituents, signed presidential photographs, presidential

52. Quoted in "Dole on the Job: Keeping the Senate Running," *Congressional Quarterly Weekly Report*, June 29, 1985, p. 1271.

53. Quoted in Sundquist, *The Decline and Resurgence of Congress*, p. 398. See also p. 401.

54. Quoted in "House, Senate Chiefs Attempt to Lead a Changed Congress," *Congressional Quarterly Weekly Report*, September 13, 1980, pp. 2696, 2698.

55. For a more thorough treatment of this topic see Edwards, *Presidential Influence in Congress*, chap. 6.

tie clasps and other memorabilia from the White House, reprints of speeches, information about government programs, pressure on agencies from the White House in favor of constituents, passage to agencies of the names of constituents nominated by members of Congress for executive branch appointments, influence on local editorial writers, ceremonial appointments to commissions, meetings with the president, and arguments that the member can use to explain votes to constituents. The president may also help members of Congress please constituents through patronage, pork-barrel projects, and government contracts, and aid with legislation of special interest to particular constituencies. The principal reason why President Reagan kept the widely criticized Clinch River breeder reactor in the budget was that it was in Tennessee, represented by Senate Majority Leader Howard Baker.

Campaign aid is yet another service the White House can provide party members, and the president may dangle it before them to attract their support.[56] This aid may come in various forms, including campaign speeches by the president and executive officials for congressional candidates, funds and advice from the party national committees, presidential endorsements, pictures with the president, and letters of appreciation from the president. Some aid is more ingenious, as when Lawrence O'Brien, then postmaster general, held a stamp dedication ceremony in a representative's hometown in 1966, complete with parade and associated festivities.[57]

When it created a Political Affairs Office, the administration of Ronald Reagan formalized an activity in which members of the White House staff had long engaged. The office's main function was to secure support for the president in Congress, and it was closely tied to the Republican National Committee and the Republican campaign committees of the House and Senate. Officials from each unit met weekly to coordinate their activities. The office was not only a liaison between the president and the campaign arena, but a place where Republicans in Congress could come for favors.[58]

All administrations are not equally active in providing services and amenities to members of Congress. The administrations of Johnson and Reagan were at the active end of the spectrum, those of Nixon and Carter at the other. Yet any such differences are relatively small in comparison with the substantial efforts made by every recent administration to develop goodwill among its party members in Congress.

56. See for example Valenti, *A Very Human President*, p. 189; Theodore Sorensen, *Kennedy* (New York: Bantam, 1966), pp. 392, 395; Laurence I. Barrett, *Gambling with History: Reagan in the White House* (New York: Penguin, 1984), p. 365.

57. O'Brien, *No Final Victories*, p. 185.

58. Dick Kirschten, "Reagan's Political Chief Rollins: 'We Help Our Friends First,'" *National Journal*, June 12, 1982, pp. 1054–1056.

Although creating goodwill is to the president's advantage, there are significant limitations to the payoffs that can be expected, even from providing seemingly major benefits such as patronage to members of the president's party. These members typically consider it their right to have the decisive say in regional federal appointments and feel the White House has an obligation to extend them this courtesy. They are unlikely to be overly grateful for receiving what they already believe to be theirs.[59]

It is also true that there is often little the president can do for members of Congress who are opposed to his policies. For example, intransigent, conservative Southern Democrats plagued President Kennedy and President Johnson, but there was little the White House could do to change their entrenched habits of voting with the Republicans. These members obtained their financial and organizational support from those opposed to the liberal policies of the New Frontier and the Great Society, and their major political battles took place in party primaries, in which they could not be helped by the presence of the president at the head of the ticket, and in which in any event the president had to remain neutral.[60]

The Stick

In 1982 one of President Reagan's aides told of how he had persuaded two Republican members of the House to vote for the president's budget cuts. The representatives feared the political repercussions in their constituencies of supporting the president, so the aide promised them the maximum campaign aid the law allowed a party to give a candidate and won their votes. When asked what would have happened if the congressmen had not given in, the aide replied: "I would have nailed them to the wall."[61]

Just as the president can offer the carrot, he can also wield the stick. The increased resources available to the White House in recent years provide increased opportunities to levy sanctions in the form of the withholding of favors. As the deputy chairman of the Republican National Committee said, there is more money than ever "to play hardball with. We're loaded for bear."[62] The threats of such actions are of course effective primarily with members of the president's party, because members of the opposition party do not expect to receive many favors from the president.[63]

59. See Nigel Bowles, *The White House and Capitol Hill* (New York: Oxford University Press, 1987), pp. 75–76.

60. See a memo from Kennedy's aide Henry Hall Wilson to Lawrence O'Brien on this point, quoted in Bowles, *The White House and Capitol Hill*, p. 69.

61. Quoted in "Playing Hardball," *Wall Street Journal*, August 18, 1982, p. 1.

62. Ibid.

63. See Kingdon, *Congressmen's Voting Decisions*, pp. 180–181, 184, 186.

Although sanctions or threats of sanctions are far from an everyday occurrence, they do happen. They may take the form of excluding a member from social events at the White House,[64] denying routine requests for tickets to tours of the White House, and shutting off access to see the president.[65] Each of these personal slights sends a signal of presidential displeasure.

Sometimes the arm-twisting is more severe and includes cutting projects in a district or state from the budget, cutting off patronage to a member, or refusing the help of the White House in fund-raising and campaign activities.[66] President Reagan's White House let it be known that campaign aid in the form of party funds and technical advice, appearances by high administration officials at fund-raisers and during campaigns, and the encouragement of contributions from political action committees (PACs) were contingent on support for the president. The White House's Political Affairs Office let junior Republicans in Congress know that it was watching their votes and public statements closely and warned them not to oppose the president. In the words of the office's director, "We will help our friends first."[67] President Reagan himself issued a rather blunt threat to Republicans on the Senate Budget Committee. The president was trying to persuade the senators to delay voting on cutting his proposals for defense spending. He told the chairman, "I'm the president and I want you to hold off for a while. People on that committee are up for reelection. They're going to be coming to me for help."[68]

Sheer psychological pressure also plays a role in presidential party leadership. One freshman congressman reported that when he told President Reagan he could not support his proposal to increase taxes in 1982, the president "got red-faced, pounded the table and yelled at me." Similarly, the director of the Political Affairs Office at the White House described the pressures the administration put on Sen. Roger Jepsen, a Republican, on the issue of selling AWACS planes to Saudi Arabia: "We just beat his brains out. That's all. We just took Jepsen and beat his brains out."[69]

64. See for example Light, *The President's Agenda*, p. 138; Ford, *A Time to Heal*, p. 90.
65. See for example Dennis Farney, "'Gypsy Moths' Feel Reagan Is up a Tree without Their Vote," *Wall Street Journal*, October 1, 1981, p. 1.
66. For a more thorough treatment of arm-twisting see Edwards, *Presidential Influence in Congress*, pp. 139–144, 176.
67. "Playing Hardball," *Wall Street Journal*, August 18, 1982, p. 1; Albert R. Hunt, "Out of the Fire," *Wall Street Journal*, October 29, 1981, p. 1; Kirschten, "Reagan's Political Chief Rollins," p. 1057; "The Tax Battle Heats Up," *Newsweek*, August 23, 1982, p. 26. See also "22 G.O.P. Senators Pressed to Back Reagan Programs," *New York Times*, March 15, 1985, sec. A, pp. 1, 13.
68. Quoted in "Reagan on the Defense," *Newsweek*, April 18, 1983, p. 22.
69. Quoted in "Playing Hardball," *Wall Street Journal*, August 18, 1982, p. 15.

Such harsh arm-twisting is unusual. The White House must take a long-run view of its relations with Congress, and intense short-term pressure on a representative or senator can alienate those whose support the president requires again and again.[70]

More typical is the orchestration of pressure by others.[71] President Reagan's White House was especially effective in this regard. Operating through party channels, its Political Affairs Office, and its Office of Public Liaison, the administration was able to generate pressure from party members' constituents, campaign contributors, political activists, business leaders, state officials, interest groups, party officials, and of course cabinet members. The Office of Legislative Affairs was also in regular communications with members of the president's party.[72] Such efforts are by no means restricted to party members, of course, but they are the primary focus because of their general proclivity to support the president.

Despite the resources available to the president, if members of his party wish to oppose him there is little he can do to stop them. The primary reason is that the parties are highly decentralized: national party leaders do not control those aspects of politics that are of vital concern to members of Congress—nominations and elections. Members of Congress are largely self-recruited, gain their party's nomination by their own efforts and not the party's, and provide most of the money and organizational support needed for their election. Presidents can do little to influence negatively the results of these activities, and usually they do not even try. As President Kennedy said in 1962, "Party loyalty or responsibility means damn little. They've got to take care of themselves first. [House members] all have to run this year—I don't and I couldn't hurt most of them if I wanted to."[73]

Bipartisanship

On July 27, 1981, President Reagan delivered an exceptionally important and effective televised address to the nation, seeking the public's support for his tax cut bill. In it he went to great lengths to present his plan as bipartisan. It was crucial that he convince the public that this controversial legislation was supported by members of both parties and was therefore by implication fair.

70. See Joseph A. Pika, "White House Boundary Roles: Marginal Men amidst the Palace Guard," *Presidential Studies Quarterly* 16 (Fall 1986): 708–709.

71. See Edwards, *Presidential Influence in Congress*, pp. 169–173, 176–179.

72. See for example Hunt, "Out of the Fire," pp. 1, 10; Robert W. Mercy, "A New GOP Congressman Tries to Resolve His Dilemma over the President's Tax Bill," *Wall Street Journal*, August 19, 1982, p. 19.

73. Quoted in Sorensen, *Kennedy*, p. 387.

He described it as "bipartisan" eleven times in the span of a few minutes! No one was to miss the point. The president required the votes of Democrats in the House to pass his bill, and he wanted their constituents to apply pressure on them to support it.

In October the president was hard at work attempting to obtain support in the Senate, then controlled by Republicans, for his decision to sell AWACS planes to Saudi Arabia. He gathered a bipartisan group of sixteen high-ranking former national security officials at the White House to state their support of his policy. He also received the backing of his predecessor, Jimmy Carter. (Carter had similarly obtained the public support of his Republican predecessor, Gerald Ford, and of other high-ranking Republican officials for ratification of the Panama Canal treaties.)

In 1982 President Reagan's most important ally in obtaining passage of a bill to increase taxes was the Democratic Speaker of the House, Tip O'Neill. When the Democrats were given free time on television to respond to the president's nationwide speech on the tax package, House Democratic Whip Thomas Foley pleaded for support of the president's proposals. This was crucial because of the large number of Republican defections from the president's coalition.

These examples illustrate the fact that despite a president's advantage in dealing with members of his party in Congress, he is often forced to solicit bipartisan support, for several reasons. First, the opposition party may control one or both houses of Congress. Even if the president received total support from all members of his party, he would still need support from some members of the opposition. For instance, between 1953 and 1988 there were sixteen years during which the Republicans controlled the executive branch while the Democrats controlled the legislative branch (1955–60, 1969–76, and 1987–88). From 1981 to 1986 the Republicans had a majority in the Senate only.

A successful bipartisan approach depends upon restraining partisanship to avoid alienating the opposition. The president must subordinate his role as a party leader to that of his role as a coalition leader. President Eisenhower, who faced a Democratic Congress in six of his eight years as president and who was not inclined toward overt partisanship, consciously attempted to follow such an approach, as did his staff.[74] He cultivated Democratic votes, especially on foreign policy.[75] When he held fund-raisers to help build the Republican

74. Wayne, *The Legislative Presidency*, p. 142; Eisenhower, *Mandate for Change*, p. 245; Holtzman, *Legislative Liaison*, p. 240; Arthur Larson, *Eisenhower: The President Nobody Knew* (New York: Charles Scribner's Sons, 1968), pp. 34–36.

75. Randall B. Ripley, *Majority Party Leadership in Congress* (Boston: Little, Brown, 1969), p. 125. See also Jewell, *Senatorial Politics and Foreign Policy*, p. 78.

party, he did so quietly so as not to contradict the impression of nonpartisanship he was trying to convey to the country.[76]

President Nixon and President Ford also faced Congresses controlled by Democrats. They tried to steer a middle course between Eisenhower's soft sell and the more partisan approaches of Kennedy and Johnson. They wanted to make the most of Republican strength while appealing to conservative Democrats by taking an issue-oriented, ideological line as well as a party line.[77] Ronald Reagan followed a similar strategy.

In his reelection campaign in 1972, Nixon did not adopt a strongly partisan line, and hoped for a majority based on principles rather than just party. He did little to help Republican candidates for Congress.[78] Likewise, President Reagan promised letters of thanks and agreed to refrain from campaigning for Republican candidates in the districts of some conservative Democrats, in return for their support on important votes.[79] To obtain bipartisan support for the MX missile, in 1985 he called off a media blitz planned for 1986 against Democrats who had won by narrow margins in 1984.[80]

A second reason for bipartisanship is that no matter how large the representation of the president's party in Congress, he cannot always depend on it for support, for members of the president's own party frequently oppose him. This is especially true of Southern Democrats. In the 1950s and 1960s their inconsistent support of Democratic presidents was especially evident in the area of civil rights legislation. Southern Democrats overwhelmingly opposed important pieces of civil rights legislation (see table 5.2), and the president would have lost the vote on each of these without the support of some Republicans.[81]

Civil rights is not the only area in which Democratic presidents have needed Republican support. For example, Lyndon Johnson realized at the beginning of his presidency that as a progressive president he would need help from the leaders of both parties to pass his domestic legislation.[82] Thus he

76. Fred I. Greenstein, "Eisenhower as an Activist President: A Look at New Evidence," *Political Science Quarterly* 94 (Winter 1979–80): 579.

77. Wayne, *The Legislative Presidency*, p. 156.

78. Ehrlichman, *Witness to Power*, p. 204.

79. See for example "Congress Clears $98.3 Billion Tax Increase," *Congressional Quarterly Weekly Report*, August 21, 1982, p. 2035; Barrett, *Gambling with History*, p. 168. See however "The GOP and the 'Boll Weevils,'" *Newsweek*, June 29, 1981, p. 17.

80. Jonathan Fuerbringer, "Pressures and Rewards Face House Members on MX Vote," *New York Times*, March 26, 1985, sec. A, p. 12.

81. See for example Charles Halleck, interview by Stephen Hess, March 22, 1965, transcript, pp. 9–14, 30, John F. Kennedy Library, Boston.

82. Joseph A. Califano, Jr., *A Presidential Nation* (New York: W. W. Norton, 1975), p. 155.

TABLE 5.2 Votes on Final Passage of Major Civil Rights Legislation Supported by Democratic Presidents

	House			Senate		
Legislation	Republicans	Northern Democrats	Southern Democrats	Republicans	Northern Democrats	Southern Democrats
24th Amendment (poll tax), 1962	132–15	132–1	31–70	30–1	39–1	8–14
1964 Civil Rights Act	138–34	141–4	11–92	27–6	43–1	3–20
1965 Voting Rights Act	112–24	188–1	33–60	30–2	42–0	5–17
1968 Open Housing Act	100–84	137–13	13–75	29–3	39–0	3–17

Figures to left of dash are yes votes, those to right are no votes.
SOURCE: Adapted from "GOP Played Key Role in Civil Rights Laws," Congressional Quarterly Weekly Report, April 29, 1978, p. 1050.

regularly consulted Republican congressional leaders and restrained evidence of partisanship in public forums.

Johnson worked very closely with the Senate Republican leader, Everett Dirksen. They had many intimate, low-key, one-to-one conferences, which Johnson regarded as essential to gaining the necessary Republican support for controversial legislation. The president gave Dirksen the same preferential treatment that he gave to the Senate Democratic majority leader, Mike Mansfield, and spoke to Dirksen frequently, sometimes as often as ten times a day.[83] Kennedy did not share the rapport with Dirksen that Johnson had but still had the senator to the White House monthly and talked to him on the telephone slightly more often.[84] In some instances the senator provided Kennedy with crucial support.[85]

Republican presidents have also had trouble gaining support from members of their party in Congress, furthering their need for a bipartisan strategy. President Eisenhower was plagued in his first term by Sen. Joseph McCarthy's irresponsible charges against his administration and by Sen. John Bricker's attempts (nearly successful) to pass a constitutional amendment limiting the president's use of executive agreements. In the House, Congressman John Taber, chairman of the Appropriations Committee, fought the president on mutual security funds (foreign aid), and Congressman Daniel Reed, chairman of the Ways and Means Committee, did the same on income tax legislation. More generally, Eisenhower had trouble gaining support from the basically conservative congressional Republicans for his internationalist foreign policy and his moderate domestic policies.[86] President Nixon went to the highly unusual step of helping to defeat Sen. Charles Goodell of New York, a Republican, in the election of 1970 because of the liberal senator's opposition to the president's policies.

In their efforts to secure bipartisan support, Republican presidents may exploit divisions within the Democratic party (tables 5.3–5.6). What is a

83. Ibid., pp. 155–156. See also Goldman, *The Tragedy of Lyndon Johnson*, pp. 83–84, 385–387; Bell, *The Johnson Treatment*, p. 40; Neil MacNeil, *Dirksen: Portrait of a Public Man* (New York: World, 1970), pp. 274, 276–281; Sanders, interview by Frantz, tape 3, transcript, p. 7; Dirksen, interview by Frantz, transcript, p. 5; Jack Valenti, interview by Joe B. Frantz, July 12, 1972, interview 5, transcript, pp. 10–13, Lyndon Baines Johnson Library, Austin, Tex.

84. MacNeil, *Dirksen*, pp. 225, 281. See also Holtzman, *Legislative Liaison*, p. 241.

85. See for example Mansfield, interview by Tillman, transcript, pp. 28, 31; Bell, *The Johnson Treatment*, pp. 38–39. According to the House Republican leader Charles Halleck, Kennedy's White House worked with him also; see Halleck, interview by Hess, transcript, pp. 14–16.

86. See for example Eisenhower, *Mandate for Change*, p. 246; Gary W. Reichard, *The Reaffirmation of Republicanism: Eisenhower and the Eighty-third Congress* (Knoxville: University of Tennessee Press, 1975), p. 121; Ambrose, *Eisenhower the President*, pp. 151–152, 155–156, 203, 218–219, 294.

TABLE 5.3   Northern and Southern Democratic Support for Republican Presidents on Nonunanimous Votes (in Percent)

	House		Senate	
Year	Northern Democrats	Southern Democrats	Northern Democrats	Southern Democrats
1953	52	36	39	46
1954	39	28	36	37
1955	47	36	39	35
1956	43	31	37	32
1957	62	30	48	38
1958	65	34	38	37
1959	36	30	24	35
1960	50	38	40	42
1969	49	46	40	45
1970	40	41	31	45
1971	33	59	26	49
1972	45	49	22	62
1973	26	43	16	46
1974	33	49	25	47
1975	33	47	29	57
1976	25	49	21	52
1981	32	58	26	52
1982	24	43	29	51
1983	21	43	38	44
1984	26	45	25	47
1985	23	40	23	37
1986	18	35	19	48

problem for Democratic presidents is an opportunity for Republican ones. On comparing table 5.5 with table 3.7, one finds that on the average Southern Democrats support Republican presidents about as often as they do presidents of their own party. In fact, the support of Southern Democratic senators for Republican presidents exceeds their support for Democratic presidents. As usual, there are not significant differences between nonunanimous votes and key votes.

Before one concludes that the narrowing of Democratic intraparty differences is due to the greatly decreased support of Northern Democrats for Republican presidents, one must look more closely at table 5.6, which shows a wide variance in the Democratic intraparty differences from one Republican president to another. The figures in table 5.5 mask substantial differences between Eisenhower and his Republican successors. He obtained higher Northern Democratic than the other presidents of his party, and lower Southern Democratic support. Equally important, he received substantially more

TABLE 5.4   Northern and Southern Democratic Support for Republican Presidents on Key Votes (in Percent)

Year	House		Senate	
	Northern Democrats	Southern Democrats	Northern Democrats	Southern Democrats
1953	48	32	35	50
1954	49	34	40	36
1955	49	27	25	30
1956	51	44	27	36
1957	77	18	61	27
1958	54	27	34	38
1959	33	30	31	35
1960	38	34	29	60
1969	40	49	37	48
1970	31	34	26	69
1971	34	64	23	54
1972	27	38	40	81
1973	24	47	18	40
1974	40	57	30	78
1975	31	41	19	47
1976	17	61	18	53
1981	21	60	36	55
1982	13	52	25	47
1983	17	46	27	57
1984	26	53	29	53
1985	28	49	23	40
1986	20	41	19	47

support from Northern Democrats than Southern Democrats in the House, and the same or nearly the same levels of support in the Senate. All other Republican presidents received substantially higher support from Southern Democrats than from Northern Democrats. This would be expected, given the essentially conservative orientation of Republican presidents and Southern Democratic members of Congress. The reverse trend during Eisenhower's years in office reflects the particularly weak support of Southern Democrats for his internationalist approach to foreign policy and for social issues and civil liberties in the 1950s, and their increasing moderation since then.[87] Much to the disappointment of the far right, Eisenhower did not attempt to dismantle the New Deal and stood strongly for an active, internationalist foreign policy.

Not only do partisan strategies often fail for lack of numbers or reliability of party cohorts, but they may also provoke the other party into a more unified

87. See Sinclair, *Majority Leadership*, pp. 11–12.

TABLE 5.5 Aggregate Northern and Southern Democratic Support for Republican Presidents (in Percent)

	House			Senate		
	Northern Democrats	Southern Democrats	Difference[a]	Northern Democrats	Southern Democrats	Difference
Nonunanimous Support	37	41	4	31	45	14
Key Votes	35	43	8	30	49	19

[a]Differences expressed in percentage points

TABLE 5.6 Northern and Southern Democratic Support for Individual Republican Presidents (in Percent)

Nonunanimous Support

President	House			Senate		
	Northern Democrats	Southern Democrats	Difference[a]	Northern Democrats	Southern Democrats	Difference
Eisenhower	49	33	16	38	38	0
Nixon[b]	39	48	9	27	49	22
Ford[c]	29	48	19	25	55	30
Reagan[d]	24	44	20	27	47	20

Key Votes

President	House			Senate		
	Northern Democrats	Southern Democrats	Difference	Northern Democrats	Southern Democrats	Difference
Eisenhower	50	31	19	35	39	4
Nixon[b]	31	46	15	29	58	29
Ford[c]	24	51	27	19	50	31
Reagan[d]	21	50	29	27	50	23

[a] Differences expressed in percentage points
[b] 1969–73
[c] 1975–76
[d] 1981–86

posture of opposition. Where there is confrontation, there can be no consensus, and consensus is often required to legislate changes on important issues. Some observers believe President Reagan hurt his chances of obtaining Democratic support for some of his proposals by his steadfast unwillingness to compromise with them early in his term.[88]

The president is also inhibited in his partisanship by pressures to be president of all the people rather than a highly partisan figure. This expectation that they be somewhat above the political fray undoubtedly constrains presidents in their role as party leader and further fuels the need for a bipartisan approach.

Despite the frequent necessity of a bipartisan strategy, it is not without costs. Bipartisanship often creates a strain with the extremists within the president's party, as a Republican president tries to appeal to the left for Democratic votes and a Democratic president to the right for Republican votes. Although the Republican right wing and Democratic left wing may find it difficult to forge a coalition in opposition to their own presidents' policies, it is not true that they must therefore support the president. Instead, they may complicate a president's strategy by joining those who oppose his policies.

It is not only in matters of ideology that a president following a bipartisan approach to coalition building may irritate his fellow partisans. Providing discrete benefits to members of the opposition instead of to members of his own party may have the same effect. In late 1981 Congressional Quarterly reported: "To keep House Republicans in line behind his economic program, Reagan appealed to their party loyalty. But to assure the necessary Democratic votes, the president agreed to modify his programs according to the Conservative Democratic Forum members' desires."[89] This strategy angered some Republicans, especially the liberals and moderates who represented constituencies hit hardest by the president's proposed reductions in spending. They were less easily swayed by appeals to party loyalty alone in the following year.[90]

Bipartisanship may also be hindered by the leaders of the president's party in Congress. Speaker Tip O'Neill and Senate Majority Leader Robert Byrd let Jimmy Carter know they would be upset if he dealt with Republicans

88. Ibid., pp. 120–121; Ornstein, "Assessing Reagan's First Year," in Ornstein, ed., *President and Congress*, p. 100; Schick, "How the Budget Was Won and Lost," p. 17; "Congress and the White House Play a Waiting Game on the 1983 Budget," *National Journal*, March 20, 1982, p. 489.

89. "'Gypsy Moths' Poised to Fly Against Reagan's New Cuts; Charge Pledges Were Broken," *Congressional Quarterly Weekly Report*, October 10, 1981, p. 1950.

90. For an example from Carter's presidency see James MacGregor Burns, *The Power to Lead: The Crisis of the American Presidency* (New York: Simon and Schuster, 1984), p. 36.

in Congress frequently. To avoid offending the Democratic party leaders, Carter therefore had fewer contacts with Republicans than he otherwise might have.[91]

The ultimate limitation on a bipartisan strategy, especially for a liberal Democratic president, is that the opposition party is generally not fertile ground for obtaining policy support. Johnson's White House, for example, directly sought Republican support only rarely, because Republicans were not often movable. Sometimes the isolation from the opposition was complete. Johnson's last chief of congressional relations recalled after leaving the White House that he had never even met Strom Thurmond, a senior Republican senator.[92] Similarly, Carter's legislative liaison aides ignored House Minority Leader John Rhodes, whom they found more partisan than his Senate counterpart, Howard Baker, and averse to bargaining with them.[93]

The Democrats are not the only ones who find it difficult to obtain bipartisan support. The task is not easy for the Republicans either. For example, only twenty-three House Democrats supported Ronald Reagan on both the big budget and tax votes in 1981, despite the president's persuasive efforts and the pull of ideology. In 1985, after Reagan's landslide reelection, the going was even tougher. Max Friedersdorf, head of the White House's congressional liaison office in both years, observed, "It's not as easy for us this time on the Democratic side."[94]

Presidential party leadership in Congress is a source of both influence and frustration for the president. Members of Congress from his party tend to give him more support than members of the opposition party. Although much of this support is a result of shared policy preferences, on some issues the pull of party affiliation provides the president with additional support. Presidents typically work hard to exploit this potential through their appeals for party loyalty, working with congressional party leaders, and the provision and withholding of favors.

Sometimes this works very smoothly, and when it does we may be inclined to share with James Sundquist the view that "the bonds of party generate centripetal forces to counter the centrifugal forces inherent in the relations

91. Carter, *Keeping Faith*, p. 67; William F. Mullen, "Perceptions of Carter's Legislative Successes and Failures: Views from the Hill and the Liaison Staff," *Presidential Studies Quarterly* 12 (Fall 1982): 522–544.

92. Sanders, interview by Frantz, tape 2, transcript, pp. 5–6, 10, 37. See also Bowles, *The White House and Capitol Hill*, p. 68.

93. Bowles, *The White House and Capitol Hill*, p. 197.

94. Bernard Weinraub, "Back in the Legislative Strategist's Saddle Again," *New York Times*, May 28, 1985, sec. A, p. 10.

between the branches; they engender impulses toward harmony to offset the natural tendencies toward dissension."[95]

Yet there are severe limitations to the responsiveness of members to appeals to party loyalty, the influence and reliability of party leaders, and the utility of favors and sanctions, and there are substantial obstacles to party unity. The president cannot always depend on support from members of his party and must often resort to bipartisan appeals for votes, even when his party is in the majority in Congress.

In such circumstances one must sympathize with Speaker Tip O'Neill's somewhat hyperbolic assertion that the Democratic party has become little more than an organizational convenience.[96] Similarly, there is a great deal of truth in one scholar's argument that congressional parties function to coordinate the legislative process rather than mobilize votes.[97]

As a result of the failure of presidential party leadership in Congress to produce reliable support from members of the president's party, promises made to the American people by winning presidential candidates have a lower probability of becoming law than if there were consistent party unity. This in turn makes majority rule less effective.

It is more difficult for voters to know whom to hold accountable for public policy when party discipline is weak. Because it is not necessarily closely tied to the president, his party in Congress can avoid responsibility for governing and focus on parochial matters and constituency interests instead. According to Tip O'Neill, members of Congress no longer have to follow the national philosophy of the party. They can get reelected on their newsletter, or on how they serve their constituents.[98] As Gerald Ford lamented, "Party responsibility does not have any real meaning any more, and that is tragic . . . the parties provide a way for the public to see who is good and who is evil and who does a job and who does not do a job. The parties today are really more or less impotent, and if you do not have party responsibility, the system does not work."[99] Debate over public policy is obscured rather than clarified under such conditions, and programs that are needed now get passed later, if at all.

Despite criticisms by party reformers, Americans seem content with the state of things. Voters evidently like to choose candidates independently of their votes for president or their opinions of the president; members of Con-

95. Sundquist, *The Decline and Resurgence of Congress*, p. 475.

96. "House, Senate Chiefs Attempt to Lead a Changed Congress," *Congressional Quarterly Weekly Report*, September 13, 1980, p. 2696.

97. Light, *The President's Agenda*, p. 213.

98. "House, Senate Chiefs Attempt to Lead a Changed Congress."

99. Ford, "Imperiled, Not Imperial," p. 30.

gress value their freedom to act in whatever ways they choose and can actually enhance their prospects for reelection by ignoring cues from the party; and party leaders at the state and local levels seem in no hurry to defer to centralized control. The big loser is the president, who in his continual efforts to persuade can only do his best to exploit the limited potential of party leadership.

Any reforms aimed at strengthening the president's party leadership must come to terms with these attitudes. Structural reforms that would alter the ways in which candidates are nominated or congressional leaders chosen depend on the acquiescence of persons who have a stake in the status quo. So do internal congressional rules that would enforce party discipline. The probability of any such reforms occurring is very low, and once reforms are made, they require the active support of these same people to ensure that the power they allocate is used on behalf of the president. But there is a little incentive in our system for this to happen. The chance of changing voters' behavior is even slimmer than that of converting party elites. Thus presidential party leadership in Congress is likely to remain just one of the many strategies presidents employ in their ceaseless efforts to obtain congressional support.

Party leadership is useful for the president. It often provides him an additional increment of support for his policies in Congress. Yet it is unlikely to provide the basis for the direction of major change. It is a resource operating at the margins of coalition building. A facilitator who exercises party leadership to exploit an opportunity presented by other factors, rather than a director who bends his fellow partisans to his will, is the type of leader most likely to arise and succeed in such a system.

CHAPTER SIX

Strategic Position of Public Approval

In his first debate with Stephen Douglas, Abraham Lincoln voiced what has become a central tenet in the contemporary study of the presidency: "Public sentiment is everything. With public sentiment nothing can fail; without it nothing can succeed."[1] In a more current analysis, Richard Neustadt argues, "While national party organizations fall away, while congressional party discipline relaxes, while interest groups proliferate and issue networks rise, a President who wishes to compete for leadership in framing policy and shaping coalitions has to make the most he can out of his popular connection."[2] Without question, public support is a primary resource for presidential leadership of Congress.

Interest in the topic of presidential support in the public has burgeoned in recent years, producing such books as *The Public Presidency*,[3] *Going Public*,[4] and *The Personal President*.[5] There can be little doubt that the White House invests enormous amounts of time and energy in its efforts to obtain public support for the president, but it is not yet clear how this potential resource is translated into a tool of presidential leadership of Congress.

Public support is different from the other resources I analyze in this book. Unlike party and legislative skills, public support involves indirect leadership

1. First debate with Stephen A. Douglas, August 21, 1858, in Roy P. Basler, ed., *The Collected Works of Abraham Lincoln* (New Brunswick, N.J.: Rutgers University Press, 1953), p. 27.

2. Richard E. Neustadt, *Presidential Power: The Politics of Leadership from FDR to Carter* (New York: John Wiley and Sons, 1980), p. 238.

3. George C. Edwards III, *The Public Presidency* (New York: St Martin's, 1983).

4. Samuel Kernell, *Going Public* (Washington: Congressional Quarterly Press, 1986).

5. Theodore J. Lowi, *The Personal President* (Ithaca, N.Y.: Cornell University Press, 1985).

of Congress. It is not an attribute of the president but involves a third factor, the public. The president needs to lead public opinion or influence perceptions of it, which in turn may influence congressional voting.

In the next three chapters I explore the relationships between the president and the public and between perceptions of public opinion and presidential support. Because of the special character of public support, I divide my discussion of this resource into separate chapters on public approval of presidential performance and electoral mandates, focusing on both strategic position and presidential efforts at leadership in the same chapter for the latter.

The Nature of the Relationship

The relationship between public approval and presidential support in Congress hinges first on why senators and representatives might respond to the public's evaluation of the president. This depends in turn on the environment of Congress and the potential for public approval to influence voting in Congress.

The Congressional Environment

Members of Congress live in a world characterized by insecurity. They depend on their constituents to retain their seats, which they usually wish to do. Yet the average representative's constituency includes about 550,000 individuals and the average senator's about five million. It is obviously not possible for any member of Congress to have direct knowledge of what more than a few of his or her constituents are thinking about politics and policy, and voters do little to help close this information gap. A relatively small, unrepresentative sample of citizens ever communicate with their representatives about policy issues.[6] To compound their problems, members of Congress are unsure of other important matters directly relevant to their reelections, such

6. *The People, Press, and Politics* (Los Angeles: Times Mirror, 1987), pp. 57–58; Lewis A. Dexter, "The Representative and His District," in *New Perspectives on the House of Representatives*, 2d ed., ed. Robert L. Peabody and Nelson W. Polsby (Chicago: Rand McNally, 1969), pp. 330; Raymond A. Bauer, Ithiel de Sola Pool, and Lewis A. Dexter, *American Business and Public Policy: The Politics of Foreign Trade* (New York: Atherton, 1963), pp. 419–420; Lewis A. Dexter, "What Do Congressmen Hear: The Mail," *Public Opinion Quarterly* 20 (Spring 1956): 16–27; Lewis A. Dexter, "Candidates Make the Issues and Give Them Meaning," *Public Opinion Quarterly* 19 (Winter 1955–56): 408–414; Donald G. Tacheron and Morris K. Udall, *The Job of a Congressman* (Indianapolis: Bobbs Merrill, 1966), pp. 282–283; Leroy N. Rieselbach, *Congressional Politics* (New York: McGraw-Hill, 1973), p. 216; John W. Kingdon, *Congressmen's Voting Decisions* (New York: Harper and Row, 1973), pp. 56–57; John S. Stolarek, Robert M. Wood, and Marcia Whicker Taylor, "Measuring Constituency Opinion in the U.S. House: Mail Versus Random Surveys," *Legislative Studies Quarterly* 6 (November 1981): 589–595.

as who voted for them in the last election, population shifts, the effects of redistricting, and the identity of their next challenger.[7]

With this lack of information comes a strong feeling of vulnerability. As one analyst put it, members of Congress perceive themselves to be "unsafe at any margin."[8] The reforms of the early 1970s brought more open meetings and roll calls, making their actions more public than ever before, and the proliferation of politically active groups puts them under more scrutiny. Any deviation from a group's perspective will be brought to the attention of relevant voters.

In addition, changes in the nature of campaigning have made it easier for challengers to mount effective campaigns in the right circumstances. Direct mail fund-raising and campaigning, political action committees, polling firms, television advertising, and national party campaigns make it possible for challengers who can meet certain thresholds of name recognition, political skills, and resources to contest what might appear to be safe seats.

In recent years much attention has focused on the large margins by which most House members win reelection. Yet one must be careful about the inferences drawn from this fact. Gary Jacobson has shown that "[House] incumbents are not safer now than they were in the 1950s, the marginals, properly defined, have not vanished, the swing-ratio has diminished little, if at all; and so competition for House seats held by incumbents has not declined."[9]

Despite appearances, House elections thus remain competitive, as the framers intended them to be. The Senate, which was designed to insulate members somewhat from the public, is even more subject to electoral competition. According to one senator, "The founding fathers gave senators six-year terms so they could be statesmen for at least four years and not respond to every whim and caprice. Now a senator in his first year knows that any vote could beat him five years later—so senators may behave like House members. They are running constantly."[10]

7. Richard F. Fenno, Jr., "U.S. House Members in Their Constituencies: An Exploration," *American Political Science Review* 71 (September 1977): 886–887. See also Richard F. Fenno, Jr., *Home Style* (Boston: Little, Brown, 1978).

8. Thomas Mann, *Unsafe at Any Margin* (Washington: American Enterprise Institute, 1978).

9. Gary C. Jacobson, "The Marginals Never Vanished: Incumbency and Competition in Elections to the U.S. House of Representatives, 1952–82," *American Journal of Political Science* 31 (February 1987): 126–141. See also Robert S. Erikson, "Is There Such a Thing As a Safe Seat?" *Polity* 8 (Summer 1976): 623–632; Melissa Collie, "Incumbency, Electoral Safety, and Turnover in the House of Representatives, 1952–1976," *American Political Science Review* 75 (March 1981): 119–131.

10. Quoted in "In the Senate of the '80s, Team Spirit Has Given Way to the Rule of Individuals," *Congressional Quarterly Weekly Report*, September 4, 1982, p. 2182.

Although more than 90 percent of House incumbents in the postwar years have won reelection, only 75 percent of senators seeking reelection have been successful. A senator's constituency is usually larger and more diverse socially, economically, and politically than a House district, and because seats in the Senate are especially attractive to potential candidates, there are often effective, well-financed challenges to incumbent senators. Senators also receive more press coverage in office than representatives and are more likely to be held accountable on controversial issues. For this reason senators indeed constantly run for reelection.[11]

As one might expect, members of Congress are well aware of their electoral insecurity and have been raising and spending more campaign funds, sending more franked mail to their constituents, traveling more to their states and districts, and staffing more local offices than ever before.[12] They realize that with the decline of partisan loyalty in the electorate, they bear more of the burden of obtaining votes.

A primary task of members of Congress is to preempt an effective challenge to their reelection by demonstrating broad support and a lack of vulnerability in their constituencies. Thus they are in most cases highly attentive to their constituents and eager to avoid votes and stands on issue that might be a catalyst for strong opponents to emerge.[13]

In such an environment, it should come as no surprise that senators and representatives are hypersensitive to the anticipated reaction of their constituents to their actions. They overestimate their visibility to their constituents and the extent to which the electorate is concerned about issues.[14] Whether or not voters follow the issues of the day or know how members of Congress vote on them, the members certainly act as if their votes make a difference in

11. Timothy E. Cook, "The Electoral Connection in the 99th Congress," *PS* 19 (Winter 1986): 16–19.

12. Glenn R. Parker, *Homeward Bound* (Pittsburgh: University of Pittsburgh Press, 1986); John R. Johannes, *To Serve the People* (Lincoln: University of Nebraska Press, 1984); Glenn R. Parker, "Is There a Political Life Cycle in the House of Representatives?" *Legislative Studies Quarterly* 11 (August 1986): 375–392.

13. Fenno, *Home Style*; and sources cited in note 12.

14. Donald E. Stokes and Warren E. Miller, "Party Government and the Saliency of Congress," *Public Opinion Quarterly* 26 (Winter 1962): 531–546; Warren E. Miller and Donald E. Stokes, "Constituency Influences on Congress," *American Political Science Review* 57 (March 1963): 45–56; Charles F. Cnudde and Donald J. McCrone, "Linkage between Constituency Attitudes and Congressional Voting Behavior: A Causal Model," *American Political Science Review* 60 (March 1966): 66–72; John W. Kingdon, *Candidates for Office* (New York: Random House, 1968), p. 145; Kingdon, *Congressmen's Voting Decisions*, pp. 59–61; Roger H. Davidson, *The Role of the Congressmen* (New York: Pegasus, 1968), p. 121.

their chances for reelection or elevation from the House to the Senate.[15]

Reinforcing this concern for public opinion are the role perceptions of members of Congress. Although good time series data on congressional role perceptions are lacking, and the way in which these perceptions affect behavior is unclear, there is some reason to believe that many senators and representatives feel they ought to reflect public opinion in their voting in Congress.[16] To the extent that this holds at any given time, it increases the sensitivity of members of Congress to the electorate.

Members of Congress thus face an environment of uncertainty and vulnerability. They want to please their constituents, yet often do not know how the voters feel about matters of public policy or politics. Looming over this arena is the public official who is the most visible and whom senators and representatives must continuously take into account: the president.

As the central figure in American politics, the president is the object of a constant stream of commentary and evaluation by all segments of society, including those that are unlikely to articulate specific policy preferences. Indeed, press coverage of the president and his policies exceeds that of all other political figures combined.[17] The president's standing in the public provides members of Congress with a guide to the public's views.

15. Gerald C. Wright, Jr., and Michael B. Berkman, "Candidates and Policy in United States Senate Elections," *American Political Science Review* 80 (June 1986): 567–590; John R. Hibbing, "Ambition in the House: Behavioral Consequences of Higher Office Goals among U.S. Representatives," *American Journal of Political Science* 30 (August 1986): 651–665; Martin Thomas, "Election Proximity and Senatorial Roll-Call Voting," *American Journal of Political Science* 29 (February 1985): 96–111; Richard C. Elling, "Ideological Change in the United States Senate: Time and Electoral Responsiveness," *Legislative Studies Quarterly* 7 (February 1982): 75–92; Richard F. Fenno, Jr., *The United States Senate: A Bicameral Perspective* (Washington: American Enterprise Institute, 1982); John R. Hibbing, "The Liberal Hour: Electoral Pressures and Transfer Payment Voting in the United States Congress," *Journal of Politics* 46 (August 1984): 846–863.

16. Davidson, *The Role of the Congressman*, pp. 79–80, 117; Thomas E. Cavanaugh, "Role Orientations of House Members: The Process of Representation" (paper delivered at the annual meeting of the American Political Science Association, Washington, August 1979).

17. See for example Richard Davis, "News Coverage of American Political Institutions" (paper presented of the annual meeting of the American Political Science Association, Washington, August 1986); Michael Baruch Grossman and Martha Joynt Kumar, *Portraying the President* (Baltimore: Johns Hopkins University Press, 1981), pp. 258–259, 265; Elmer E. Cornwell, Jr., "Presidential News: The Expanding Public Image," *Journalism Quarterly* 36 (Summer 1959): 275–283; Alan P. Balutis, "The Presidency and the Press: The Expanding Presidential Image," *Presidential Studies Quarterly* 7 (Fall 1977): 244–251; Norman Ornstein and Michael Robinson, "The Case of Our Disappearing Congress," *TV Guide*, January 11, 1986, pp. 4–6, 8–10. See also Herbert J. Gans, *Deciding What's News* (New York: Vintage, 1979), p. 9.

Because of the high visibility and frequency of presidential approval polls, it is safe to assume that members of Congress are aware of the president's standing with the public. In addition, senators and representatives learn of the public's opinion of the president from other political elites, political activists, leaders of interest groups, the press, attentive publics, and constituents. Some of what they hear may be echoes of their own actions in government.

The public's evaluations of the president are important not only as surrogates for broader opinions on politics and policy, but also as influences on congressional behavior. Members of Congress must anticipate the public's reaction to their decisions to support or oppose the president and his policies. Depending on the president's public standing, they may choose to be close to him or independent from him to increase their chances of reelection. Polls find that a significant percentage of voters see their votes for candidates for Congress as support for the president or opposition to him.[18]

One study found that members of Congress spent more time in their constituencies when the president's approval ratings were low, explaining how they differed from him.[19] Similarly, members of the president's party try to distance themselves from him during election periods if he is low in the polls. This anticipation of the voter's reaction to their support for the president is quite sensible. Members of Congress defeated in the election of 1974, for example, had supported Richard Nixon more than their colleagues had who won reelection.[20] Another study found that regardless of party, representatives who do not support the president's programs are not punished by the voters if the president's policies are perceived as unsuccessful, but strong supporters of the president are less fortunate.[21]

The White House encourages members of Congress to infer from the president's approval levels the public's support for his policies. Ultimately, the effectiveness of this strategy is tied to the potential for making the support of a senator or representative a campaign issue. Presidents high in the polls are in a position to make such threats. According to an aide to Reagan, for example, the president's contacts with members of Congress before the tax

18. See for example *CBS News/The New York Times Poll* (news release, October 30, 1986), tables 21, 27.

19. Glenn R. Parker, "Cycles in Congressional District Attention," *Journal of Politics* 42 (May 1980): 547.

20. Walter D. Burnham, "Insulation and Responsiveness in Congressional Elections," *Political Science Quarterly* 90 (Fall 1975): 418; "1974 Support in Congress: Ford Low, Nixon Up," *Congressional Quarterly Weekly Report*, January 18, 1975, p. 148.

21. John R. Alford and John R. Hibbing, "The Conditions Required for Economic Issue Voting: Actions Speak More Loudly than Partisan Affiliation" (paper presented at the annual meeting of the Midwest Political Science Association, Chicago, April 1984).

vote of 1981 were "merely a device to keep the congressmen thinking about what could happen next year. I'm sure Mr. Reagan is charming as hell, but that isn't what is important. It's his reminding these people that they could lose their jobs next year."[22]

Members of Congress may also use the president's standing in the polls as an indicator of his ability to mobilize public opinion against his opponents. Senators and representatives are especially likely to be sensitive to this possibility after a successful demonstration of the president's ability to mobilize the public, as appears to have occurred in response to the efforts of Reagan's White House in 1981.[23] As Richard Neustadt put it, "Washingtonians . . . are vulnerable to any breeze from home that presidential words and sighs can stir. If he is deemed effective on the tube, they will anticipate."[24]

Looking at the matter from another perspective, low presidential approval ratings free members of Congress from supporting the president if they are otherwise inclined to oppose him. A senior political aide to President Carter noted:

> When the President is low in public opinion polls, the Members of Congress see little hazard in bucking him. . . . After all, very few Congressmen examine an issue solely on its merits; they are politicians and they think politically. I'm not saying they make only politically expedient choices. But they read the polls and from that they feel secure in turning their back on the President with political impunity. Unquestionably, the success of the President's policies bear a tremendous relationship to his popularity in the polls.[25]

Similarly, Lyndon Johnson found fewer members of Congress eager to attend White House receptions or discuss matters of policy with him when his standing in the polls declined.[26]

Views from the White House
Thus there are solid theoretical reasons for expecting members of Congress to be responsive to the president's standing in the public. What about the view from the White House? What do the participants have to say?

22. Quoted in Paul C. Light, *The President's Agenda: Domestic Policy Choice from Kennedy to Carter (with Notes on Reagan)* (Baltimore: Johns Hopkins University Press, 1983), p. xiii.

23. See Kernell, *Going Public*, pp. 115–123.

24. Neustadt, *Presidential Power*, p. 238.

25. Quoted in Dom Bonafede, "The Strained Relationship," *National Journal*, May 19, 1979, p. 830.

26. Nigel Bowles, *The White House and Capitol Hill* (New York: Oxford University Press, 1987), pp. 99, 102, 104.

Dwight Eisenhower, one of our most popular postwar presidents, went to considerable lengths to nurture his public support. According to Fred Greenstein, Eisenhower "was fully aware that his popularity was essential to his ability to exercise influence over other leaders. As he once noted, 'one man can do a lot . . . at any particular given moment, if at that moment he happens to be ranking high in public estimation.'"[27]

Lyndon Johnson understood well the advantage public support afforded him. In his memoirs he declared that "Presidential popularity is a major source of strength in gaining cooperation from Congress."[28] Johnson's aide Harry McPherson agrees, remembering that members of Congress "listened hard for evidence of how the President stood in their states in order that they might know how to treat him."[29]

Richard Nixon agreed with his predecessor about the importance of the president's standing in the public. On the evening of his second inauguration he recorded in his diary his concern over the drop he expected in his approval levels in response to the extensive Christmas bombing of North Vietnam. The polls could affect his ability to lead, "since politicians do pay attention to them."[30] Earlier, Nixon also expressed his concern at his dependence on his general support from the public when he wrote, "No leader survives simply by doing well. A leader survives when people have confidence in him when he's not doing well."[31]

President Carter's aides were quite explicit about the importance of the president's public approval in their efforts to influence Congress. One stated that the "only way to keep [Congress] honest is to keep our popularity high."[32] The president's legislative liaison officials generally agreed that their effectiveness with Congress ultimately depended upon the president's ability to influence public opinion. As one of them said, "When you go up to the Hill and the latest polls show Carter isn't doing well, there isn't much reason for a member to go along with him. There's little we can do if the member isn't persuaded on the issue."[33] Another aide at the White House was even more

27. Fred I. Greenstein, *The Hidden-Hand Presidency* (New York: Basic Books, 1982), p. 99.
28. *Lyndon B. Johnson, The Vantage Point: Perspectives of the Presidency, 1963–1969* (New York: Popular Library, 1971), p. 443.
29. Harry McPherson, *A Political Education* (Boston: Little, Brown, 1972), pp. 246–247.
30. Richard M. Nixon, *RN: The Memoirs of Richard M. Nixon* (New York: Grosset and Dunlap, 1977), p. 753.
31. Quoted in William Safire, *Before the Fall: An Inside View of the Pre-Watergate White House* (New York: Doubleday, 1975), p. 284.
32. Quoted in "Run, Run, Run," *Newsweek*, May 2, 1977, p. 38. See also the statement of Hamilton Jordan in the same article.
33. Quoted in "Carter Seeks More Effective Use of Departmental Lobbyists' Skills," *Congressional Quarterly Weekly Report*, March 4, 1978, p. 585.

explicit: "No president whose popularity is as low as this President's has much clout on the Hill."[34]

President Reagan's administration was especially sensitive to the president's public approval levels. According to David Gergen, the head of the White House Office of Communication in Reagan's first term, "Everything here is built on the idea that the president's success depends on grassroots support."[35]

Potential for Influence

There is reason to expect members of Congress to respond to the president's support from the public. Yet we should not conclude that this relationship is either simple or direct. Many scholars who examine the impact of public support for the president on the support he receives in Congress approach it on a tactical level. In other words, they view public support for the president as increasing the probability that members of Congress will vote for the president's proposals. According to the argument, senators and representatives include the president's public standing in their decision-making calculus and are more inclined to support the president when the people do. The essence of this relationship is conversion.

Yet one should not expect public approval to translate directly into support in Congress. No matter how low a president's standing with the public or how small the margin of his election, he still receives support from a substantial number of senators and representatives. Similarly, no matter how high his approval levels climb or how large his winning percentage of the vote, a significant portion of the Congress still opposes his policies.

The president's public support must compete for influence with other, more stable factors that affect voting in Congress, including ideology, party, personal views and commitments on specific policies, and constituency interests. Although constituency interests may seem to overlap with presidential approval, they should be viewed as distinct. It is quite possible for constituents to approve of the president but oppose him on particular policies, and it is opinions on these policies that will ring most loudly in congressional ears. The opposition of farmers to Ronald Reagan's agricultural policies in 1985 and 1986 is a case in point.

The responsiveness of members of Congress to public approval for the president results from the interaction of several factors: (1) congressional fear of the reactions of constituents; (2) the disposition of members of Congress to

34. Quoted in "Slings and Arrow," *Newsweek*, July 31, 1978, p. 20.

35. Quoted in Sidney Blumenthal, "Marketing the President," *New York Times Magazine*, September 13, 1981, p. 110.

support the president; (3) the potential movement of congressional support; and (4) the potential movement of public opinion.

Members of the president's party in Congress typically give him much higher support than do members of the opposition. As a result, they have the greatest potential to lower their support in response to a decrease in the president's standing among their constituents, the most important of whom are their party's identifiers (discussed below). Such a decrease does not normally occur, however. Further, these members of Congress will be in general agreement with much of what their party leader proposes, and therefore this potential is unlikely to be realized. They want to support the chief executive and have incentives to fight any responsiveness to decreases in his public approval.

On the other hand, the already high levels of support of these members of Congress preclude them from increasing their support very much in response to an increase in the president's approval rate. At the same time there will always be some intraparty opposition to the president, and presidential supporters have a clear record of backing the White House that they can exhibit to their constituents to ward off possible primary challenges based on their personal lack of support for the president.

In addition, because the president is typically reasonably high in the polls among members of his own party in the public, there is limited potential for him to rise much higher. Only three presidents increased their support among party members in the public over the levels that they enjoyed in their first year in office (table 6.1): Eisenhower (1955, 1956, and 1959: 6, 4, and 1 percentage point), Nixon (1972: 3 percentage points), and Reagan (1984–86: 4, 3, and 1 percentage point).

Members of the opposition party generally accord the president low support and therefore cannot decrease their support much if his approval ratings slip. They will certainly agree with at least some of what he proposes, and there is much less room for the president's approval to fall among members of the opposition party than among those in his own party. Typically the president stands 38 percentage points lower in the polls among members of the opposition than among members of his own party.

In the interest of electoral survival, the opposition party can substantially increase its support for the president in response to a notable rise in his standing among its electoral constituency, but such increases are rare. In fact, there is no instance since World War II in which the president's approval ratings among opposition party members in the public in a given year exceeded the ratings in his first year in office (table 6.1). In addition, members of the opposition party typically do not want to support the White House and will respond to increases in presidential approval only under duress. This sometimes occurs, but it is not a reliable basis for obtaining congressional support.

TABLE 6.1   Average Yearly Presidential Approval (in Percent)

Year	Party of President	All Respondents	Democrats	Republicans	Independents
1953	R	68	56	87	68
1954	R	66	50	88	69
1955	R	71	56	90	74
1956	R	73	56	93	76
1957	R	64	47	86	66
1958	R	55	37	82	56
1959	R	64	48	88	66
1960	R	62	46	88	65
1961	D	75	87	58	71
1962	D	72	86	49	69
1963	D	65	79	46	62
1964	D	74	84	62	67
1965	D	66	79	49	60
1966	D	51	67	32	44
1967	D	44	59	26	38
1968	D	42	57	26	35
1969	R	61	49	82	60
1970	R	57	41	82	57
1971	R	50	35	79	48
1972	R	56	40	84	57
1973	R	42	26	70	42
1974	R	35	24	58	35
1975	R	43	32	65	44
1976	R	48	36	69	50
1977	D	62	73	46	60
1978	D	46	57	28	42
1979	D	37	46	24	34
1980	D	41	53	25	35
1981	R	58	40	85	59
1982	R	44	23	79	46
1983	R	44	24	78	47
1984	R	55	28	89	58
1985	R	60	36	88	60
1986	R	60	40	86	61

R = Republican
D = Democrat
SOURCE: Gallup Poll

The standard deviation of presidential support for the typical president is quite small (table 6.2). Much of the variance that does exist is a result of the deviant years of 1959, 1964, and 1968. Public approval is more volatile (see table 6.3), but for most of the period under study the range of opinion is modest. The principal exceptions relate to the unusual circumstances of Johnson's inflated approval in the wake of the assassination of President Ken-

TABLE 6.2   Standard Deviations of Presidential Support

| | Nonunanimous Support | | | |
| | *House* | | *Senate* | |
Presidents	*Democrats*	*Republicans*	*Democrats*	*Republicans*
Eisenhower	6.6	9.5	5.0	3.1
Kennedy	1.5	4.5	2.6	3.5
Johnson	6.0	5.9	7.4	7.7
Nixon[a]	6.6	5.7	6.4	1.1
Ford[b]	3.5	0.7	4.9	3.5
Carter	1.7	3.4	3.0	1.4
Reagan[c]	5.3	4.3	4.9	3.7

| | Key Votes | | | |
| | *House* | | *Senate* | |
Presidents	*Democrats*	*Republicans*	*Democrats*	*Republicans*
Eisenhower	6.2	8.0	6.2	5.2
Kennedy	3.2	1.5	6.7	7.1
Johnson	8.4	6.1	6.5	7.3
Nixon[a]	6.6	3.3	10.7	9.9
Ford[b]	3.5	8.5	0.7	0.7
Carter	5.7	1.4	4.6	11.1
Reagan[c]	4.5	3.5	5.6	7.8

[a]1969–73
[b]1975–76
[c]1981–86

nedy, Nixon's losses in public support as a result of the Watergate scandal, and Carter's mercurial support during the Iranian hostage crisis.

On reexamining table 3.1, one finds that Senate Republicans have varied little in their presidential support within presidential terms, except in 1964. Senate Democratic support has been similarly stable, except in 1959 and 1968. House Democrats provided stable intraterm support except in 1973. House Republicans were the most volatile in their support, especially under Republican presidents, and even here the standard deviations are not large.

Because of constraints on the movement of public approval of the president and congressional support for the president, and because of differences in the disposition to support the chief executive, only some members of Congress are likely to respond to changes in the president's standing with the public. The president's strategic position is such that a fundamental leadership resource is useful primarily at the margins of coalition building.

TABLE 6.3   Standard Deviations of Presidential Approval

Presidents	All Respondents	Democrats	Republicans	Independents
Eisenhower	7.0	9.2	4.6	7.7
Kennedy	6.9	5.4	10.9	7.9
Johnson	13.0	11.3	14.7	13.4
Nixon	13.7	13.4	12.7	14.1
Ford	7.1	8.3	5.7	7.8
Carter	12.1	12.2	11.7	13.2
Reagan (1981–86)	7.7	8.7	5.7	8.1

A more useful orientation than that of conversion is Richard Neustadt's view that public approval operates mostly in the background and sets limits on what Congress will do for the president or to him. Widespread support gives him leeway and weakens resistance to his policies.[36] Lack of public support strengthens the resolve of those inclined to oppose the president and narrows the range in which he receives the benefit of the doubt.

A president with strong public support provides a cover for members of Congress to cast votes to which their constituents might otherwise object. They can defend their votes as having been made in support of the president rather than on substantive policy grounds alone. Of course, a president without public support loses this advantage and may find himself avoided by members of Congress who will certainly not articulate their decisions as having been made in support of the president if the president is caught in the depths of the polls.

In addition, low ratings in the polls may create incentives to attack the president, further eroding his already weakened position. For example, after the arms sales to Iran and the diversion of funds to the contras became a cause célèbre in late 1986, it became more acceptable in Congress and in the press to raise questions about Ronald Reagan's capacities as president. Disillusionment is a dangerous force for the White House.

The impact of public approval for the president on congressional support for the president occurs at the margins, within the confines of other influences. Members of Congress are unlikely to vote against the clear interests of their constituents or the firm tenets of their ideology solely in deference to a widely supported chief executive. Approval gives a president leverage, but not control.

Thus studies that search for a relationship between presidential approval and presidential support in Congress within or between short periods of time

36. Neustadt, *Presidential Power*, chap. 5.

are theoretically irrelevant. They also have severe methodological weaknesses, including a failure to recognize the lack of variability in the independent variable.[37] There is no theoretical reason to expect such close associations. The impact of public approval is at once broader and more subtle.

The Impact of Public Approval

In recent years there has been substantial interest in the impact of public approval on the president's success in Congress. Studies have found approval related to the rate of victories on roll calls,[38] the probability that there will be attempts to override presidential vetoes and the probability that they will succeed,[39] and congressional support in general.[40] One must of course be cautious in studying this relationship.

Nixon's Decline

In 1973 President Nixon won only 51 percent of the votes in Congress on which he took a stand, fewer than any president in this study; his second-lowest percentage, 66, came in the preceding year. Nixon's record for 1973 would have been even lower without the many routine votes that took place at the end of the year. According to the measured Nonunanimous Support, his support decreased among all members of Congress, especially Democrats (table 6.4).

Why did this happen? Nixon had just won one of the greatest landslide victories in history, carrying every state except Massachusetts (and the District of Columbia). There were twelve more Republicans in the House and two more in the Senate in 1973 than in 1972, when he received considerably more support.

American military involvement in Vietnam had virtually ended at the time of Nixon's second inauguration and therefore should have been less of an

37. Jon R. Bond and Richard Fleisher, "Presidential Popularity and Congressional Voting: A Reexamination of Public Opinion as a Source of Influence in Congress," *Western Political Quarterly* 37 (June 1984): 291–306; Harvey G. Zeidenstein, "Varying Relationships Between Presidents' Popularity and Their Legislative Success: A Futile Search for Patterns," *Presidential Studies Quarterly* 13 (Fall 1983): 530–550.

38. Charles W. Ostrom, Jr., and Dennis M. Simon, "Promise and Performance: A Dynamic Model of Presidential Popularity," *American Political Science Review* 79 (June 1985): 349; Douglas Rivers and Nancy L. Rose, "Passing the President's Program: Public Opinion and Presidential Influence in Congress," *American Journal of Political Science* 29 (May 1985): 183–196.

39. David W. Rohde and Dennis M. Simon, "Presidential Vetoes and Congressional Response: A Study of Institutional Conflict," *American Journal of Political Science* 29 (August 1985): 397–427.

40. George C. Edwards III, *Presidential Influence in Congress* (San Francisco: W. H. Freeman, 1980), chap. 4.

TABLE 6.4   Nonunanimous Support for President Nixon, 1972–73
(in Percent)

	1972	1973	Difference
House			
Democrats	46	31	−15
Republicans	68	65	−3
Senate			
Democrats	34	24	−10
Republicans	66	64	−2

irritation to Congress. Bob Haldeman and John Ehrlichman, who were disliked for their arrogance and formed the cornerstone of the so-called Berlin Wall around the president, were early victims of Watergate. The ineffective vice president, Spiro Agnew, fell to his own tragedy, and the president brought Bryce Harlow and Melvin Laird into the White House and nominated Gerald Ford as Agnew's successor. These three men were experienced in dealing with Congress, which liked and respected them. The chief congressional liaison aide, William Timmons, reported that the president held more meetings with the leaders of both parties and with the Republican rank and file, and had more social contact with members of Congress than ever before.[41] All these actions should have increased rather than lowered Nixon's support in Congress. What explains the decline in support for the president?

One might argue that Congress was angered by Nixon's arrogant approach toward it and his unique conception of the separation of powers, which involved the impoundment of a large amount of appropriated funds, the waging of an undeclared war, and an expansive claim of executive privilege. Nevertheless, just because members of Congress may have been alienated by certain actions by the president, they would not necessarily oppose him on legislation unrelated to these actions (as almost all legislation was). In addition, Nixon's activity regarding impoundment, undeclared war, and executive privilege was prevalent well before 1973. The most reasonable explanation for Richard Nixon's substantial decline in support among members of Congress in 1973 is his equally substantial decline in public approval, primarily because of the Watergate affair. In December 1972 his overall approval stood at 59 percent; one year later it had fallen to 29 percent. Without public support his legislative program languished.

In 1974 the president largely withdrew as a legislative leader. He added only five proposals to his domestic legislative agenda, took positions on fewer

41. "White House Study of Nixon Support in 93rd Congress . . . Finds Only 100 Votes at Present for Impeachment," *Congressional Quarterly Weekly Report*, January 19, 1974, p. 81.

than a fifth of congressional roll calls, vetoed only two bills, and generally avoided controversy that might antagonize Congress. In contrast, Gerald Ford vetoed twenty-four bills in the last five months of 1974 alone.[42]

Reagan's Blitzkrieg

The fundamental basis for Ronald Reagan's success in Congress in 1981 was his support from the public. Although he began his tenure with a modest approval rating of 51 percent, he climbed steadily in the polls, peaking at 68 percent in mid-May, just in time for the crucial votes on his spending and tax proposals.

Much of this increase was due to the assassination attempt against him on March 30. His dignity and good humor under adverse conditions endeared him to the American people and gave his approval ratings a significant boost. Although it is somewhat macabre to argue that being shot was a political asset, the assassination attempt provided the president with a substantial increase in public support at a crucial juncture in the policy-making process.

Public approval reinforced perceptions of an electoral mandate (see chapter 8) and was quickly translated into legislative victories on budget and tax cuts. Members of Congress were clear as to its impact. According to Congressman Kent Hance of Texas, the Conservative Democratic Forum's point man on the tax bill, "Reagan won 72 percent of the vote in my district and he's a lot more popular now than he was on Election Day. It's mighty tough to go against a popular president in a district like mine."[43]

Democratic leaders agreed with Hance's analysis. Regarding the president's proposed reductions in expenditures, Speaker Tip O'Neill declared that legislators "go along with the will of the people, and the will of the people is to go along with the President."[44] Similarly, the Senate's Democratic leader, Robert Byrd, justified voting for the president's budget by saying that "people want the President to be given a chance."[45]

Unfortunately for the president, his honeymoon with the public soon ended. By November his approval was below 50 percent, a fall of 19 percentage points since May. The impact of this drop was immediately evident. A bill

42. Richard W. Boyd and David J. Hadley, "Presidential and Congressional Response to Political Crisis: Nixon, Congress, and Watergate," *Congress and the Presidency* 10 (Autumn 1983): 195–218; Light, *The President's Agenda*, p. 41.

43. Quoted in "Conservative Southerners Are Enjoying their Wooing as Key to Tax Bill Success," *Congressional Quarterly Weekly Report*, June 13, p. 1024.

44. Quoted in "Budget Fight Shows O'Neill's Fragile Grasp," *Congressional Quarterly Weekly Report*, May 9, 1981, p. 786.

45. Quoted in Barbara Kellerman, *The Political Presidency* (New York: Oxford University Press, 1984), p. 244.

TABLE 6.5   Nonunanimous Support for President Reagan, 1981–82
             (in Percent)

	1981	1982	Difference
House			
Democrats	39	30	−9
Republicans	72	61	−11
Senate			
Democrats	33	35	+2
Republicans	81	72	−9

from the White House asking for additional budget cuts never even made it to the floor in either chamber. According to a special assistant to the Republican Senate leader, Howard Baker, "When all's well, when the president's policies are popular, senators attach themselves to him for all to see; when things aren't so rosy, senators suddenly become more independent. It's the survival instinct at work."[46]

In 1982 the president's approval ratings were below 50 percent for the entire year and fewer Americans approved of his performance than disapproved. His budget was largely ignored by Congress. All elements in Congress reduced their support markedly, except for Senate Democrats, who were already giving him little (table 6.5). By 1983 House Republicans refused even to propose the president's budget, much less vote for it. In the absence of public support for the president, Congress took a more independent path.

Regression Analysis

A more rigorous and systematic examination of the influence of presidential approval on presidential support in Congress may be made with regression analysis. There are two premises that require discussion. First, I have assumed that members of Congress follow public opinion about the president rather than shape it. If the reverse were true, then support for the president among members of Congress could not be a response to public approval of the president. That some members of Congress, particularly key members, do affect public opinion seems plausible, but the extent is unmeasured and perhaps unmeasurable. Most members of Congress are not highly visible to their constituents,[47] and are unlikely to influence greatly their constituents' approval of the president.

46. James A. Miller, *Running in Place* (New York: Simon and Schuster, 1986), pp. 76–77.

47. See Stokes and Miller, "Party Government and the Saliency of Congress"; George C. Edwards III, *The Public Presidency* (New York: St. Martin's, 1983), p. 25 and sources cited therein.

Another possibility is that a third factor influences both congressional support and public support for the president. If so, the relationship between the two variables will be spurious. The president's party may have such an impact, which I discuss below. Or members of each party among the public and in Congress may react to the president on the basis of his legislative proposals. In this case presidential programs rather than approval determine presidential support. This reasoning assumes however, that the public and members of Congress respond to presidential programs similarly, which is unlikely given their differences in background, responsibilities, and access to information on presidential proposals. In addition, this line of reasoning assumes that public and congressional evaluations of the president are based solely on his legislative programs. Presidential approval and support would be little influenced by the president's failure to propose programs, his policies that are not voted on by Congress (such as administrative decisions and much foreign policy), and his handling of other matters (Watergate, State of the Union messages, and so on). These assumptions are difficult to accept.

The possibility that both the public and members of Congress respond similarly to the president's general performance seems equally unlikely. The differences between the two groups preclude such an assumption. Representatives would have to translate their general evaluations into specific votes on legislative proposals, which in turn would match changes in the public's general approval of the president. This is hardly likely.

The results of regressing presidential support on overall presidential approval appear in table 6.6.[48] Of primary interest in this and the following tables are the regression coefficients (B). They indicate a modest positive relationship between presidential approval and presidential support, as would be expected. On the average, the president receives about an additional 1.5 percentage points in congressional support for every 10 percentage points of public approval he achieves.

Employing overall presidential approval as the independent variable may not be the best strategy. If members of Congress respond to the president's standing in the public to increase the probability that they will be reelected, they should be most concerned with their reelection constituen-

---

48. See Gary King, "How Not to Lie with Statistics: Avoiding Common Mistakes in Quantitative Political Science," *American Journal of Political Science* 30 (August 1986): 666–687 for an excellent discussion of the use and presentation of data in regression analysis.

In table 6.6 and the following tables the symbol * in the column for the Durbin-Watson statistic indicates that the original equation had positive autocorrelation at the .01 level. First-order autocorrelation is the type most likely to arise with this type of data, and corrections were made by including a lagged (one-year) value of the dependent variable as an explanatory variable. It is the results from the corrected equations that appear in the tables.

TABLE 6.6   Relationship between Presidential Approval and Presidential Support, 1953–86

	Support	B	SE	Level of Significance	SED	Constant	Durbin-Watson
House	NS	.13	.06	.03	3.58	23.6	*
	KV	.15	.06	.02	4.03	41.3	1.76
Senate	NS	.17	.07	.02	4.19	21.4	*
	KV	.14	.10	.17	6.54	45.1	1.59

N   = 34
NS = Nonunanimous Support
KV = Key Votes
SE = Standard Error
SED = Standard Error of the Disturbances
*   = Corrected for autocorrelation

cies. There is substantial evidence that senators and representatives do not pay equal heed to all the voters they represent. Those to whom they are most responsive are generally part of their electoral coalitions. In addition, members of Congress are likely to receive communications from their electoral supporters more frequently than from other constituents.[49]

Party identification is the best predictor of sources of support for members of Congress. One would expect members of Congress to be more responsive to presidential approval among members of the electorate who share their party affiliation and compose the core of their electoral bases. Democratic members of Congress should be most responsive to Democratic party identifiers and Republican members to Republican party identifiers.

49. See Kingdon, *Congressmen's Voting Decisions*, p. 34; Miller and Stokes, "Constituency Influence on Congress"; Dexter, "The Representative and His District"; Duncan MacRae, *Dimensions of Congressional Voting* (Berkeley: University of California Press, 1958), p. 264; Aage R. Clausen, *How Congressmen Decide: A Policy Focus* (New York: St. Martin's, 1973), pp. 126–127, 182, 188; Morris P. Fiorina, *Representatives, Roll Calls, and Constituencies* (Lexington, Mass.: Lexington Books, 1974); Fenno, *Home Style*; Stolarek, Wood, and Taylor, "Measuring Constituency Opinion in the U.S. House"; Keith T. Poole and Howard Rosenthal, "The Polarization of American Politics," *Journal of Politics* 46 (November 1984): 1061–1074; Amihai Glazer and Marc Robbins, "Congressional Responsiveness to Constituency Change," *American Journal of Political Science* 29 (May 1985): 259–273; Gregory Markus, "Electoral Coalitions and Senate Roll-Call Behavior: An Ecological Analysis," *American Journal of Political Science* 18 (August 1974): 595–608; Bruce I. Oppenheimer, "Senators' Constituencies: Suggestions for Redefinition" (paper presented at the annual meeting of the American Political Science Association, Chicago, September 1971); Christopher H. Achen, "Measuring Representation," *American Journal of Political Science* 22 (August 1978): 475–510; Charles S. Bullock III and David W. Brady, "Party, Constituency, and U.S. Senate Voting Behavior" (paper presented at the annual meeting of the Southern Political Science Association, New Orleans, November 1977).

As is the case with presidential support, a failure to disaggregate presidential approval may lead to puzzling data and inappropriate inferences. For example, in 1984 President Reagan's approval rating averaged 55 percent for the year. This figure masks considerable variance, however: the approval rating was 89 percent among Republicans, 29 percent among Democrats. An analyst who compares the president's meager congressional support levels from Democrats that year to his overall approval ratings may erroneously conclude that there was no relationship at all, and the strong Republican support in Congress may seem equally baffling.

In addition, the correlation (r) of .81 between Democratic and Republican approval indicates that although the variables are closely related, they are conceptually distinct. (It is not appropriate to correlate partisan opinion with overall opinion, because the former is a large component of the latter. To do so would be to correlate opinion with itself.) Moreover, the relationships (not shown) between overall presidential approval and presidential support among party groups in Congress are weaker than the figures shown in table 6.7. By matching senators and representatives with their electoral constituencies, one obtains a better sense of the relationship between public approval and congressional support.

Table 6.7 gives the results of regressing presidential approval among party-identified groups with the presidential support of their fellow partisans in Congress. The president's party is controlled for because of the large changes in presidential approval and presidential support associated with changes in the party of the president, which could artificially inflate the relationship between the two (fig. 1).

In the House the coefficients for Democrats (for both Nonunanimous Support and Key Votes) are impressive and indicate that an increase of 10 percentage points in presidential approval among Democrats among the public is associated with a 3 or 4 percentage point increase in Democratic support for the president in Congress. In the Senate the Democratic coefficients are

FIGURE 1   Paths of Influence among Presidential Party, Presidential
            Approval, and Presidential Support

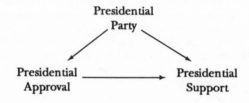

TABLE 6.7 Relationship between Presidential Approval and Presidential Support within Parties, 1953–86

Party Group	Support	B	SE	House Level of Significance	SED	Constant	Durbin-Watson
D	NS	.32	.09	.00	6.07	68.5	1.51
D	KV	.42	.09	.00	6.39	55.5	1.84
R	NS	−.02	.10	.84	6.36	−9.8	2.29
R	KV	−.15	.11	.21	6.87	−15.5	1.39

Party Group	Support	B	SE	Senate Level of Significance	SED	Constant	Durbin-Watson
D	NS	.19	.08	.03	5.39	69.0	1.72
D	KV	.15	.10	.13	6.71	79.4	2.54
R	NS	.28	.10	.01	6.00	11.82	*
R	KV	.08	.16	.61	9.66	10.10	1.65

N   = 34
NS   = Nonunanimous Support
KV   = Key Votes
SE   = Standard Error
SED = Standard Error of the Disturbances
D   = Democrat
R   = Republican
*   = Corrected for autocorrelation

more modest, but still indicate a positive relationship between presidential approval and presidential support.

The figures for Republicans are quite different. In the House they are much weaker than those for the Democrats and are actually negative. The Senate results are mixed. The coefficient for Nonunanimous Support is strong whereas that for Key Votes is not.

It is possible that aggregating all thirty-four years of the study in one equation masks different relationships between public approval and congressional support in Democratic and Republican presidential years. Thus it is worthwhile to examine the relationship between presidential approval among identifiers with each party in the public and presidential support among the corresponding party members in the House and Senate, and to do so separately in Democratic and Republican presidential years (table 6.8).

In the House, Democrats show some responsiveness to presidential approval under both Democratic and Republican presidents. The presidential support of House Republicans continues to show no positive relationship with

TABLE 6.8   Relationship between Presidential Approval and Presidential
Support by Party of the President, 1953–86

Party Group	Support	PP	B	SE	House Level of Significance	SED	Constant	Durbin-Watson
D	NS	D	.30	.08	.01	3.97	48.1	1.64
D	NS	R	.34	.14	.03	7.01	24.6	1.40
D	KV	D	.48	.12	.00	5.84	33.5	1.89
D	KV	R	.36	.14	.02	6.75	22.0	1.70
R	NS	D	−.11	.11	.32	4.94	32.2	1.69
R	NS	R	.10	.17	.58	6.96	57.4	2.25
R	KV	D	−.30	.12	.03	5.31	38.2	1.41
R	KV	R	.06	.18	.75	7.29	62.7	1.24

Party Group	Support	PP	B	SE	Senate Level of Significance	SED	Constant	Durbin-Watson
D	NS	D	.16	.13	.26	6.17	50.1	1.32
D	NS	R	.21	.10	.05	5.07	25.8	1.66
D	KV	D	.14	.11	.26	5.31	55.3	2.88
D	KV	R	.17	.15	.28	7.46	28.3	2.41
R	NS	D	.10	.15	.53	6.82	35.3	1.30
R	NS	R	.45	.15	.01	5.14	27.7	*
R	KV	D	−.28	.25	.30	11.59	50.5	1.74
R	KV	R	.55	.17	.00	6.79	24.7	1.67

N   = 12 for Democratic presidential years, 22 for Republican presidential years
PP   = President's party
D   = Democrat
R   = Republican
NS   = Nonunanimous Support
KV   = Key Votes
SE   = Standard Error
SED = Standard Error of the Disturbances
*   = Corrected for autocorrelation

presidential approval, although it is worth noting that the coefficients are negative when a Democrat occupies the White House.

Senate Democrats are less responsive than their House colleagues, but they display no differences between Democratic and Republican presidential years: the results are similar to those for all years combined. On the other hand, Republicans reveal marked differences between the administrations of different parties. Although the coefficients for Democratic presidential years indicate a lack of relationship between presidential approval and presidential support, the figures are robust under Republican presidents, showing a gain in Senate support for the president of 4 or 5 percentage points for every increase in public approval of 10 percentage points.

The findings shown in table 6.8 bolster the Democratic results in table 6.7 and reveal no separate interaction between presidential approval and presidential support among Democrats. The coefficients also disclose a strong relationship for Senate Republicans when one of their party occupies the White House.

A related way of investigating different rates of interaction between presidential approval and presidential support is to examine differences between the in and out parties over all thirty-four years. One might argue that members of Congress belonging to the president's party would be most responsive to his approval levels because they had to run for reelection on his record.

The coefficients for in and out years turn out to be virtually identical (table 6.9). The distinction between in party and out party is therefore not useful, except for Senate Republicans.

TABLE 6.9   Relationship between Presidential Approval and Presidential Support by In and Out Party, 1953–86

Party Group	Support	B	SE	House Level of Significance	SED	Constant	Durbin-Watson
In	NS	.20	.08	.02	5.43	55.3	2.18
Out	NS	.22	.09	.02	5.75	53.1	2.14
In	KV	.16	.10	.11	6.44	57.4	1.88
Out	KV	.19	.11	.11	7.45	56.6	1.36

Party Group	Support	B	SE	Senate Level of Significance	SED	Constant	Durbin-Watson
In	NS	.18	.09	.05	5.62	32.9	*
Out	NS	.13	.10	.20	6.31	32.8	*
In	KV	.21	.10	.05	6.46	20.6	*
Out	KV	.23	.11	.05	7.24	55.0	1.43

N   = 34
NS   = Nonunanimous Support
KV   = Key Votes
SE   = Standard Error
SED = Standard Error of the Disturbances
*   = Corrected for autocorrelation

Perhaps Republican senators have to be especially sensitive to their constituencies. Throughout most of the period in question they operated in a hostile environment, in which the public typically cast Democratic votes for Congress. On the one hand, they are often more moderate than their fellow partisans in the House, who represent smaller constituencies. On the other, Republicans in the public, the core of their reelection constituencies, are extremely supportive of Republican presidents, more so than are Democrats of Democratic presidents. Republican senators may have to adjust their presidential support away from their normal inclinations, more so than do Democratic senators.

Under Democratic presidents, however, the political landscape has a different configuration. Democratic presidents are typically not popular with Republican voters (who gave them 32 percent approval or less in half the Democratic years in question), so there is less pressure to respond to high presidential approval. At the same time, there is a danger in being too responsive to strong disapproval of Democratic presidents, because this may alienate moderate constituents whose support Republican senators need for reelection. These members of the upper chamber are caught in the middle of contending forces, and one finds no relationship between presidential approval and congressional support under these conditions.

In sum, presidential approval does influence the presidential support of Democrats in both the House and Senate, and of Republicans in the Senate under Republican presidents. Each ten percentage points in presidential approval brings the president about 2 to 5 percentage points of additional support in Congress. This is a valuable resource for the chief executive when it is available.

On the other hand, House Republicans are not systematically responsive to presidential approval under any of the conditions examined here, and Senate Republicans are unresponsive under Democratic presidents. High presidential approval ratings do not always lead to high levels of congressional support, as in the case of House Republicans in 1955, 1957, and 1958. Conversely, presidents can sometimes obtain abnormally high levels of congressional support in the absence of high levels of public approval. President Johnson did this among Senate Republicans in 1967–68, and President Eisenhower (1958) and President Carter (1979) did well among House Democrats in spite of notable drops in approval among Democrats in the public.

Presidential approval is likely to have its greatest positive impact on Congress when members of the legislature sense that the public supports the chief executive for his positions on issues as well as his general leadership or other characteristics. The strongest negative influence is likely to occur when there is a dramatic, rapid decline in the president's approval level, undermining other sources of support. Neither of these situations is typical.

The strategic position of presidential approval is mixed. It accords the president useful leverage in dealing with Congress. As the most volatile resource for leadership, public approval is the factor most likely to determine whether or not an opportunity for change exists. Public approval makes other resources more efficacious. The president's party is more likely to be responsive if the president is held in high public esteem, the public is more easily moved, and legislative skills become more effective. Public approval is therefore the resource with the greatest potential to turn a typical situation into one favorable for change.

Despite its utility, presidential approval is not a resource that in most instances will dominate executive-legislative relations. Like party leadership, it works at the margins, within the confines of other influences on Congress, yet it is an important background resource for leadership.

CHAPTER SEVEN

Leading the Public

Assuming that public support can be a useful resource for the president, is he in a position to call upon it when he needs to move Congress? Commentators on the presidency often assume that the White House can persuade or even mobilize the public if the president is a skilled enough communicator. Before accepting this premise, however, one must critically examine the chief executive's efforts at leading the public.

Certainly presidents are not passive followers of public opinion. As Theodore Roosevelt proclaimed, "People used to say of me that I . . . divined what the people were going to think. I did not 'divine' . . . I simply made up my mind what they ought to think, and then did my best to get them to think it."[1] In a similar view, John Kennedy's closest aide, Theodore Sorensen, remembered that "no problem of the Presidency concerned him more than that of public communication—educating, persuading and mobilizing that opinion."[2]

Attempting to lead is not the same as succeeding, and American history is not replete with examples of a mobilized public pressuring Congress on behalf of the president's proposals. Presidential leadership of the public is no easier or more reliable than leadership in other areas of American politics.

Public Activity

The White House is caught in a virtual whirlwind of public relations activity. One can get a sense of the level of presidential public activity from table 7.1.[3]

1. Quoted in Emmet John Hughes, "Presidency vs. Jimmy Carter," *Fortune*, December 4, 1978, pp. 62, 64.
2. Theodore C. Sorensen, *Kennedy* (New York: Bantam, 1966), p. 346.
3. See also William W. Lammers, "Presidential Attention-Focusing Activities," in Doris

TABLE 7.1   Level of Public Activities of Presidents[a]

President	Total Activities	Yearly Average	Monthly Average
Eisenhower	901	113	9
Kennedy	784	277	23
Johnson	1,649	319	27
Nixon	1,084	195	16
Ford	1,228	503	42
Carter	1,350	338	28
Reagan[b]	1,482	371	31

[a]Includes all domestic and foreign appearances by a president.
[b]1981–84
SOURCE: Gary King and Lyn Ragsdale, *The Elusive Executive* (Washington: Congressional Quarterly Press, 1988), pp. 270, 274, 275.

John Kennedy, the first "television president," considerably increased the rate of public appearances of his predecessor. His successors have been even more active in making public appearances, with the notable exception of Richard Nixon: they have averaged more than one appearance for every weekday of the year.

There are many means to obtain public support, ranging from directly asking for it to public relations efforts fashioned after those of advertising agencies. A thorough examination of presidential efforts at leading the public is well beyond the scope of this book, and I have examined such matters in some detail elsewhere.[4] The focus here is on the probability that the president will succeed in leading public opinion.

Much of the activity in the White House is aimed at producing long-term, broad-based support for the president. Just what explains presidential approval is one of the most complex and challenging questions in the study of the presidency. In recent research I found that presidential approval was the product of many factors.[5] At the base of evaluations of the president is the predisposition of many people to support him. Political party identification provides the basic underpinning of approval or disapproval and mediates the impact of other factors. The positivity bias and bandwagon effect buttress approval levels, at least early in a new president's term.

A. Graber, ed., *The President and the Public* (Philadelphia: Institute for the Study of Human Issues, 1982), pp. 145–171, and Samuel Kernell, *Going Public* (Washington: Congressional Quarterly Press, 1986), chap. 4.
    4. George C. Edwards III, *The Public Presidency* (New York: St. Martin's, 1983), chap. 2.
    5. See Ibid., chap. 6.

Changes in approval levels appear to be due primarily to the public's evaluation of how the president is handling policy areas such as the economy, war, energy, and foreign affairs. Citizens seem to focus on the president's efforts and his stands on issues rather than on his personality, how his policies affect them, or even whether his policies are successful in the short run. Personal characteristics of the president related to his job also play an important role in influencing presidential approval. Conversely, incidents that cause the public to rally around the flag, such as the taking of American hostages in Iran in 1979, may provide an occasional increment of support, but in general they do not seem to be very significant.

Policy efforts, stands on issues, and personal characteristics are nebulous matters subject to a wide range of interpretations, few of which will be based on first-hand experience. The modern White House engages in extraordinary efforts to influence public perceptions of the president by attempting to control the manner in which he presents himself to the public and the way he is portrayed by the press.

Despite these exertions, presidents are frequently not high in the polls and frequently fail to obtain majority approval. Even Ronald Reagan, often viewed as having enjoyed great public support, averaged only 50 percent approval in his first term, just 3 percentage points more than his defeated predecessor, Jimmy Carter.[6]

There is much that is not yet understood about how people arrive at their perceptions of the president, but it is certain that presidents prefer to be high in the polls. That they frequently are not is testimony to the limits imposed on leadership of the public and the importance of such stabilizing influences as party identification. Samuel Kernell, a close student of the public presidency, concludes, "The supply of popular support rests on opinion dynamics over which the president may exert little direct control."[7]

Presidents are also interested in obtaining short-term support for specific policies, and they may directly seek the public's backing. They frequently attempt to influence public opinion with speeches on television or radio or to large groups. Not all presidents are effective speakers, however, and not all look good under the glare of hot lights and the unflattering gaze of television cameras. Also, the public is not always receptive to the president's message.

Presentation

Certainly one factor that affects the president's ability to obtain public support is the quality of his presentations to the people. Although this emphasis on

6. George C. Edwards, "Comparing Chief Executives," *Public Opinion*, June-July 1985, pp. 50–51, 54.

7. Kernell, *Going Public*, p. 137.

style rather than substance may offend the sensibilities of some, it is a part of political life. In a national poll preceding the presidential election of 1984, 76 percent of the respondents agreed that a "candidate's way of speaking to people" influenced their votes and an equal percentage agreed that being a "great communicator" was necessary to being a good president.[8] One need only think of the extensive commentary on President Reagan's speaking style to be reminded of the prominence of presentation in the public's mind.

Given the importance of presentation, how well have recent presidents fared on this dimension? The speeches of Harry Truman, the first president to be televised, were not impressive. He eschewed style and simply stood before a lectern reading from his text while staring into the cameras. His media adviser tried in vain to change the president's flat Missouri accent and rapid delivery.[9] Dwight Eisenhower's staff, sensing that more efforts would have to be made to exploit the potential of the new medium, hired the actor Robert Montgomery as a consultant for the president's television appearances. The results were an improvement over the style of Eisenhower's predecessor, but his speeches were rarely memorable.

John Kennedy came across more effectively on television. His youthful attractiveness, vigor, easy manner, intelligence, and well-crafted speeches helped him to project a favorable image to the country. Yet he was not a gifted speaker, possessing "a peculiar Boston cadence, letting his voice fall just when it should have risen to gain maximum effect."[10] Projecting charm but little passion, Kennedy was not able to arouse the country behind his legislative program. One memorable and risky failure was a rousing stump speech to a cheering crowd at Madison Square Garden carried over national television on behalf of his Medicare proposal in 1962. He pleased his supporters but did not succeed in converting others.

President Johnson had notable problems speaking on television. He greatly feared making mistakes as he gave speeches before large audiences. He read stiffly from a formal text, attempting to cloak some of his rougher edges. According to one of his biographers, when he gave a public speech, "he projected an image of feigned propriety, dullness, and dishonesty." The contrast between the earthy man described in the press and the image of the pious preacher he projected was too great to accept.[11] Johnson tried contact lenses, makeup, and a variety of electronic prompting devices to improve his television image, but nothing seemed to help.[12]

8. *CBS News/The New York Times Poll* (news release, February 5, 1984), table 5.

9. Newton Minow, John B. Martin, and Lee M. Mitchell, *Presidential Television* (New York: Basic Books, 1973), p. 33; Ken Hechler, interview, April 3, 1987, Princeton University.

10. George W. Ball, *The Past Has Another Pattern* (New York: W. W. Norton, 1982), p. 168.

11. Doris Kearns, *Lyndon Johnson and the American Dream* (New York: Harper and Row, 1976), p. 303. See also John Roche, remarks delivered at Princeton University, April 3, 1987.

12. Minow, Martin, and Mitchell, *Presidential Television*, p. 47.

It may seem strange that a person with Johnson's finely honed political skills who was overpowering in personal conversation could not speak effectively to mass audiences. As one close aide put it, "I've never seen him lose [a debate] in the Oval Office and I've never seen him win one in a formal speech or even in an extemporaneous speech to a large number of people."[13]

Presidents are inevitably prisoners of their pasts. Johnson was "an old Southwest politician who has been shouting to courthouse crowds all his life," someone whose intensity did not come over well in less intimate gatherings. Harry McPherson commented on the president's approach in small meetings:

> He used arguments and told stories and made analogies that just simply would not do on thirty minutes of television. Sometimes he goes, after touching first base . . . to left field, climbs into the bleachers, sells hot dogs, runs back down on the field, and circles the bases and comes home. You think he's never going to get to the point, but it all comes back with tremendous force and with great comprehensive power when he ends his argument, and it's damned near irresistible when he's at his best. This can't be done on television. You need a straight kind of approach, very logical and cool and dispassionate almost, that has some humor and some genuine self-reflection that he's not good at projecting.[14]

Richard Nixon was better at speaking to a live audience than to a camera. He liked to get immediate reactions to his words and then respond to his listeners. Because he could not do this on television, he tended to freeze into a pose that he thought appropriate.[15] In addition, his general appearance and graceless mannerisms were distracting. Nixon even hired his own television producer as a special assistant. One of the special assistant's contributions was to have the television camera aimed at the front of Nixon's face during press conferences instead of providing less flattering profile shots.[16]

Gerald Ford's efforts were flat and uninspiring, even though he hired a former television writer and stand-up comedian as a special consultant on the White House staff. This consultant had the president dress less conservatively, shorten his speeches, and make them more humorous and less filled with jargon. Ford also practiced his speeches, as when he videotaped a re-

13. Harry McPherson, interview by T. H. Baker, January 16, 1969, interview 3, tape 1, transcript, p. 27, Lyndon Baines Johnson Library, Austin, Tex.

14. Harry McPherson, interview by T. H. Baker, December 5, 1968, interview 2, tape 1, transcript, p. 19, Lyndon Baines Johnson Library, Austin, Tex.

15. William Safire, *Before the Fall: An Inside View of the Pre-Watergate White House* (New York: Doubleday, 1975), p. 537.

16. David Wise, *The Politics of Lying: Government Deception, Secrecy, and Power* (New York: Vintage, 1973), pp. 377–378.

hearsal of a speech on his economic and energy proposals and then had his "kitchen cabinet" evaluate its content and delivery.[17]

Jimmy Carter's televised speeches suffered from his soft, soporific tone and an unusual cadence that caused him to misplace his emphases and pauses and swallow his best lines. Few people seemed to feel stirred by his words. He made little effort to improve his presentation,[18] although he did consciously attempt to sound more authoritative in his "crisis of confidence" speech in 1979, in which he raised his voice and pounded on his desk. The impact of these theatrics did not appear to be longlasting.

President Reagan's experience as an actor may have won him few plaudits for his movie performances, but it helped him to understand how he appeared on television and how his gestures and the use of his voice affected his audience. His televised addresses to the nation in 1981 seem to have been quite effective in arousing support for his policies.

All presidents since Truman have had advice from experts on lighting, makeup, stage settings, camera angles, clothing, pacing of delivery, and other facets of making speeches. Despite this aid and the experience that politicians inevitably have in speaking, presidential speeches aimed at directly leading public opinion have typically not been very impressive.

Content

Presidents have to contend with not only the medium, but also their messages. Not all presidents are adept at producing speeches that will gain them support. Nixon's speech-writer William Safire remembers the president making a "courageous" decision on the invasion of Cambodia and then wrapping "it in a pious and divisive speech" that "only Nixon could do."[19]

The most effective speeches seem to be those aimed at building general support and image rather than specific support. They focus on simple themes rather than complex details. This is how Calvin Coolidge used his successful radio speeches, and Franklin Roosevelt did the same with his famous fireside chats. Roosevelt was more concerned with long-range objectives than specific policies. He tried to educate the public and build his image, placing events and policies in their broader context. (The only time he sought support for a specific policy in a fireside chat was for his "court-packing" bill, and this was a

17. Gerald R. Ford, *A Time to Heal* (New York: Harper and Row, 1979), pp. 261–262, 376–377.

18. James Fallows, "The Passionless Presidency: The Trouble with Jimmy Carter's Administration," *Atlantic Monthly*, May 1979, p. 44.

19. Safire, *Before the Fall*, p. 187. See also Henry Kissinger, *White House Years* (Boston: Little, Brown, 1979), pp. 504–505, 515.

notable failure.) His approach was light and subtle, not hard-sell. All this was aided by his personality and natural flair for public speaking. He empathized with the people, explained what was being done to alleviate their problems, and instilled renewed confidence in the populace.[20] The limitation of such an approach is of course that general support cannot always be translated into public backing for specific policies.

Presidents may be hindered by their inability to project clear visions of public policy. The need for simplicity places a premium on coherence and consistency in the presentation of the administration's goals and the means for meeting them. Yet presidents often find this demand on their rhetoric difficult to satisfy. For example, Jimmy Carter faced a great deal of criticism for lacking a unifying theme and cohesion in his programs, and for failing to inspire the public with a sense of purpose, an idea to follow. Instead of providing the country with a sense of his vision and priorities, he emphasized discrete problem solving. He had an "analytic but not synthetic approach to government."[21]

In an interview after the presidential election of 1980, Carter's chief of staff, Hamilton Jordan, seemed to agree with the criticism of Carter's administration when he reflected: "My most basic regret is that, in doing so many things, we never clearly fixed in the public mind a sense of our priorities. We had our priorities. . . . But we never clearly presented to the American people a short agenda of our country's problems and our solutions to those problems."[22]

Ronald Reagan, in contrast, narrowed his rhetorical focus and persisted in articulating consistent themes and goals, even in the face of apparent deviations in his policies. Thus he remained a dedicated budget-balancer despite presiding over by far the largest deficits in history, and he opposed all tax increases while supporting revenue "enhancements." The images he created of his administration's policies were strong enough to overcome criticism of what appeared to many commentators as evident digressions from his chosen path.

Public's Receptivity

No matter how effective a president may be as a speaker or how well his speech is written, he still must contend with the receptivity of his audience.

20. Minow, Martin, and Mitchell, *Presidential Television*, p. 30; Elmer E. Cornwell, Jr., *The Presidency and the Press* (Morristown, N.J.: General Learning Press, 1974), p. 10.

21. Bert A. Rockman, "Constants, Cycles, Trends, and Persona in Presidential Governance" (paper presented at the annual meeting of the American Political Science Association, Washington, August 1979), p. 44. See also Fallows, "The Passionless Presidency," pp. 42–43.

22. "Jordan Takes Stock as He Packs Up His Memories," *New York Times*, December 4, 1980, p. 22.

The first problem he faces is that Americans are rarely attentive listeners, and most people are not very interested in politics. The relative importance the typical citizen attaches to a president's address is illustrated by the attention President Carter gave to setting the date for his State of the Union message in 1978. He had to be careful to avoid preempting prime-time programming on the night that the season's most popular shows, "Laverne and Shirley," "Happy Days," and "Three's Company,"[23] were shown, so as not to irritate the shows' loyal viewers.

The public's lack of interest in politics constrains the president's leadership of public opinion in the long run as well as on a given day. Although he has unparalleled access to the American people, the president cannot make too much use of it. If he does, his speeches will become commonplace and lose their drama and interest. This is why presidents do not make appeals to the public on television very often. Despite the fame and success of Franklin Roosevelt's fireside chats, which were broadcast over the radio, he made no more than thirty of them in his twelve years in office.[24] He knew he had to maintain their uniqueness, and other presidents have followed the same principle. President Nixon and President Reagan turned to radio and midday addresses and reserved prime-time television for their most important speeches.[25]

A clearer picture of the reluctance of presidents to use the airwaves for a formal presentation can be obtained from table 7.2. Despite the substantial increase in public presidential activities overall, there has been little variance among recent presidents in their use of nationally televised addresses to the nation.[26] The principal exception is Richard Nixon, owing primarily to his increased exposure during the Watergate period.

Television is a medium in which visual interest, action, and conflict are most effective, and presidential speeches are unlikely to have these characteristics. Although some addresses to the nation occur at moments of high drama, such as President Johnson's televised demands for a voting rights act before a joint session of Congress in 1965, this is not typical. Style can sometimes give way to substance because of circumstances, but usually it is an uphill battle.

The public's lack of interest in political matters can be very frustrating for the White House. It is difficult to get a message through. A national poll in

23. "Prime Concern," *Newsweek*, December 19, 1977, p. 17.

24. Arthur M. Schlesinger, Jr., *A Thousand Days: John F. Kennedy in the White House* (Boston: Houghton Mifflin, 1965), p. 715. Roosevelt, his wife, and his aides made hundreds of traditional speeches over the radio, however. See Minow, Martin, and Mitchell, *Presidential Television*, pp. 30–32.

25. Herbert G. Klein, *Making It Perfectly Clear* (Garden City, N.Y.: Doubleday, 1980), p. 428. See Richard Nixon's fifth television interview with David Frost for the former president's view on going to the people too often.

26. See also Lammers, "Presidential Attention-Focusing Activities," p. 152–153.

TABLE 7.2   Major Presidential Speeches[a]

President	Total Speeches	Average Interval Between Speeches (in Months)
Eisenhower	41	2.4
Kennedy	15	2.3
Johnson	23	2.7
Nixon	36	1.9
Ford	12	2.4
Carter	17	2.8
Reagan[b]	20	2.4

[a]Defined as live, nationally televised and broadcast addresses to the country that preempt all major network programming. They include inaugural addresses, State of the Union messages, other addresses to joint sessions of Congress delivered during prime time, and prime-time addresses to the nation.
[b]1981–84
SOURCE: Gary King and Lyn Ragsdale, *The Elusive Executive* (Washington: Congressional Quarterly Press, 1988), p. 262.

May 1982 found that only 27 percent of the public knew that the inflation rate had fallen. Thirty-four percent thought it had gone up, although the inflation rate had in fact fallen sharply.[27] It was not until April 1983 that a majority of respondents felt inflation was less of a problem than it had been a year earlier,[28] although the drop in the inflation rate, the greatest success in economic policy of Ronald Reagan's administration, was being constantly articulated in public forums.

The public may misperceive or ignore even the most basic facts regarding a presidential policy. After President Reagan's nationwide televised speech on the invasion of Grenada, only 59 percent of the people could even identify the part of the world in which the island was situated.[29] As late as 1986, 62 percent of Americans did not know which side the United States supported in Nicaragua, despite extensive, sustained coverage of the president's policy by virtually all the news media.[30] Similarly, in June 1986 only 40 percent of the public had heard or read at least something about Reagan's highest domestic priority, the tax reform bill before the Senate.[31]

27. *CBS News/The New York Times Poll* (news release, May 27, 1982), p. 3.
28. *ABC News/The Washington Post Poll*, cited in "Knowing the Cost of Almost Everything," *National Journal*, May 5, 1984, p. 894.
29. *CBS News/The New York Times Poll* (news release, October 28, 1983), table 4.
30. *CBS News/The New York Times Poll* (news release, April 15, 1986), table 16.
31. *CBS News/The New York Times Poll* (news release, June 24, 1986), table 9.

This ignorance on the part of the public can have direct consequences for the president. For example, although 40 percent of those who knew which side the United States supported in Nicaragua were willing to support the president's policy of aiding the contras, this was true of only 16 percent of those who did not know.[32]

Americans are difficult to persuade and mobilize not only because of their apathy but also because of their predispositions. Most people usually hold views and values anchored in like-minded social groups of family, friends, and fellow workers. Both their cognitive needs for consistency and their uniform (and protective) environments pose formidable challenges for political leaders to overcome. In the absence of a national crisis, which fortunately is a rare occurrence, most people are not open to political appeals.[33]

Instead, citizens have psychological defenses that screen the president's message and reinforce their predispositions. A study of persons watching Ronald Reagan speak on television found that those who were previously supportive of him had a positive response to his presentation, while those previously disapproving became irritated.[34]

In addition, the public is not overly gullible, in spite of what some cynical observers believe. For example, in a conversation about the brewing Watergate scandal with his chief of staff on April 25, 1973, President Nixon commented: "Bring it out and fight it out . . . we'll survive. . . . Despite all the polls and the rest, I think there's still a hell of a lot of people out there, and from what I've seen . . . they want to believe, that's the point, isn't it?"[35] Although the president remained in office for more than a year, the public's faith was limited.

Finally, although Americans are attracted to strong leaders, they do not seem to feel a corresponding obligation to follow their leadership. In his memoirs, Richard Nixon argues that the public cannot be aroused behind the president when it has high expectations and the president must tell the public that these expectations have not been met.[36] Cultural predispositions continue to bedevil presidential leadership.

As a result of the hurdles over which the president must pass in his attempts to lead public opinion, one would not expect the White House to

32. "Polls Show Confusion on Aid to Contras," *New York Times*, April 15, 1986, sec. A, p. 6.

33. For a recent discussion of the social flow of information see Robert Huckfeldt and John Sprague, "Networks in Context: The Social Flow of Political Information," *American Political Science Review* 81 (December 1987): 1197–1216.

34. Roberta Glaros and Bruce Miroff, "Watching Ronald Reagan: Viewers' Reactions to the President on Television," *Congress and the Presidency* 10 (Spring 1983): 25–46.

35. Quoted in Theodore H. White, *Breach of Faith* (New York: Dell, 1976), pp. 415–416.

36. Richard M. Nixon, *RN: The Memoirs of Richard Nixon* (New York: Grosset and Dunlap, 1978), pp. 726, 731–732.

influence large segments of the public at any one time. Yet even a seemingly modest shift in public opinion can be very useful to the president. For example, a change of 6 percentage points could transform a split in public opinion to an advantage of 56 percent to 44 percent for the president. Presidential leadership operates at the margins of the basic configurations of American politics, but the margins can be vital to the president's success.

Success of Appeals

The cards are stacked against a president who tries to influence public opinion. John Kennedy once sardonically suggested an exchange from *King Henry IV, Part 1*, as an epigraph for Clinton Rossiter's famous work *The American Presidency*:

> *Glendower.* I can call spirits from the vasty deep.
> *Hotspur.*   Why, so can I, or so can any man.
>   But will they come when you do call for them?[37]

In October 1983, 241 American marines were killed in their barracks in Beirut, Lebanon. A few days later the United States invaded the island of Grenada. President Reagan made a nationwide televised address to the public, reporting on these events and seeking support. One national poll found that after the speech, approval of his handling of the events in Lebanon increased from 41 percent to 52 percent and of those in Grenada from 53 percent to 63 percent.[38] Another national poll found that approval of his handling of the situation in Grenada increased from 46 percent to 55 percent. Of those who had heard the president's speech, 65 percent approved, whereas only 47 percent of those who had not heard the speech approved.[39] This show of support was extremely useful for Reagan. It preempted congressional criticism, which had been building until poll results indicating public approval of the president were released.

Aside from their rarity, before-and-after comparisons are inherently limited in evaluating the impact of presidential leadership on public opinion. Sampling errors of plus or minus 3 percent in large national polls are enough to make even differences of 10 percentage points seem insignificant (polls with smaller samples have even larger margins of error). Or opinions may change as part of a long-range process or owing to stimuli from sources other than the

37. Sorensen, *Kennedy*, p. 440.

38. Barry Sussman, "Reagan's Talk Gains Support for Policies," *Washington Post*, October 30, 1983, sec. A, pp. l, 18. For another example of foreign policy see Kernell, *Going Public*, pp. 153–167.

39. *CBS News/The New York Times Poll* (news release, October 28, 1983), p. 2.

president. Further, recorded opinions on issues are sometimes distorted by the wording of questions.[40]

Using a different technique, in a survey taken just after the American invasion of Cambodia in 1970, the Gallup Poll found dramatic evidence that the public sometimes took its cues on public policy issues from the president. When asked if they "approved of President Nixon's decision," 51 percent of the respondents replied in the affirmative. When asked in the same poll if they approved of sending American troops into Cambodia, 58 percent disapproved and only 28 percent approved.[41] When the sample of the public was asked about the same specific action without mentioning the president's name, many more disapproved. Another study described the Family Assistance Plan and asked a sample of citizens whether they favored it. Forty-eight percent did, 40 percent opposed it, and 12 percent were undecided. When another sample was told that the plan was President Nixon's, support increased slightly to 50 percent, and, more significantly, opposition decreased to 25 percent and 24 percent fell into the undecided category.[42]

Such studies are rare, and it is difficult to rule out the possibility that the public is in fact aware of the president's actions and thus already influenced by them. In an effort to overcome this problem, Lee Sigelman directed a poll in Lexington, Kentucky, in December 1979. First he ascertained public opinion on six potential responses to the hostage crisis in Iran. Then he asked those who opposed each option if they would change their views "if President Carter considered this action necessary" (table 7.3).[43]

In each case a substantial percentage of the public changed its opinion in deference to the supposed opinion of the president. Between 40 percent and 63 percent of those originally opposed to each option altered their views in light of the hypothetical support of the president, and the greater the initial level of opposition, the more change that took place (there being a greater number of people who could potentially change their views).

Similarly, a poll of residents of Utah found that two-thirds of them opposed basing MX missiles in Utah and Nevada. But an equal number said they would definitely or probably support President Reagan if he proceeded to base the missiles there.[44]

40. Lee Sigelman, "Gauging the Public Response to Presidential Leadership," *Presidential Studies Quarterly* 10 (Summer 1980): 428–429; idem, "Rallying to the President's Support: A Reappraisal of the Evidence," *Polity* 11 (Summer 1979): 542–561.

41. Michael Wheeler, *Lies, Damn Lies, and Statistics: The Manipulation of Public Opinion in America* (New York: Liveright, 1976), pp. 146–147.

42. Carey Rosen, "A Test of Presidential Leadership of Public Opinion: The Split-Ballot Technique," *Polity* 6 (Winter 1973): 282–290.

43. Sigelman, "Gauging the Public Response."

44. "Most Utah Residents Say 'No' to MX Missile Deployment," Bryan-College Station (Texas) *Eagle*, September 15, 1981, sec. A, p. 5.

TABLE 7.3   Reconsidering Policy Opinions in Response to the President
(in Percent)

Policy	Original Approval	Approval after Reconsideration	Change Due to President
Wait and see	58	83	25
Return Shah to Iran	21	53	32
Send Shah elsewhere	74	87	13
Naval blockade	62	85	23
Threaten to send troops	43	73	30
Send troops	29	62	33

SOURCE: Lee Sigelman, "Gauging the Public Responses to Presidential Leadership," *Presidential Studies Quarterly* 10 (Summer 1980): 431.

Another study employing an experimental design found that support for hypothetical policy proposals varied with the public's knowledge of the person who had made them and its support for the person. When informed that President Reagan was the source of the proposals, enthusiastic supporters of Reagan evaluated the proposals favorably, but when the source was withheld, these same proposals were unfavorably evaluated by Reagan's supporters. This innovative research shows the impact of cognition, information, and psychological identification on presidential attempts to obtain the public's support for policy.[45]

Not all results are so positive. In one study different samples were asked whether they supported a domestic policy proposal dealing with welfare and a proposal dealing with foreign aid. One of the groups was told President Carter supported the proposals. The authors found that attaching the president's name to either proposal not only failed to increase support for it, but actually had a negative effect, because those who disapproved of Carter reacted strongly against proposals they thought were his.[46]

In perhaps the most famous presidential public appeal, Woodrow Wilson took his case on behalf of the League of Nations directly to the American people in a nationwide tour. His goal was to pressure the Senate into ratifying

45. Dan Thomas and Lee Sigelman, "Presidential Identification and Policy Leadership: Experimental Evidence on the Reagan Case," in George C. Edwards III et al., eds., *The Presidency and Public Policy Making* (Pittsburgh: University of Pittsburgh Press, 1985), pp. 37–49.

46. Lee Sigelman and Carol K. Sigelman, "Presidential Leadership of Public Opinion: From 'Benevolent Leader' to Kiss of Death?" *Experimental Study of Politics*, no. 3 (1981): 1–22. See also Pamela Johnston Conover and Lee Sigelman, "Presidential Influence and Public Opinion: The Case of the Iranian Hostage Crisis," *Social Science Quarterly* 63 (June 1982): 249–264.

the Treaty of Versailles, which contained provisions for setting up the league. He failed in his goal, however, and permanently damaged his health when he suffered a severe stroke en route.

A point to keep in mind is that none of the studies discussed so far measures the firmness of any opinion changes that occur. Because the public generally does not have firm opinions on issues, it may be swayed in the short run, providing the president succeeds in obtaining its attention. This volatility also means however that any opinion change is subject to slippage. As issues fade into the background or positions on issues confront the realities of daily life, opinions that were altered in response to presidential leadership may quickly be forgotten.

Presidents do have a difficult time moving public opinion in the long run. Shortly after becoming president, Jimmy Carter made a televised appeal to the American people on the energy crisis, calling it the "moral equivalent of war." One year later the Gallup Poll found exactly the same proportion of the public felt the energy situation was "very serious" as before Carter's speech (41 percent).[47]

Ronald Reagan was certainly interested in policy change and went to unprecedented lengths to influence public opinion. Nevertheless, numerous national surveys of public opinion have found that support for regulatory programs and spending on health care, welfare, urban problems, education, environmental protection, and aid to minorities has increased rather than decreased during Reagan's tenure.[48] On the other hand, support for increased defense expenditures was decidedly lower at the end of his administration than when he took office.[49] In the realm of foreign policy, near the end of 1986 only 25 percent of the public favored the president's cherished aid to the

47. "Carter Fails to Educate Public on Energy Crisis," *New Orleans Times Picayune*, April 30, 1978, sec. 1, p. 21. For examples relating to other presidents see Walter Bunge, Robert Hudson, and Chung Woo Suh, "Johnson Information Strategy for Vietnam: An Evaluation," *Journalism Quarterly* 45 (Autumn 1968): 419–425; Halford Ross Ryan, "Harry S Truman: A Misdirected Defense for MacArthur's Dismissal," *Presidential Studies Quarterly* 11 (Fall 1981): 576–582.

48. William Schneider, "The Voters' Mood 1986: The Six-Year Itch," *National Journal*, December 7, 1985, p. 2758; "Supporting a Greater Federal Role," *National Journal*, April 18, 1987, p. 924; "Opinion Outlook," *National Journal*, April 18, 1987, p. 964; Seymour Martin Lipset, "Beyond 1984: The Anomalies of American Politics," *PS* 19 (Spring 1986), p. 223; "Federal Budget Deficit," *Gallup Report*, August 1987, pp. 25, 27. See also *CBS News/The New York Times Poll* (news release, October 27, 1987), tables 16, 20.

49. Lipset, "Beyond 1984"; "Supporting a Greater Federal Role," p. 924; "Defense," *Gallup Report*, May 1987, pp. 2–3. See also "Opinion Outlook," *National Journal*, June 13, 1987, p. 1550; *CBS News/The New York Times Poll* (news release, October 27, 1987), table 15.

contras in Nicaragua.[50] Finally, Americans did not move their general ideological preference to the right.[51]

Foreign policy is more distant from the lives of most Americans than is
domestic policy and is therefore seen as more complex and based on spe-
cialized knowledge. People tend to defer more to the president on these
issues than on domestic issues that they can directly relate to their own
experience. Studies have shown public opinion undergoing changes in line
with presidents' policies on testing nuclear weapons,[52] relations with the
People's Republic of China,[53] and both escalating and de-escalating the war in
Vietnam.[54] Nevertheless, as we saw above, there are notable exceptions.

There is another vital factor to consider when examining presidential
leadership of the public's policy preferences: his approval level. One innovative study found that despite the mythology surrounding the bully pulpit, a
president's ability to influence the policy preferences of the public depends on
his standing. Presidents low in the polls have little success in leading opinion.[55] The ability to influence public opinion simply cannot be assumed as a
given.

Sometimes merely changing public opinion is not sufficient, and the
president feels that the public must communicate its views directly to Congress. Mobilizing the public may be the ultimate weapon to influence Congress in the president's arsenal. When the people speak, especially when they
speak clearly, Congress listens attentively.

Mobilizing the public involves overcoming formidable barriers and accepting substantial risk. It entails the double burden of obtaining both support
and political action from a generally inattentive and apathetic public. If the
president tries to mobilize the public and fails, the lack of response speaks

50. *CBS News/The New York Times Poll* (news release, December 1, 1986), table 5. See also
CBS News/The New York Times Poll (news release, October 27, 1987), table 17; "Americans on
Contra Aid: Broad Opposition," *New York Times*, January 31, 1988, sec. 4, p. 1. For a broader
comparison of public opinion and the Reagan administration's policies see John E. Reilly, ed.,
American Public Opinion and U.S. Foreign Policy 1987 (Chicago: Chicago Council on Foreign
Relations, 1987), chaps. 5–6.

51. See for example John A. Fleishman, "Trends in Self-identified Ideology from 1972 to
1982: No Support for the Salience Hypothesis," *American Journal of Political Science* 30 (August
1986): 517–541.

52. Eugene J. Rossi, "Mass and Attentive Opinion on Nuclear Weapons Tests and Fallout,
1954–1963," *Public Opinion Quarterly* 29 (Summer 1965): 280–297.

53. Robert S. Erikson, Norman R. Luttbeg, and Kent L. Tedin, *American Public Opinion:
Its Origins, Content, and Impact*, 2d ed. (New York: John Wiley and Sons, 1980), p. 144.

54. John E. Mueller, *War, Presidents and Public Opinion* (New York: John Wiley and Sons,
1973), pp. 69–74.

55. Benjamin I. Page and Robert Y. Shapiro, "Presidential Leadership Through public
Opinion," in George C. Edwards III et al., *The Presidency and Public Policy Making* (Pittsburgh:
University of Pittsburgh Press, 1985), pp. 22–36. See also Kernell, *Going Public*, pp. 155–161.

eloquently to members of Congress, who are highly attuned to public opinion.

Perhaps the most notable recent example of a president mobilizing public opinion to pressure Congress is Ronald Reagan's effort to obtain passage of his bill to cut taxes in 1981. Shortly before the crucial vote in the House, the president made a televised plea for support of his tax cut proposals and asked the public to let their representatives in Congress know how they felt. Evidently this worked, for thousands of phone calls, letters, and telegrams poured into congressional offices. How much of this represented the efforts of the White House and its corporate allies rather than individual expressions of opinion will probably never be known. But on the morning of the vote Speaker Tip O'Neill declared, "We are experiencing a telephone blitz like this nation has never seen. It's had a devastating effect."[56] With this kind of response, the president easily carried the day.

The White House is of course not content to rely solely on a presidential appeal for a show of support. It may take additional steps to orchestrate public pressure on Congress. For example, Samuel Kernell describes the auxiliary efforts at mobilization of Reagan's White House in 1981:

> Each major television appeal by President Reagan on the eve of a critical budget vote in Congress was preceded by weeks of preparatory work. Polls were taken; speeches incorporating the resulting insights were drafted; the press was briefed, either directly or via leaks. Meanwhile in the field, the ultimate recipients of the president's message, members of Congress, were softened up by presidential travel into their states and districts and by grass-root lobbying campaigns, initiated and orchestrated by the White House but including RNC and sympathetic business organizations.[57]

Reagan's White House tapped a broad network of constituency groups. Operating through party channels, its Political Affairs Office, and its Office of Public Liaison, the administration generated pressure from the constituents of members of Congress, campaign contributors, political activists, business leaders, state officials, interest groups, and party officials.[58] Television adver-

56. Quoted in "Tax Cut Passed by Solid Margin in House, Senate," *Congressional Quarterly Weekly Report*, August 1, 1981, p. 1374. See also Kernell, *Going Public*, pp. 120–121.

57. Samuel Kernell, *Going Public*, p. 137. See also p. 116.

58. For examples of other presidents mobilizing interest groups see Carl Albert, interview by Dorothy Pierce McSweeny, August 13, 1969, interview 3, transcript, p. 22, Lyndon Baines Johnson Library, Austin, Tex.; Harold (Barefoot) Sanders, interview by Joe B. Frantz, March 24, 1969, tape 2, transcript, p. 42, Lyndon Baines Johnson Library, Austin, Tex.; Martha Joynt Kumar and Michael Baruch Grossman, "The Presidency and Interest Groups," in Michael Nelson, ed., *The Presidency and the Political System* (Washington: Congressional Quarterly Press, 1984), pp. 282–312; Joseph A. Pika, "White House Relations with Interest Groups: Eisenhower and Carter in Context" (unpublished paper).

tisements, letters, and attention from the local news media helped focus attention on swing votes. Although these pressures were directed toward Republicans, Southern Democrats received considerable attention as well, which reinforced their sense of electoral vulnerability.

The administration's effort at mobilizing the public on behalf of the tax cut of 1981 is significant not only because of the success of presidential leadership but also because it appears to be a deviant case—even for Ronald Reagan. His next major legislative battle was over the sale of AWACS planes to Saudi Arabia. The White House decided it could not mobilize the public on this issue, however, and adopted an "inside" strategy to prevent a legislative veto.[59]

In the remainder of his tenure the president went repeatedly to the people regarding a wide range of policies, including the budget, aid to the contras in Nicaragua, and defense expenditures. Despite his high approval levels for much of the time, he was never again able to arouse many in his audience to communicate their support of his policies to Congress. Most issues hold less appeal to the public than substantial tax cuts.

Even with elaborate campaigns supporting overt presidential efforts at mobilization, the odds of success are not in the White House's favor. For example, in 1985 the Republican National Committee sent a mailing to constituents of eight members of the House Ways and Means Committee asking them to urge their representatives to support President Reagan's tax reform plan, the highest domestic policy priority of his second term. Instead of eliciting additional support, however, this effort at mobilizing the public evoked anger and resentment among those at whom it was aimed. One Republican member complained of the "sleazy, underhanded attempts to influence my votes."[60]

Leading the public is perhaps the ultimate tool of the political leader. It is difficult for others who hold power to deny the legitimate demands of a president with popular support. As a result, the president constantly endeavors to obtain the public's support for him and his policies. Despite this activity, the public does not reliably respond to his leadership. The content and style of the president's public presentations, his standing in the polls when he appeals for support, the impact of factors beyond his control, and the public's frequent lack of receptivity to his efforts at leadership often present significant obstacles to the achievement of his goal.

59. See "Reagan's Legislative Strategy Team Keeps His Record of Victories Intact," *National Journal*, June 26, 1982, p. 1130.

60. "Partisan Pressures Building as Tax Bill Markups Continue," *Congressional Quarterly Weekly Report*, October 12, 1985, pp. 2046–2047.

Public support is not a dependable resource for the president, and it is not one that he can easily create when he needs it to influence Congress. Leading the public is leading at the margins. Most of the time the White House can do no more than move a small portion of the public from opposition or neutrality to support for the president, or from passive agreement to active support. Sometimes this may be enough to influence a few wavering senators or representatives to back the president, and occasionally this may have a critical impact. More typically the consequences of attempting to lead the public will be of modest significance.

There are also some occasions on which the president may wish to keep a low public profile. To attract fence sitters in Congress on issues of relatively low visibility, the White House may choose to "stay private." By doing so the president may be able to avoid arousing opposition to some of his proposals. He may also avoid the appearance of defeat if he loses. Finally, staying private eases the path of reaching agreement with Congress, because to eschew public posturing provides maneuvering room for concessions and avoids the appearance of inconsistency when compromises are made.[61]

61. Cary R. Covington, "'Staying Private': Gaining Congressional Support for Unpublicized Presidential Preferences on Roll-Call Votes," *Journal of Politics* 49 (August 1987): 737–755.

CHAPTER EIGHT

Mandates and Misperceptions

Presidential elections are a cornerstone of American politics and justifiably receive a great deal of scholarly attention. In general, this research focuses on understanding and explaining mass political behavior. At the same time, it is important that elections not be studied in isolation as though they were merely some sort of democratic ritual. The entertainment value of politics aside, it is because of public policy that we care about elections.

This is the essential question: What difference do presidential elections make? What is their impact on support for the winner's program in Congress? Of course presidential elections determine who will serve as president, but not all elections leave their mark on public policy.

The elections of 1980 and 1984 offer a striking paradox: in 1980 Ronald Reagan received only 51 percent of the vote. His first approval rating in the Gallup Poll after his inauguration was lower than that of any postwar president, again only 51 percent. Yet there is general agreement that in the areas of defense, taxes, and domestic programs he and his supporters significantly altered American public policy.

By contrast, in 1984 Reagan won a great electoral victory with 59 percent of the vote. Public opinion polls at the time of the election showed that the voters viewed him in a very positive light as a strong, effective leader and strongly supported his performance on the economy and national security policy.[1] Moreover, the first Gallup poll after the inauguration found that Reagan enjoyed an approval rating of 62 percent. Yet the president immediately faced strong opposition in Congress to his proposals on domestic and

1. See for example CBS News/The New York Times Poll (news release, January 21, 1985), tables 1–3; "Opinion Roundup," Public Opinion, December-January 1985, p. 37.

foreign policy. As an example, in the Congress of 1985-86 the president won no real increase at all in his cherished defense budget. Much of the time he was on the defensive, as in his embarrassing defeat on sanctions against South Africa. Why did Reagan encounter such difficulty in obtaining support in Congress when he seemingly had the support of the people?

This example raises a fundamental issue of the role of public opinion in presidential leadership in Congress. Without question, presidential elections are the most dramatic and salient expressions of public opinion that occur in the United States. What remains to be understood is how presidential elections influence policy and why some elections have so much more impact than others.

Structuring Choices

Past work on the impact of presidential elections on congressional support for the president has focused on comparing the president's vote in a congressional district with the support of the district's representative for the president's policies. Such an orientation is attractive, because presidential election returns are the only data available at the level of the congressional district that reflect at least in part the public's evaluation of the president, and the sample of public opinion is very large indeed.

These studies have found significant but varied relationships between the president's electoral performance and subsequent congressional support.[2] All are based on the premise that individual members of Congress will alter their decisions in response to the president's showing in their constituencies. Conversion is constrained by a number of factors, however, and the orientation of research into the subject must be altered if it is to lead to an understanding of the role of public support in presidential leadership of Congress.

2. George C. Edwards III, *Presidential Influence in Congress* (San Francisco: W. H. Freeman, 1980), chap. 4; Kathryn Newcomer Harmon and Marsha Braun, "Joint Electoral Outcomes as Cues for Congressional Support of U.S. Presidents," *Legislative Studies Quarterly* 4 (May 1979): 281–299; Loren K. Waldman, "Liberalism of Congressmen and the Presidential Vote in Their Districts," *Midwest Journal of Political Science* 11 (February 1967): 73–85; Marvin G. Weinbaum and Dennis R. Judd, "In Search of a Mandated Congress," *Midwest Journal of Political Science* 14 (May 1970): 276–302; Milton Cummings, *Congressmen and the Electorate* (New York: Free Press, 1966); J. Vincent Buck, "Presidential Coattails and Congressional Loyalty," *Midwest Journal of Political Science* 16 (August 1972): 460–472; Jeanne Martin, "Presidential Elections and Administration Support among Congressmen," *American Journal of Political Science* 20 (August 1976): 483–490; John E. Schwarz and Barton Fenmore, "Presidential Election Results and Congressional Roll Call Behavior: The Cases of 1964, 1968, and 1972," *Legislative Studies Quarterly* 2 (November 1977): 409–422.

One should also keep in mind that substantial improvement or erosion in the president's standing with the public can occur in a relatively short period. Members of Congress can hardly be expected to ignore these changes and respond only to election returns.

Further, the president typically receives a lower percentage of the vote in a congressional district than the district's representative. Even in the landslide election of 1984, for example, Ronald Reagan received a smaller percentage of the vote than the winning candidate for the House in three-fourths of all congressional districts.

Finally, presidential election victories may actually be detrimental to conversion. Party voting and thus party polarization may actually increase after an election such as those of 1964 and 1980, as the winning party stakes out new ground.

Conversion is not the only way in which public opinion may influence presidential-congressional relations. Public support for the president may influence Congress in a more fundamental, more strategic manner than by simply changing probabilities of support. If a president can structure the choices faced by Congress, he can influence not only those open to conversion on issues, but everyone who votes on them as well. By framing issues in ways that favor his programs, the president sets the terms of the debate on his proposals and thus the premises on which members of Congress cast their votes.

Distinguishing between conversion and the structuring of choices lends a new understanding to the topic at hand. When a president is successful in framing issues to his advantage, he has won half the battle. He has established the premises or direction of a policy or set of policies. Attempts at conversion take place within this context, and even if they fail, the president can still significantly alter the course of public policy.

It is important to distinguish the structuring of choices from the setting of the agenda. Changes in the agenda may occur without changes in public policy. Agenda setting is only one stage in the policy-making process and by itself does not determine the outcomes of the process. In the structuring of choices the same issues remain on the agenda, but the questions asked about them change.

Although there are occasions when a president can exploit an external event such as arms control negotiations to structure legislators' choices on a single issue (see chapter 10), he cannot rely on his environment to be so accommodating. The White House must also advocate the passage of many proposals at roughly the same time, further complicating its strategic position.

In addition, opponents of the president's policies are unlikely to defer to his attempts to structure choices on issues. Policies are very complex and typically affect many different interests, which inevitably evaluate programs from their diverse perspectives. Interests in the United States are more numerous, more politically active, and in possession of more resources than ever before. The rise of single-issue groups has only exacerbated this situation. Organized interests are ready and able to fight vigorously, so that they can be heard and can show how the trade-offs involved in policy choices involve far more than the dimensions of evaluation proposed by the president. One can hardly project decreases in aid for college students and call them merely a means of reducing the deficit. Opponents immediately raise other aspects of the issue, from equity to economic growth.

Thus the president faces numerous obstacles in structuring choices for Congress. The most effective means of setting the terms of debate on many issues at once and overcoming opposition is by creating the perception of an electoral mandate, an impression that the voters want to see the winner's programs implemented. Indeed, large-scale changes in policy virtually never occur in the absence of such perceptions, such as those of 1932, 1964, and 1980.

Mandates can be powerful symbols in American politics. They accord added legitimacy and credibility to the newly elected president's proposals. Concerns for representation and political survival encourage members of Congress to support the president if they feel the people have spoken. And members of Congress are susceptible to such beliefs. According to David Mayhew, "Nothing is more important in Capitol Hill politics than the shared conviction that election returns have proven a point."[3] Members of Congress also need to believe that voters have not merely rejected the losers in elections but positively selected the victors and what they stand for.

More important, mandates change the premises of decision. Following the presidential election of 1932 the essential question became how government should act to fight the Depression rather than whether it should act. Similarly, following the election of 1964 the dominant question in Congress was not whether to pass new social programs, but how many to pass and how much to increase spending.

In 1981 the tables were turned. Ronald Reagan's victory placed a stigma on big government and exalted the unregulated marketplace and large defense budgets. More specifically, the terms of the debate over policy changed from which federal programs to expand to which ones to cut; from which civil rights rules to extend to which ones to limit; from how much to regulate to how little; from which natural resources to protect to which to develop; from how

3. David R. Mayhew, *Congress: The Electoral Connection* (New Haven and London: Yale University Press, 1974), pp. 70–71.

little to increase defense spending to how much; and from how little to cut taxes to how much.

When Jim Jones, the chairman of the House Budget Committee, and his allies drafted a Democratic budget resolution as an alternative to Reagan's, it proposed a more modest tax cut, a smaller increase for the Pentagon, and less of a decrease in social programs. Nevertheless, Jones's plan followed the general outlines of the administration's. Reagan had won a major victory even before the first vote.

Perceptions of Mandates

Assuming that presidential elections can structure choices for Congress, do all presidential elections do so? The answer is clearly no. Merely winning an election does not provide a president with a mandate. Every election produces a winner, but mandates are much less common.

If mandates are infrequent, under what conditions do they occur? Are the conditions objective or is there room for misperception? Perceptions are often more important than reality, because it is how political elites interpret the presidential vote that affects how they respond to the president and his proposals. As one examines perceptions of mandates, presidential leadership should be kept in mind. Ultimately, what can the president do to influence perceptions of a mandate? Can he turn his election into a resource for his leadership of Congress?

Nature of Elections

The most straightforward explanation of perceptions of a mandate is that a clear majority of the populace has shown through its votes that it supports certain policies proposed by the winning candidate. Yet by their very nature, elections rarely provide clear indications of the public's thinking on individual proposals.

If presidential elections are to provide majority support for specific policies, the following conditions must be met: (1) voters must have opinions on policies; (2) voters must know candidates' stands on the issues; (3) candidates must offer voters the alternatives the voters desire; (4) there must be a large turnout of voters; (5) voters must vote on the basis of issues; and (6) one must be able to correlate voter support with voters' policy views.

Although political commentators seldom hesitate to talk of mandates for policies (it took Dan Rather only five minutes after CBS had begun its coverage on election night in 1984 to proclaim a mandate for President Reagan), careful students of politics know better. The first five conditions of the six enumerated above are rarely met, if ever.[4] For this reason it is very difficult to discern the relationship between voters' policy preferences and a president's victory at the polls. When asked about his mandate in 1960, John F. Kennedy reportedly replied, "Mandate, schmandate. The mandate is that I am here and you're not."[5]

Even landslide elections are difficult to interpret. For example, Stanley Kelley found that in Lyndon Johnson's victory in 1964, issues gave the president his base of support and concerns over the relative competence of the candidates won the swing vote for him. In 1972, however, the question of competence dominated the election. Although traditional domestic issues associated with the New Deal were salient, they actually favored George McGovern, not the landslide winner, Richard Nixon.[6]

In addition, there are two complicating factors. First, there may be no majority opinion on an issue, even among those who have an opinion. Public opinion polls often force respondents to choose one of a restricted number of possible answers. But opinion on any issue is probably quite fragmented, providing no majority opinion to identify. For example, in fall 1984, 40 percent of the people felt that the United States should do more to stop the spread of communism in Central America, whereas 36 percent disagreed. At the same time, 44 percent were more worried about a communist takeover there, but 39 percent were more concerned about a war.[7]

Second, voters may be concerned with several issues in an election, but they have only one vote with which to express their views. Citizens may support one candidate's position on some issues yet vote for another candidate because of concern for other issues or general evaluations of performance. In 1984 voters preferred Walter Mondale to Ronald Reagan on the issues of defense spending, aid to the contras, environmental protection, protection of civil rights, and helping the poor and disadvantaged, but most voted for Reagan for president.[8] When they cast their ballots, voters signal only their choice of candidate, not their choice of the candidates' policies. One should be cautious in inferring support for specific policies from the results of this process, for the vote is a rather blunt instrument for expressing one's views.

4. See for example George C. Edwards III, *The Public Presidency* (New York: St. Martin's, 1983), pp. 18–23.
    5. Quoted in Everett Carll Ladd, *The Ladd Report #1* (New York: W. W. Norton, 1985), p. 3.
    6. Stanley Kelley, Jr., *Interpreting Elections* (Princeton: Princeton University Press, 1983), pp. 72–125.
    7. *CBS News/The New York Times Poll* (news release, October 19, 1984), p. 3.
    8. *Los Angeles Times* poll, October 12–15, 1984; Martin P. Wattenberg, *The Decline of American Political Parties, 1952–1984* (Cambridge: Harvard University Press, 1986), p. 154.

Although a candidate's overt avoidance of stands on issues during a campaign can undercut claims of a mandate after the election, the key to structuring choices for Congress is not through popular referenda on specific policies. It is directions, not details, priorities, not particulars, that establish the premises of decisions and the terms of debate.

Winning Big

Winning a large percentage of the popular vote or a large majority in the Electoral College certainly lends credibility to claims of a mandate. To be able to show that the public's support of the president is both deep and widespread adds legitimacy to the White House's demands for congressional support of the president's program.

Yet there is no guarantee that others, including members of Congress, will interpret election results as the White House views them. The reasons voters support candidates are by no means always clear, and in ambiguous situations a wide range of factors influence perceptions of mandates.

As a result, presidents who win election by large margins frequently find that their victories are not accompanied by perceptions of support for the president's proposals. In the presidential elections held between 1952 and 1984, most of the impressive electoral victories (Richard Nixon's 61 percent in 1972, Ronald Reagan's 59 percent in 1984, and Dwight Eisenhower's 57 percent in 1956) did not elicit perceptions of mandates (table 8.1). Equally important, a relatively small percentage of the vote does not necessarily preclude perceptions of a mandate. For example, Ronald Reagan was perceived as having won a mandate with only 51 percent of the vote in 1980 (although he

TABLE 8.1   Presidential Election Results

Year	Winner	Percentage of Popular Vote	Electoral Vote
1952	Eisenhower	55	442
1956	Eisenhower	57	457
1960	Kennedy	50	303
1964	Johnson	61	486
1968	Nixon	43	301
1972	Nixon	61	520
1976	Carter	50	297
1980	Reagan	51	489
1984	Reagan	59	525

did very well in the Electoral College). There is more to perceptions of mandates than a straightforward summing of the presidential election results.[9] To understand more fully why this is so, one must examine less direct influences on the way election outcomes are interpreted.

Party Seats Won

The addition of a large number of new seats for the president's party in Congress is an indicator used by commentators, and certainly by members of Congress, in evaluating the significance of a president's electoral victory. If observers attribute long coattails to the president, they are likely to see the election as especially meaningful, because the people appear to be sending strong signals of support for the chief executive. This is also an area in which the potential for misinterpretation is great, however.

An excellent example of an election in which coattails were misperceived is that of 1980. Immediately after the election a consensus seemed to develop among the public and political leaders that the results indicated enormous change in opinion and perhaps a major political realignment in the direction of conservatism and the Republican party. Much of this was due to the stunning gain of twelve seats for the Republicans in the Senate. The GOP won twenty-two of the thirty-four Senate seats up for election and defeated nine incumbent Democrats in the process. Conversely, the Democrats won no new seats at all.

In reality these races were very close. In eleven the Republican winners received 52.1 percent of the vote or less. A shift of only fifty thousand strategically placed votes would have left the Democrats with a Senate majority of fifty-four to forty-six. But "the margins of victory were overshadowed by the victories themselves,"[10] and many commentators magnified the outcomes because they were so unexpected.

This emphasis had great advantages for the newly elected president. Many of the Republican Senate victories were attributed to his coattails, on the basis of little or no evidence. Much later some scholars concluded that nationwide Reagan's coattails were worth about 3 percentage points to Re-

9. Robert E. Goodwin, "The Importance of Winning Big," *Legislative Studies Quarterly* 2 (November 1977): 399–407. Goodwin found no relation between popular electoral majorities in presidential elections and the president's subsequent success as measured by the box score of Congressional Quarterly.

10. Thomas E. Mann and Norman J. Ornstein, "Sending a Message: Voters and Congress in 1982," in Thomas E. Mann and Norman J. Ornstein, eds., *The American Elections of 1982* (Washington: American Enterprise Institute, 1983), pp. 135–137.

publican candidates for the House.[11] Others found a smaller impact.[12] Using the more generous estimate for the sake of argument, if it is accurate for all congressional candidates and if the advantage of 3 percentage points was spread evenly across the country, then each of the eleven Republicans who won election by a margin of 6 percentage points or less owed his or her seat to Reagan. (If these candidates each had received 3 percentage points fewer votes and his or her opponent 3 percentage points more, they would have been tied.)

Things are not so straightforward, however. It is unlikely that 3 percentage points should be attributed to the president in every race, especially where he ran relatively poorly, which was often the case in the states in which Republicans won narrow Senate victories. There are also many other factors that influence elections; at the least these put Republican candidates in the range of victory, where coattails might affect the outcome of their races.

Of the twenty-two Republican winners, Reagan ran ahead of only ten, behind eleven, and equal with one. In the nine races in which Republicans defeated Democratic incumbents, Reagan ran ahead of his party's candidate in only five. Although it is possible to have coattail effects while running behind a senatorial candidate, in the absence of more supportive data one can hardly attribute these Republican victories to presidential coattails, and one should hesitate before attributing an advantage of 3 percentage points to Republicans in these elections.

In two of the five races in which Reagan ran ahead of Republican challengers, the challengers won by such large margins (in South Dakota 19 percentage points, in Indiana 8 percentage points) that it is improbable that his coattails were crucial. In addition, both Democratic senators in these races, George McGovern and Birch Bayh, were vulnerable targets. They had won their last elections by narrow margins (53 percent and 51 percent), despite the advantages enjoyed by Democrats in the election of 1974, which was influenced by the Watergate scandal. Bayh's largest share of the vote in three previous elections had been only 52 percent.

This leaves only three seats in which Reagan ran ahead of a Republican challenger who won narrowly. One was in Georgia, where the Democrat

11. Alan I. Abramowitz, "National Issues, Strategic Politicians, and Voting Behavior in the 1980 and 1984 Congressional Elections," *American Journal of Political Science* 28 (November 1984): 710–721.

12. Randall L. Calvert and John A. Ferejohn, "Coattail Voting in Recent Presidential Elections," *American Political Science Review* 77 (June 1983): 407–419; John A. Ferejohn and Morris P. Fiorina, "Incumbency and Realignment in Congressional Elections," in John E. Chubb and Paul E. Peterson, eds., *The New Direction in American Politics* (Washington: Brookings Institution, 1985), p. 111.

Herman Talmadge lost his safe seat after being censured by the Senate for financial improprieties. Without the scandal Talmadge would easily have won reelection, although it is possible that Reagan's coattails provided the crucial margin for the Republican, Mack Mattingly, in this close race.

In New Hampshire John Durkin also lost his seat to a Republican challenger. It is hard to imagine a more vulnerable seat. In the election in 1974 he virtually tied his opponent in the closest race in the history of the U.S. Senate, despite a probable boost from Watergate. The Senate was unable to resolve the issue and Durkin eventually won his place in the Senate in a bitter special election in 1975. He became only the second Democrat to occupy the seat since the Civil War (the previous Democrat served in 1933–38). Again, Reagan's coattails may have provided the margin of victory in 1980, but Durkin seemed destined to lose anyway.

The remaining Democratic incumbent to go down to defeat was Frank Church of Idaho, running for his fifth term. He lost a very close race while Reagan carried the state with 66 percent of the presidential vote—this may have been a coattail victory for the Republicans.

It should also be noted that two-thirds of the defeated Democratic incumbents were running for at least their fourth term, and U.S. senators have traditionally been vulnerable in such elections. One who was not, John Culver of Iowa, had won only 52 percent of the vote in his previous campaign in 1974.

Of the six Republicans who won reelection, Reagan ran ahead of only two. One, Paul Laxalt of Nevada, still obtained 59 percent of the vote and thus is not likely to have won because of coattails. The remaining incumbent was Barry Goldwater, who garnered only 50 percent of the vote to Reagan's 61 percent. Thus, the Republican nominee of 1980 may have saved the seat of his predecessor from 1964. Goldwater was also the only Republican incumbent to win reelection by a margin of less than 8 percentage points.

In the seven open seats that the Republicans won, the coattail theory fares no better. In North Dakota Mark Andrews ran ahead of Reagan and won 70 percent of the vote. In Oklahoma Don Nickles trailed Reagan by 8 percentage points with 53 percent of the vote, but still defeated his principal opponent by a safe margin of 10 percentage points. Arlen Specter won a Senate seat in Pennsylvania with 51 percent of the vote, but Reagan won only 50 percent. Alfonse D'Amato won in New York by 1 percentage point with 45 percent of the vote, yet Reagan won only 47 percent, and the explanation for D'Amato's victory seems to have been the 11 percent of the vote that Jacob Javits received on the Liberal party's line.

In the three remaining open seats in which the party holding the seat changed, the Democratic candidates had first defeated incumbent senators (Donald Stewart in Alabama, Mike Gravel in Alaska, and Richard Stone in

Florida) in divisive primaries that undoubtedly diminished the party's chances in November.[13] Further, the winning Republican in Alabama, Jeremiah Denton, ran ahead of Reagan, and Frank Murkowski of Alaska ran even with Reagan and won his race by 8 percentage points.

Data are lacking that would make it possible to determine precisely the extent and impact of Ronald Reagan's coattails in the Senate elections of 1980, and one must be cautious in drawing any conclusions. Nevertheless, it seems safe to argue that in most instances where in theory the president's coattails might have made the critical difference in the outcomes of the elections, other factors such as divisive primaries, weak political bases, scandals, or third-party candidates were primarily responsible for Republican Senate victories. One can certainly conclude that it was not support for Ronald Reagan and his policies that was responsible for the weak candidacies of so many Democrats in 1980. In these circumstances, whatever coattails Reagan may have had look much less impressive than what was portrayed in the press.

Important though less dramatic changes in the president's favor also took place in the House in the election of 1980. The Republicans gained thirty-four seats, cutting the Democrats' margin by sixty-eight. Yet in earlier work I found that Reagan's coattails were responsible for only five of these victories.[14] Once again, attributions of coattails were frequent but greatly exaggerated.

The president was not as fortunate in his reelection in 1984 as he had been in 1980. Republicans lost two seats in the Senate and gained only fourteen in the House (this was very similar to Richard Nixon's experience in 1972). Because these results occurred in the face of Reagan's sweeping victory, it was easy to conclude that the voters were sending mixed signals on election day, and that the basis of Reagan's victory was more personal than political. The results of the congressional election also demonstrated to members of Congress that their electoral fortunes were not connected with the president's. All this was eloquent evidence countering the thesis of a mandate.

There is reason to believe that the president's coattails were actually longer in 1984 than in 1980, at least in terms of the percentage of the congressional vote they influenced.[15] The Republicans simply had a high swing ratio

13. Patrick J. Kenney and Tom W. Rice, "The Effect of Primary Divisiveness in Gubernatorial and Senatorial Elections," *Journal of Politics* 46 (August 1984): 904–915; Robert A. Bernstein, "Divisive Primaries Do Hurt: U.S. Senate Races, 1956–1972," *American Political Science Review* 71 (June 1977): 540–545.

14. Edwards, *The Public Presidency*, pp. 83–93.

15. Ferejohn and Fiorina, "Incumbency and Realignment in Congressional Elections," p. 111.

TABLE 8.2   Net Party Gains in House and Senate Seats in Presidential
Election Years

Year	President's Party	House	Senate
1952	R	22R	1R
1956	R	2D	1D
1960	D	22R	2R
1964	D	37D	1D
1968	R	5R	6R
1972	R	12R	2D
1976	D	1D	0
1980	R	34R	12R
1984	R	14R	2D

D = Democrat
R = Republican

in 1980, as a result of which a shift of 3.2 percent in the national vote brought them a shift of 7.8 percent in House seats. In 1984, on the other hand, a shift of 3.8 percent of the vote gained them only a 3.6 percent increase in seats.[16]

Although misperception can support the president's claims of a mandate, more typically his coattails will appear unimpressive. What is especially striking about the net party gains in Congress in presidential election years is that after the dust has settled there has usually been only a small change in party balance (table 8.2). In the House over the nine presidential elections held between 1952 and 1984, the party of the winning presidential candidate has gained a total of 125 seats and lost twenty-four (1956 and 1960) for a net of 101 seats, or only about eleven seats per election on average. In the Senate the opposition party gained seats in four of the nine elections (1956, 1960, 1972, and 1984), and there was no net change in 1976. The net gain of thirteen seats averages out to about one and a half seats per election.

The absence of notable gains for the president's party in Congress detracts from the euphoria of victory and inserts an unsettling element into analyses that follow the election. Perhaps surprisingly, this is particularly evident after landslide victories. In 1956 the Democrats gained seats in both houses despite Eisenhower's success. They repeated this performance in 1972 and 1984 in the Senate in the face of Nixon's and Reagan's landslides, and Republican gains in the House in those years were quite modest. The Democrats did gain thirty-seven seats in the House in 1964, the year of Johnson's

16. Gary Jacobson, "National Forces in Congressional Elections" (paper delivered of the Annual Meeting of the American Political Science Association, Washington, August, 1986), table 8.

landslide victory, but only one in the Senate. Therefore, although gains in party seats in Congress provide welcome reinforcement for assertions of presidential mandates, they seldom do so.

Media Hyperbole

Another factor that contributes to misperceptions of mandates is the analyses of election results that appear immediately after the election. Most such interpretations of election outcomes are made by journalists in the news media. Although most are based on superficial readings of the aggregate data available right after the election, they dominate the attention of the public and elites. They also appear at a time when the meaning of the outcome may be ambiguous and members of Congress are highly attuned to understanding what voters meant by their votes. In this environment, news reports loom large and go a long way toward establishing the framework within which others view the results of the election.

Unfortunately the news media often get the story wrong. Reports of the election of 1980 illustrate this problem. Press reports typically exaggerated the one-sidedness of Reagan's victory and the supposed collapse of the traditional Democratic coalition. Journalists dwelt largely on influences on voters that worked for Reagan and against Carter and gave little attention to the opposite influences. As Stanley Kelley remarked, "A foreign reader of some reports might have found it mysterious that anyone had voted against the new president, but almost half the electorate did."[17]

Many commentators were also in error when they announced a turn toward conservatism. Despite Reagan's lead over Carter of 10 percentage points, polls showed that there was not a substantial shift to the right in the public's thinking on issues of policy.[18] Polls also indicated that a large percentage of Reagan's supporters voted for him because he was seen as the lesser of evils, because they opposed Carter, or because they felt it was time for a change. These vague responses, not particularly oriented toward policy, reveal that the election was more a rejection of Jimmy Carter than a vote of confidence in Ronald Reagan.[19]

17. Kelley, *Interpreting Elections,* p. 223.

18. *CBS News/The New York Times Poll* (news release, November 15, 1980), p. 45. See also Kathleen A. Frankovic, "The Public Opinion Trends," in Marlene Michaels Pomper, ed., *The Election of 1980* (Chatham, N.J.: Chatham House, 1981), pp. 103, 113–117; Gerald M. Pomper, "The Presidential Election," in *The Election of 1980,* p. 87; Kelly, *Interpreting Elections,* chap. 9.

19. *CBS News/The New York Times Poll* (news release, November 15, 1980), table 4; Frankovic, "Public Opinion Trends," pp. 97–99, 103; Everett Carll Ladd, "The Brittle Mandate: Electoral Dealignment and the 1980 Presidential Election," *Political Science Quarterly* 96 (Spring 1981): 1–26; Arthur H. Miller and Martin P. Wattenberg, "Throwing the Rascals Out: Policy and Performance Evaluations of Presidential Candidates, 1952–1980," *American Political*

Perhaps the most notable policy proposal Reagan made early in his term was for a substantial tax cut. Yet before the election almost twice as many people were in favor of the smaller tax cut proposed by President Carter than the larger one proposed by candidate Reagan.[20] Similarly, the public did not support decreased spending on domestic policy at election time.[21] Thus by inferring support for specific policies from victory at the polls one risks substantially misreading public opinion.

Nevertheless, interpretations of widespread opinion change were common, and they undoubtedly affected perceptions among members of Congress, who are inherently susceptible to such influence. Sen. Alan Simpson, who viewed Reagan as having received "an awesome depth of support,"[22] seems representative of many other Senate Republicans.

Equally important, at least in 1981, many Democrats defected to Reagan's side in the fear of what they perceived as strong, clear signals from their constituents to support the new president.[23] This perception is dramatically illustrated by the comment in 1981 of a leading political adviser to Speaker of the House Tip O'Neill: "What the Democrats did . . . was to recognize the *cataclysmic* nature of the 1980 election results. The American public wanted this new President to be given a chance to try out his programs. We weren't going to come across as being obstructionists."[24] That the Democrats' perception was in error is less important than that they held it, owing in part to mistaken interpretations by the news media.

Orientation of the Campaign

The winning candidate's inclination to present policy alternatives during the campaign may also affect perceptions of a mandate. Often, in the interests

Science Review 79 (June 1985): 359–372; William Schneider, "The November 4 Vote for President: What Did It Mean?" in Austin Ranney, ed., *The American Elections of 1980* (Washington: American Enterprise Institute, 1981), pp. 247–248; Gregory B. Markus, "Political Attitudes During an Election Year: A Report on the 1980 NES Panel Study," *American Political Science Review* 76 (September 1982): 538–560; Douglas A. Hibbs, Jr., "President Reagan's Mandate from 1980 Elections: A Shift to the Right?" *American Politics Quarterly* 10 (October 1982): 387–420; Martin P. Wattenberg, *American Politics Quarterly* 14 (July 1986): 219–246.

20. *CBS News/The New York Times Poll* (news release, September 27, 1980), p. 4, tables 19, 23.

21. Miller and Wattenberg, "Political Performance Voting in the 1980 Election," p. 8.

22. Television interview, 1980.

23. Barbara Sinclair, *Majority Leadership in the U.S. House* (Baltimore: Johns Hopkins University Press, 1983) pp. 196–197, 242. See also Barbara Sinclair, "Agenda Control and Policy Success: Ronald Reagan and the 97th House," *Legislative Studies Quarterly* 10 (August 1985): 312; Patricia A. Hurley, "Electoral Change and Policy Consequences: Representation in the 97th Congress," *American Politics Quarterly* 2 (April 1984): 189–190.

24. Quoted in Laurence Barrett, *Gambling with History* (New York: Penguin, 1984), p. 147.

of building a broad electoral coalition, a candidate avoids specifics to such a degree that he undercuts future claims of policy mandates. In American politics the electoral and governing processes are often quite separate.

All four of the elections in which the winner obtained more than 55 percent of the vote (1956, 1964, 1972, 1984) were races in which the incumbent won reelection (table 8.1). With the exception of Lyndon Johnson, who had been in office only a year, the presidents used their campaigns to appeal as broadly as possible and run up the score. Yet in producing impressive personal victories they undermined their ability to govern after the election. Eisenhower, Nixon, and Reagan each experienced considerable difficulties with Congress in the two years immediately following their landslide victories.

The election of 1984 illustrates how winning candidates can compromise their ability to govern after the election. Ronald Reagan's rhetorical style, marked by the repetition of uplifting generalities, was well-suited to a medium that places a premium on straightforward communication of broad, simple ideas. He appealed to shared, basic values and invoked themes of leadership and opportunity that stirred the emotions of his audience. Some may term this the politics of mood elevation. In addition, the dazzling technical competence of his campaign staff in lighting, sound, and the creation of backdrops painted to complement his skin tones created outstanding visual images. The repetition, simplicity, and consistency of the president's message served him well in obtaining support, but it did little to encourage interpretations of a mandate.

President Reagan consistently sidestepped Walter Mondale's challenge to spell out his future economic program. The White House went so far as to instruct the administration's officials to postpone normal preparation of the coming year's budget out of fear that leaks of impending reductions would offend various groups of voters. Of course the president also denied repeatedly that there was any economic problem that current policies would not remedy. The Reagan campaign asked voters to make retrospective rather than prospective choices.

What is perhaps most remarkable about the administration's efforts to obscure its policies was its blatancy. According to the White House spokesman Larry Speakes, "The press can ask nine different ways what we are going to do about the budget next year. We're just not going to answer." In March the president gave an interview in the Oval Office to two reporters from the *New York Times*. They asked him five times to be specific about how he would make further reductions in domestic spending. Each time, Reagan refused to answer. To do so, he argued, would invite "demagoguery" from the Democrats.[25] Regarding questions from the press about charges from Mondale, James Lake, press secretary of Reagan's reelection committee, argued that "it would be foolish of us to let Ronald Reagan respond to him."[26] The president simply held no press conference after July.

All this was not lost on the public. A poll late in the campaign found that 39 percent of the public felt Reagan avoided discussing the issues, a figure that included 30 percent of Reagan's probable voters.[27]

What *did* the president say? During the campaign the *New York Times* published what is called "the speech" for each candidate.[28] This was the common body of material that the candidates repeated in most of their speeches throughout the campaign. A careful reading of Reagan's presentation reveals that his only specific proposals were for low-tax "enterprise zones" and a lower minimum wage for youth, both of which he had proposed earlier in his term and failed to pass Congress. He also made general references to simpler, fairer, and lower taxes.

Another outlet for the candidates was the presidential debates. In the first debate, on domestic policy, the candidates squared off on only three issues: tax increases, a constitutional amendment to allow prayer in the public schools, and a constitutional amendment to prohibit abortions. It is worth noting that the president has no direct role in the passage and ratification of amendments to the Constitution.

In the rest of the debate Reagan essentially argued for a continuation of his previous policies. This discussion was highly general, as were the many comments that raised symbols or dealt with matters such as religious beliefs. Naturally, each candidate spent much time criticizing his opponent.

It is of course an exaggeration to argue that there were no obvious policy differences between the candidates. They differed fundamentally on a range of policies, as anyone reading the party platforms could easily discern. The candidates rarely referred to their party's platforms, however, and the White House disavowed the Republican platform shortly after it was written. Probably the most notable reference to either platform was Walter Mondale's inaccurate claim that Jerry Falwell would screen Reagan's nominations to the federal bench.

25. Quoted in Steven R. Weisman, "The President and the Press: The Art of Controlling Access," *New York Times Magazine*, October 14, 1984, sec. 1, pp. 74, 80.

26. Quoted in Howell Raines, "Reagan Appears to Succeed by Avoiding Specific Issues," *New York Times*, September 23, 1984, sec. 1, p. 14.

27. *CBS News/The New York Times Poll* (news release, October 6, 1984), table 18a.

28. "The Speech: President Reagan," *New York Times*, September 27, 1984, sec. A, p. 14; "The Speech: Walter F. Mondale," *New York Times*, October 11, 1984, sec. A, p. 13.

Equally important, very few people ever read party platforms. Their knowledge of them is rudimentary at best. Despite the substantial publicity surrounding the Republican party's decision to take no stand on the Equal Rights Amendment in its platform in 1980, a poll after the convention found that only 1 percent of registered voters knew what position the GOP had taken.[29]

By steadfastly refusing to deal with specific questions of policy and relying on broad generalities, Reagan undercut later claims for a mandate. His failure to present a blueprint for a second term wasted political capital that would have been necessary for generating a major change in policy. His landslide appeared as more a personal victory than one based on policy.

The election of 1964 was unusual. President Johnson had a reasonably clear platform of proposals, most of which had been on the agenda for several years. Further, he had not served in office long enough to see many of his programs become law, despite his success in Congress in 1964. Thus observers were aware of Johnson's proposals and could tie them directly to the election. The Eighty-ninth Congress was very responsive to the president's legislative requests.

Continuity vs. Change

Related to the orientation of the campaign is the relative impact of continuity and change on perceptions of the outcome of the election. Once again, the contrast between the elections of 1980 and 1984 nicely illustrates the point.

The results of the election of 1984 were less explosive than those of 1980, despite their far more impressive proportions, because the outcome represented continuity rather than change. In 1984 the incumbent was reelected; in 1980 the incumbent was thrown out of office, which had not happened to an elected president since Herbert Hoover. According to a strong supporter of Reagan, Sen. James McClure, a Republican, "The president doesn't have the automatic fealty, being reelected, as he had in 1981 repudiating the previous administration. We don't have a new president and a new mandate sweeping the country."[30]

As a candidate in 1980 Reagan advocated major changes in public policy. Although he did not always specify the details of these changes, few observers were unaware of the thrust of his commitments. Four years later, however,

29. Michael J. Malbin, "The Conventions, Platforms, and Issue Activists," in *The American Elections of 1980*, p. 138 n. 38.

30. Quoted in "Senate Republicans See Obstacles for Reagan," *New York Times*, November 28, 1984, sec. A, p. 11.

President Ronald Reagan asked for continuity. He wanted voters to reward him for a successful term. It is not surprising that members of Congress interpreted the two elections differently. It is easier for members of Congress to oppose programs without appearing to oppose a popular president if the incumbent frames the campaign as a referendum on his qualities as a leader and does not associate himself with new policies.

Further, the results in 1984 were easy to anticipate and surprised virtually no one. They also reinforced the status quo. Continuity has considerably less psychological impact than change, especially if the change appears to be substantial. Thus the proportions of a victory may be less important than its predictability and emotional impact.

What is crucial is not just change, but a combination of change, a substantial defeat of the leading opponent, and a sense of new directions in policy. This combination is unusual. Dwight Eisenhower entitled the first volume of his memoirs *Mandate for Change*, but he chose not to present a legislative program to Congress in 1953. His campaign slogan of "Communism, Corruption, and Korea" was catchy, but it had little legislative content. The next three changes in the party in control of the White House were by excruciatingly thin margins. Kennedy, Nixon, and Carter beat their opponents by less than 1 percent of the vote in 1960, 1968, and 1976. The impact of their victories was diminished by their indecisive nature. Although Ronald Reagan obtained only 51 percent of the vote in 1980, he beat his principal opponent, Jimmy Carter, by 10 percentage points.

The Tides of Opinion

In his study of agenda setting in the national government, John Kingdon found that people in and around government believed strongly that there was such a thing as a "national mood," that they could measure it, and that it had consequences for policy.[31] Every president must work within the confines of public opinion. Although they may influence its texture, they rarely if ever can shape its basic contours. If perceptions of a mandate are to take hold, the directions in which the president desires to move must be consistent with the national mood.

Things often do not work out that way. Some presidents, such as Harry Truman, may fight the grain of opinion, whereas others, such as John F. Kennedy, may be waiting for it to mature. Conversely, a president such as Franklin D. Roosevelt arrives at the crest of a wave of opinion and can ride it freely.

31. John W. Kingdon, *Agendas, Alternatives, and Public Policies* (Boston: Little, Brown, 1984), pp. 153–157.

Some presidents may move with the grain of history but against the dominant perspective of their own party. Kingdon spent several years in the late 1970s interviewing policy makers in Washington. He found a consensus on a conservative national mood, characterized for example by opposition to regulation and large government expenditures and support for reducing the size of government.[32]

Jimmy Carter's views were congruent with this national mood. His campaign themes in 1976 were the most conservative of any Democratic candidate since the Depression, stressing fiscal restraint, economic deregulation, bureaucratic efficiency, and traditional moral values. By the last half of his term he also advocated substantial increases in defense expenditures.

Nevertheless, Carter's ability to promote perceptions of a mandate was undermined by the constant opposition he faced from the vocal and powerful liberal wing of his own party. His press secretary, Jody Powell, reports that a survey of the press found that 75 percent of the critical commentary on the administration reported in 1977 had come from Democrats, mostly liberals.[33] In 1980 the president had to deal with the challenge of Senator Edward Kennedy for the Democratic nomination for president.

Four years after Jimmy Carter's election, Ronald Reagan was elected with a similar percentage of the vote. Yet the new president did not face the same constraints as his predecessor. His party was overwhelmingly conservative and included few who actively and vocally opposed the president.

Presidential Influence on Perceptions

What can presidents do to lead others to perceive their electoral victories as mandates? The answer is that most of the factors that influence perceptions of mandates are not under the president's control. The president can do little to change the nature of elections. How much voters think about issues, know of them, or vote on the basis of them may be influenced to some degree by the president's emphasis on issues in the campaign, but there is little evidence that campaigns affect large segments of the voting population at all.[34]

Similarly, presidents have not been successful in moving people to go to the polls and cast their votes. Despite large-scale efforts by both parties to encourage and facilitate voting in the elections of 1984, for example, the

32. Ibid., p. 154.

33. Jody Powell, *The Other Side of the Story* (New York: William Morrow, 1984), p. 186. See also pp. 182–192.

34. See for example Herbert Asher, *Presidential Elections and American Politics*, rev. ed. (Homewood, Ill.: Dorsey, 1980), pp. 316–317; Kathleen A. Frankovic, "The 1984 Election: The Irrelevance of the Campaign," *PS* 18 (Winter 1985): 39–47.

TABLE 8.3   Ticket Splitting between Presidential and House Candidates

Year	Number of Split Districts	Percentage of All Districts[a]
1952	84	19.3
1956	130	29.9
1960	114	26.1
1964	145	33.3
1968	139	32.0
1972	192	44.1
1976	124	28.5
1980	143	32.8
1984	190	43.7

[a]437 districts in 1960, 435 in all other years
SOURCE: Norman J. Ornstein et al., *Vital Statistics on Congress, 1984–1985 Edition* (Washington: American Enterprise Institute, 1984), p. 56.

turnout remained the same as in 1980, 53 percent. The figure from 1980 represented a steady decrease from the several preceding elections. Although the puzzle of voter participation remains to be solved, turnout seems to be due to factors beyond the reach of the White House.[35]

It is therefore inevitable that correlating the support of voters with their views on policy will be difficult. Opinion in a populace as heterogeneous as that of the United States will be diverse. Finally, barring drastic changes in our electoral system, citizens will continue to have one vote with which to express their views on a range of topics. The president's impact on the nature of elections is marginal at best.

Naturally, candidates for the presidency try to win election by as large a margin as possible and desire to carry their party's congressional candidates into office with them. Winning big is not a matter of choice, however: candidates simply do the best they can. Yet coattails are typically short, and evidence is lacking that suggests presidents are successful in encouraging straight-ticket voting. Split-ticket voting has been increasing for years as party identification has declined, and the presidential vote has had a decreasing influence on the congressional vote.[36] The number of congressional districts carried by a presidential candidate of one party and a House candidate of another party is large, and the trend is in the direction of increasingly split results (table 8.3).

35. See for example Paul R. Abramson, John H. Aldrich, and David W. Rohde, *Change and Continuity in the 1984 Elections* (Washington: Congressional Quarterly Press, 1986), chap. 4 and sources cited therein.

36. Ferejohn and Fiorina, "Incumbency and Realignment in Congressional Elections," p. 99.

In addition to being influenced by the nature of elections and the electorate, perceptions of mandates are subject to broad historical forces largely beyond the president's control. What I have termed the tides of opinion are a vital part of the environment in which presidential candidates seek election and serve in office. Presidents may rise or fall with the tide, but they are unlikely to alter fundamentally the basic configuration of American politics in the short period in which perceptions about the election outcomes take hold. Likewise, whether a candidate topples an incumbent president or seeks reelection (maintaining the status quo) is not a matter of leadership strategy. Candidates simply seek to win in the context of the conditions extant at the time.

Presidents are of course not without means to influence perceptions of their victories at the polls. They have substantial discretion in orienting their campaign and stressing policy change. In theory they could make their positions on issues crystal clear, increasing the probability that observers will connect the votes they receive with these positions. Nevertheless, presidential candidates typically strive to minimize the possibility of alienating voters who might otherwise support them, to increase their chances of winning the election or of winning by as large a margin as possible. They tend to emphasize general goals and images in their presentations to the public, such as peace and prosperity, while remaining obscure on more specific issues.[37]

One might assume that the policies of incumbent presidents seeking reelection would be clear to the public. Yet their current policies are not always clear to voters or necessarily accurate guides to the future. Incumbent presidents are usually more vague than their challengers on issues, and they rarely present detailed plans for future policy on the campaign trail, as was made clear in the campaign of 1984. In addition, incumbents usually have to defend their records rather than emphasize the future. In some instances, such as in 1972, 1976, and 1980, incumbent presidents simply employ the "Rose Garden strategy" and do not campaign very actively.[38]

The president also attempts to influence appraisals of his electoral victory in the aftermath of the election. As one aide to Ronald Reagan declared in early 1981, "We are going to push the mandate as far as possible. If you don't hear us say the public has spoken again and again, we won't be doing our job.

---

37. See Benjamin I. Page, *Choices and Echoes in Presidential Elections* (Chicago: University of Chicago Press, 1978), pp. 160, 178; Edward G. Carmines and J. David Gopian, "Issue Coalitions, Issueless Campaigns: The Paradox of Rationality in American Presidential Elections," *Journal of Politics* 43 (November 1981): 1170–1189.

38. Page, *Choices and Echoes in Presidential Elections*, pp. 168–169; Gerald M. Pomper with Susan S. Lederman, *Elections in America*, 2d ed. (New York: Longman, 1980), pp. 134–135.

The strategy is to keep the pressure on the Democrats, to keep jolting them back to November 4, 1980."[39]

Another official at the White House confessed that the "mandate" of 1980 was "a carefully created illusion." He added, "We were never quite as strong as we gave the impression of being. We pretended we had a mandate that was very much larger than it was."[40] Because these claims reinforced the conventional wisdom, they were especially persuasive.

In addition, Reagan's strategist Richard Wirthlin honestly felt his candidate had received a mandate from the electorate in 1980.[41] He repeated this in many forums and undoubtedly influenced the perceptions of the election held by a number of elites. That Wirthlin's inferences were based on a rather generous definition of mandate probably was less important than his position close to the new president and his role as Reagan's chief pollster.

The White House did not hesitate to declare a broad mandate from the voters once again in 1984. Sometimes these claims were extraordinary. Shortly after the election, for example, Larry Speakes contended that the voters had mandated that Congress limit budget procedures to a "single up or down vote."[42]

A month after his second inauguration, President Reagan began a press conference by informing his television audience, "As for those who will tell us that growth and expansion are not even, that spending restraint is politically impossible, that higher taxes are necessary, our answer is simple. That issue was debated and decided on November 6th. We intend to proceed with the mandate we've been given by the people."[43] Evidently, the voters had selected an economic theory as well as a president.

These assertions did not fall on receptive ears among policy makers in Washington. The president immediately faced strong opposition in Congress to his domestic and foreign policy proposals. Because public officials, journalists, and other elites employ the criteria discussed above in evaluating the outcomes of elections, the White House's claims of a mandate were not accepted at face value.

39. Quoted in Paul C. Light, *The President's Agenda* (Baltimore: Johns Hopkins University Press, 1982), p. 30.

40. Quoted in C. T. Hanson, "Gunsmoke and Sleeping Dogs: The Prez's Press at Midterm," *Columbia Journalism Review*, May–June 1983, pp. 30–31.

41. Interview with Richard Wirthlin, April 4, 1987, Princeton.

42. Quoted in "Reagan Reported to Lean to Freezing Budget Figure," *New York Times*, November 30, 1984, sec. A, p. 8.

43. Quoted in "Text of Press Conferences," *Congressional Quarterly Weekly Report*, March 2, 1985, p. 405.

Presidential elections may play a vital role in changing policy by helping to structure the choices faced by members of Congress. By setting the terms of the debate over issues and the premises of decision, presidents can influence a large number of senators and representatives and obtain a large portion of what they want from them.

At the same time, it must be kept in mind that perceptions and not necessarily reality determine how political elites react to the outcomes of elections. Significant change relies on the serendipitous confluence of several reinforcing perceptions. This is a constraint on the president, because he is not in a position to influence the way in which others view his election.

There are also limits to what perceptions of mandates can do for a president. For example one of the most difficult and important votes in President Reagan's first year was on what was known as Gramm-Latta II, the final budget resolution for fiscal year 1982. Despite the perception of a mandate, there were fewer Democratic defections in the House than on any final budget resolution vote in previous years. Once again effective leadership consists of exploiting opportunities rather than creating them.

CHAPTER NINE

Strategic Position of Legislative Skills

In 1981 Ronald Reagan's dramatic budget and tax proposals passed Congress largely unscathed. Many observers commented on his personal skills in dealing with Congress and offered them as at least a major part of the explanation of the president's success.[1] Yet in 1983 House Republicans refused even to propose the president's budget, much less vote for it. This presents a fascinating puzzle. Had President Reagan's legislative skills diminished substantially over the preceding two years, or were they in fact not very significant in his early victories? More broadly, are these skills at the core of presidential leadership or are they important only at the margins of coalition building, taking a back seat to more fundamental contextual factors such as party strength in Congress and public support? Can legislative skills provide a foundation for the role of director or can they serve only to support a facilitator?

There is more involved here than merely an isolated, albeit important, empirical question. The emphasis on personal skills, what James MacGregor Burns calls the "skill mystique,"[2] has important consequences for the way we evaluate the president and, more broadly, how we orient ourselves to politics. If problems of leadership are simply personal failures, then one need not look far for a solution: all that is needed is to find a president more skillful at persuasion and manipulation. With a strong and effective leader at the helm, the ship of state will sail smoothly. One need not be concerned with broader

---

1. See for example the essays in Norman J. Ornstein, ed., *President and Congress: Assessing Reagan's First Year* (Washington: American Enterprise Institute, 1982).

2. James MacGregor Burns, *The Power to Lead* (New York: Simon and Schuster, 1984), p. 38.

forces in the polity that may influence public policy making. Because these forces may be complex and perhaps intractable, the focus on leadership skills simplifies the analysis and evaluation of remedies for problems of governing.

If on the other hand presidential leadership skills are one of many factors that influence congressional policy making, and not necessarily the most important one, our understanding of the presidency must be richer and our expectations of it less demanding. Attention should not be devoted exclusively to the chief executive. Instead, the focus must be on the context in which the president seeks to achieve his goals, and one should be always mindful of the other institutions and actors with independent power involved in policy making. It follows directly from this orientation that there are significant constraints on what presidential skills can accomplish. For this reason, change must usually involve more than an upgrading of skills through on-the-job training or a change in the occupant of the Oval Office.

In examining the strategic position of presidential legislative skills, my goal is to evaluate their overall impact on congressional support for the president, and to place the role of legislative skills as tools of presidential leadership in their proper perspective.

The Conventional Wisdom

Attributing significance to presidential legislative leadership skills is a well-entrenched aspect of much of the writing, both popular and scholarly, on presidential-congressional relations. Scholars chronicle and study presidential acts, and it is only natural to ascribe importance to them. The tendency of the press to focus on the more unique aspects of these relationships, such as presidential bargaining and arm twisting, and to imply that what it is presenting is typical, only reinforces the conventional wisdom.

Further, most reporters and correspondents are trained to focus on individual personalities and what is new rather than on patterns of behavior, and they perceive presidential success in Congress as resulting from the president's legislative skills.[3] For example, Robert Pierpoint, an experienced network correspondent covering the White House, recently described how he thought Lyndon Johnson would have garnered support for the nomination of Theodore Sorensen as director of the CIA in 1977:

> Good mornin', Mr. Chairman, this is yore President. . . . Not too well, thank you. I'm a mite unhappy that you don't seem to like my new

3. Similarly, Thomas E. Patterson found that the press emphasized electoral skills rather than issues in covering elections, believing that the skills were what made the difference. See *The Mass Media Election* (New York: Praeger, 1980), pp. 51–52. F. Christopher Arterton found that reporters viewed elections as contests between individuals. See *Media Politics* (Lexington, Mass.: D. C. Heath, 1984) pp. 63–64.

Director of the CIA. At least that's what I read in the press. . . . Yeah, Senator, I know all that. Knew it before I nominated him. Senator, I want to tell you something I been thinkin' about. You know all them military bases you got out there in Hah-wai-ee? Well, I been wonderin' if some of them bases might not be better off somewhere else . . . say Alaska . . . or Gu-Wam. . . . No, Senator, I haven't made any decisions yet. But I do know those bases are pretty important to your people out there. . . . Oh, is that right, you've changed your mind about my appointment to head the CIA? Thank you, Senator, I thought yu'd see it my way!

Pierpoint then concludes that "that's the kind of power a president has" and criticizes President Carter for not exploiting it.[4]

The statements of participants in the legislative process also sometimes buttress the view that legislative skills are central factors in explaining presidential success in Congress. According to Lyndon Johnson, for example, "There is only one way for a President to deal with the Congress, and that is continuously, incessantly, and without interruption."[5] He believed that "merely placing a program before Congress is not enough. Without constant attention from the administration most legislation moves through the congressional process at the speed of a glacier."[6]

Some scholars also emphasize personal legislative skills.[7] Paul Light engaged in a more systematic study of the question than most other commentators, and concluded that legislative skills were intervening variables operating within the boundaries of presidential success set by presidential approval in the public and party strength in Congress. He found presidents more likely to obtain passage of their proposals when they introduced their programs early and lobbied for them than when they introduced them late and failed to lobby for them.[8]

Reason for Skepticism

Despite these assertions and findings, there are a number of reasons to doubt the significance of presidential legislative skills in influencing Congress to support the White House's proposals. In comparing the presidential support

4. Robert Pierpoint, *At the White House: Assignment to Six Presidents* (New York: Putnam's, 1981), p. 119.

5. Doris Kearns, *Lyndon Johnson and the American Dream* (New York: Harper and Row, 1976), p. 226.

6. Lyndon B. Johnson, *The Vantage Point* (New York: Popular Library, 1971), p. 448.

7. See for example Barbara Kellerman, *The Political Presidency* (New York: Oxford University Press, 1984).

8. Paul Light, "Passing Nonincremental Policy: Presidential Influence in Congress, Kennedy to Carter," *Congress and the Presidency* 9 (Winter 1981–82): 61–82.

scores of various groups in Congress in earlier research, I found that there was little variance between presidents who were highly skilled, such as Lyndon Johnson, and others, who had reputations for being much less skilled, such as Jimmy Carter.[9]

The authors of a recent study provide a strong critique of the use of case studies to test the importance of presidential legislative skills. They employ systematic data from 1953–84 on the success of presidents in winning votes and find that skilled presidents were no more likely to win than less skilled ones.[10]

Although Light's research is important as a step toward placing a president's legislative skills in the proper perspective, one must be cautious in accepting its specific findings. The study is limited to nonincremental domestic policy, attempts to explain only the passage of legislation (like a box score) rather than the support of members of Congress, and lacks clear operational definitions for crucial terms such as "nonincremental" and "lobbying." The number of programs involved is also quite small, and the author tests the impact of the White House's lobbying by comparing the success of proposals that were lobbied for with those that were not lobbied for at all. Because it is difficult to imagine a significant, that is, "nonincremental," presidential policy proposal that the White House simply ignores, it is unlikely that much can be learned about the importance of legislative skills from such a comparison.

Light points out an interesting and seemingly paradoxical phenomenon. The essence of his argument (for the purposes of this study) is that presidents are more successful when they are less skilled and less successful when they have refined their skills.[11] The reasonable conclusion to draw from this analysis is not the perverse one that legislative skills are detrimental to obtaining legislative support. Instead, one might infer that legislative skills are of relatively modest significance in explaining congressional behavior in relation to other factors.

Misperceptions of history may also contribute to an undue emphasis on presidential legislative skills. This is especially true regarding two of the most prolific periods of presidential legislative success, Franklin Roosevelt's "hundred days" and Lyndon Johnson's Eighty-ninth Congress. The first piece of legislation Roosevelt proposed in 1933 was a bill to control the resumption of

9. George C. Edwards III, *Presidential Influence in Congress* (San Francisco: W. H. Freeman, 1980), chap. 7.

10. Richard Fleisher and Jon Bond, "Presidential Leadership Skill and Success in Congress" (paper presented at the annual meeting of the Southern Political Science Association, Atlanta, November 1986).

11. Paul C. Light, *The President's Agenda: Domestic Policy Choice from Kennedy to Carter* (Baltimore: Johns Hopkins University Press, 1982).

banking. According to James MacGregor Burns, "The milling representatives could hardly wait to act." Even during the forty minute debate in the House, shouts of "Vote! Vote!" echoed from the floor. The Republican leader, Bertrand H. Snell, exclaimed in support, "The House is burning down and the President of the United States says this is the way to put out the fire."[12] There was little need for personal legislative skills in this environment.

Yet even in 1933 Roosevelt faced congressional resistance to his programs. The second bill he proposed gave the federal government the power to effect government economies to cut the deficit. The prospects of such a policy frightened veterans' organizations, which deluged Congress with telegrams in opposition. There was open revolt against the president in Congress on his second bill. It passed the House only when sixty-nine fiscally conservative Republicans voted with the president. Ninety Democrats, including seven party leaders, deserted FDR at this early stage in the hundred days. Things were not any better in the Senate, and it took the first fireside chat and the popular proposal to repeal Prohibition to solidify Democratic ranks.[13] The president, in other words, took his case to the people rather than the Congress in order obtain to passage of his legislation.

Roosevelt went on to serve in the White House longer than anyone else, but most of these years were not legislatively productive. Burns entitles his discussion of presidential-congressional relations in the late 1930s "Deadlock on the Potomac."[14] Either Roosevelt had lost his legislative skills, which is not a reasonable proposition, or other factors were more significant in determining congressional support.

John Kennedy and Lyndon Johnson are generally viewed as having had substantially different legislative skills and relationships with Congress. Yet their visible differences were not considered important by the leading participants in legislative process. According to the White House's chief liaison aide for the House under both Kennedy and Johnson, Henry Hall Wilson, the approach of the two presidents to the House was "practically identical."[15] Similarly, the White House liaison to the Senate for both presidents, Mike Manatos, argues that it did not make any difference on the Hill which president he represented. His appeals for support were treated the same.[16]

12. James MacGregor Burns, *Roosevelt: The Lion and the Fox* (New York: Harcourt, Brace and World, 1956) pp. 166–167.

13. Ibid., pp. 167–168.

14. Ibid., pp. 337–342.

15. Henry Hall Wilson, interview by Joe B. Frantz, April 11, 1973, transcript, pp. 6–7, Lyndon Baines Johnson Library, Austin, Tex.

16. Mike Manatos, interview by Joe B. Frantz, August 25, 1969, transcript, pp. 13–14, Lyndon Baines Johnson Library, Austin, Tex.

The congressional leaders John McCormack, Carl Albert, Charles Halleck, and Everett Dirksen, Johnson's aides Lawrence O'Brien, Joseph Califano, and Mike Manatos, the executive branch official James Sundquist, and numerous scholars agree that had Kennedy lived and won by a large margin in 1964, he would have got much the same from Congress as Johnson did, and that the basic explanation for Johnson's phenomenal success in 1965 and 1966 was the increase in the number of liberal Democrats in Congress as a result of the elections of 1964.[17] Significantly, Kennedy and Johnson legislative liaison aides do not argue to the contrary in their published memoirs or their oral histories in the Kennedy and Johnson presidential libraries.

Arthur Schlesinger, Jr., a historian and White House aide to President Kennedy, is also skeptical about the significance of legislative skills. Comparing President Kennedy and President Johnson he concludes:

> When Johnson lost 48 Democratic House seats in the 1966 election, he found himself, despite his alleged wizardry, in the same condition of stalemate that had thwarted Kennedy and, indeed, every Democratic President since 1938. Had the sequence been different, had Johnson been elected to the Presidency in 1960 with Kennedy as his Vice President, and had Johnson then offered the 87th Congress the same program actually offered by Kennedy, the probability is that he would have had no more success than Kennedy—perhaps even less because he appealed less effectively to public opinion. And, if Johnson had died in 1963 and Kennedy had beaten Goldwater by a large margin in 1964, then Kennedy would have had those extra votes in the House of Representatives, and the pundits of the press would have contrasted his cool management of Congress with the frenetic and bumbling efforts of his predecessor. In the end, arithmetic is decisive.[18]

17. John McCormack, interview by T. Harrison Baker, September 23, 1968, transcript, pp. 20, 39–40, Lyndon Baines Johnson Library, Austin, Tex.; Carl Albert, interview by Dorothy Pierce McSweeny, July 9, 1969, interview 3, transcript, p. 4, Lyndon Baines Johnson Library, Austin, Tex.; Eric F. Goldman, *The Tragedy of Lyndon Johnson* (New York: Dell, 1974), p. 68; Charles Halleck, interview by Stephen Hess, March 22, 1965, transcript, p. 27, John F. Kennedy Library, Boston; Lawrence F. O'Brien, *No Final Victories* (New York: Ballantine, 1974), pp. 106, 145–149, 188–189; Richard Bolling, *Power in the House* (New York: Capricorn, 1974), pp. 218, 229; Joseph A. Califano, Jr., *A Presidential Nation* (New York: W. W. Norton, 1975), p. 155; Manatos, interview by Frantz, pp. 14, 29–30, 57–58 (see also p. 32); James L. Sundquist, *Politics and Policy* (Washington: Brookings Institution, 1968), pp. 476–482; Joseph Cooper and Gary Bombardier, "Presidential Leadership and Party Success," *Journal of Politics* 30 (November 1968): 1012–1027; Aage R. Clausen, *How Congressmen Decide* (New York: St. Martin's, 1973) p. 146. See also Rowland Evans and Robert Novak, *Lyndon B. Johnson: The Exercise of Power* (New York: New American Library, 1966), p. 364.
18. Arthur M. Schlesinger, Jr., *Robert Kennedy and His Times* (New York: Ballantine, 1978), p. 742.

Similarly, party remained the dominant factor in the relations with Congress of Reagan's administration. In contrasting President Reagan's difficulties with Congress in 1983–84 with his more productive experience in 1981–82, Tom Loeffler, the House Republican chief deputy whip, commented, "The difference is that in 1981 and 1982 the White House was more capable of pushing the president's program through Congress simply because the makeup of the House was different."[19]

Ronald Reagan also benefited from the nature of the times. Although 1981 was hardly a repeat of 1933, there was a definite sense of the need for immediate action to meet urgent problems. In its first issue after Reagan's inauguration, the *Congressional Quarterly Weekly Report* declared that "one of Reagan's biggest advantages is the sense of both parties in Congress that the nation's problems are now very serious indeed."[20]

Similarly, David Stockman, a principal architect and proponent of Reagan's budgeting and tax proposals, remembers that when the president announced his "Program for Economic Recovery" to a joint session of Congress in February 1981, "the plan already had momentum and few were standing in the way." Reagan was "speaking to an assembly of desperate politicians who . . . were predisposed to grant him extraordinary latitude in finding a new remedy for the nation's economic ills . . . not because they understood the plan or even accepted it, but because they had lost all faith in the remedies tried before."[21] Paul Craig Roberts, a founder of supply-side economics and a principal advocate of it in the administration, recalled, "By the time Ronald Reagan entered the White House, only an incompetent administration could have lost the tax-cut battle."[22]

Scholars examining congressional leadership from within Congress have reached conclusions about the relative importance of skills and party seats similar to those articulated in this section. In their innovative examination of leadership in the House of Representatives, Joseph Cooper and David Brady conclude that institutional context is more important than personal skills or traits in determining the influence of leaders. They found no relationship between leadership style and effectiveness. They argue that style is determined more by the institutional context in which leaders find themselves than by their own personal traits. In the end the impact of institutional context on a

19. "White House Lobbyists Find Congress Is Less Supportive," *Congressional Quarterly Weekly Report*, June 16, 1984, p. 1429.

20. "Numerous Factors Favoring Good Relationship Between Reagan and New Congress," *Congressional Quarterly Weekly Report*, January 24, 1981, p. 172.

21. David A. Stockman, *The Triumph of Politics* (New York: Harper and Row, 1986), pp. 79–80; see also p. 120.

22. Paul Craig Roberts, *The Supply Side Revolution* (Cambridge: Harvard University Press, 1984), p. 88.

leader's power and style is determined primarily by party strength.[23]

Like public support, presidential skills must compete with other, more stable factors that affect voting in Congress in addition to party. These include ideology, personal views and commitments on specific policies, and the interests of constituencies. By the time a president tries to exercise influence on a vote, most members of Congress have made up their minds on the basis of these other factors. As Lawrence O'Brien wrote to Lyndon Johnson in 1965, "Normally we enter into a tough count with a minimum of 175 votes, about which we need not worry."[24] O'Brien's memo indicates that Johnson could depend on 175 votes out of the 218 necessary for a majority. If not everyone voted, which was usually the case, the number of votes needed to win was of course less than 218. So Johnson needed to add at most forty-three votes to his dependable coalition, or only about one-fifth of the total needed. One should keep in mind also that these figures are for "tough counts," not the typical vote. On less controversial measures he undoubtedly needed even fewer votes, if he needed any at all.

Thus a president's legislative skills are likely to be critical only for those members of Congress who remain open to change after other influences have had their impact. Although the size and composition of this group vary from issue to issue, it will almost always be a minority in each chamber. Sometimes the number will be large enough to make a notable difference, but often it will not. At times a few votes will be crucial in affecting the outcomes on issues. Whatever the circumstances, the impact will usually be relatively modest. Therefore, although potentially important, legislative skills are not likely to be at the core of policy change.

In an interview near the end of President Reagan's first two years in office, Richard Cheney, the chairman of the House Republican Policy Committee and President Ford's chief of staff, attributed the president's success in 1981 to the results of the 1980 election, public support, the attempted assassination of the president, and Reagan's having proposed policies in which Republicans in Congress believed, not to the White House's personal deal-

23. Joseph Cooper and David W. Brady, "Institutional Context and Leadership Style: The House from Cannon to Rayburn," *American Political Science Review* 75 (June 1981): 411–425. See also David W. Rohde and Kenneth A. Shepsle, "Leaders and Followers in the House of Representatives: Reflections on Woodrow Wilson's *Congressional Government*," *Congress and the Presidency* 14 (Autumn 1987): 111–133; Barbara Sinclair, "Party Leadership and Policy Change," in Gerald C. Wright, Jr., Leroy N. Rieselbach, and Lawrence C. Dodd, eds., *Congress and Policy Change* (New York: Agathon, 1986), pp. 175–200.

24. John F. Manley, "White House Lobbying and the Problem of Presidential Power" (paper presented at the annual meeting of the American Political Science Association, Washington, September 1977), p. 27. For a similar argument regarding the Eighty-seventh Congress see Neil MacNeil, *Forge of Democracy* (New York: David McKay, 1963), pp. 258–259.

ings with members.[25] There were actually fewer Democratic defections in the House from the party's stand on Gramm-Latta II, the final vote on the budget resolution, than on any such vote in previous years. It did not matter, however, because the president had sufficient votes within his own party as a result of the election of 1980.

In sum, despite the conventional wisdom that attributes substantial importance to a president's legislative skills in determining support for the president on congressional votes, there is good reason to be cautious in accepting this conclusion at face value. Other factors are likely to exercise more influence on congressional voting.

Evaluating the Impact of Legislative Skills

If a president's legislative skills have limited impact on congressional voting, one should not expect to find systematic differences in the support that presidents with different legislative skills received in Congress. If on the other hand legislative skills are an important tool of presidential leadership in Congress, then presidents with the most highly developed legislative skills should consistently receive more support than less skilled presidents.

To evaluate the importance of presidents' legislative skills, one would ideally measure the extent to which presidents exercised these skills on each member of a Congress or on the same members over several Congresses. After controlling for other sources of influence, one would determine whether members of Congress on whom a president's legislative skills were exercised provided more support than other members, or whether members' support over time fluctuated with the degree to which the president exercised his skills on them.

Unfortunately, there is no way to obtain data on the exercise of presidential legislative skills on each member of Congress, especially when it occurred in earlier decades. There is a substantial amount of information on the legislative activities of various presidents, however, and it is known how members of Congress voted on presidential proposals.

I employ an aggregate approach to evaluating the impact of legislative skills. The goal is to determine whether legislative skills have a systematic influence on support for the president's program in Congress (not whether they ever do), to place legislative skills in perspective, and to search for patterns of behavior. In the following chapter I examine presidents' efforts at exercising specific types of skills and the likely consequences of doing so.

25. Interview with Richard Cheney, November 19, 1982, Princeton.

Although some observers view legislative skills almost solely in terms of the president's personal interactions with members of Congress, and thus advocate evaluating skills by studying only those bills on which the president was intimately involved in lobbying, such a focus is too narrow. Much of the White House's liaison with members of Congress is aimed not at obtaining a discrete vote on a specific policy but at creating a favorable environment in which support for a policy can be requested from all members of Congress at once, or at generating a general climate of goodwill.

It is important to emphasize the use of Key Votes, which average only ten per year in the House and nine in the Senate. This exclusive index of presidential support might be expected to highlight the differences in the success of presidents with different legislative skills. Key Votes, which may well focus on issues about which the president cares the most and on which he tries the hardest, may reveal differences in support that broader indexes mask.

The most productive analysis is a comparison of presidential support among different groups of members of Congress. One can control for the factors of party representation in Congress and region by comparing the support that similar groups gave different presidents. Naturally, the party of the president also plays an important role in determining the level of support given by various groups in Congress. Thus formal comparisons must be restricted to presidents of the same party.

Democratic Presidents

According to the conventional wisdom, Lyndon Johnson would have received more support in the House than either Kennedy or Carter. Johnson was the master legislative technician, giving Congress highest priority and leaving no stone unturned in his efforts to exercise his influence. If there is no clear evidence of the significance of legislative skills for Johnson, there is not likely to be any for anyone. Kennedy, on the other hand, had more nonlegislative concerns and lacked Johnson's fascination with the legislative process. Carter lacked his predecessors' experience in Washington and was widely criticized for his maladroit handling of congressional relations from the very beginning of his term.

Table 9.1 summarizes the records of support in the House on each index for Kennedy, Johnson, and Carter. The figures in the table, for each index, do not support the hypothesis that Johnson's legislative skills were significant in influencing representatives to support his policies. Kennedy received more support from both Northern and Southern Democrats than did Johnson, whereas Johnson received more support from Republicans. Carter's support is similar to Johnson's among Republicans, greater among Southern Democrats, and lower only among Northern Democrats (consequently, the per-

TABLE 9.1   House Support for Democratic Presidents (in Percent)

| | Kennedy, 1961–63 | |
| | *Nonunanimous* | *Key* |
	Support	*Votes*
Democrats	73	74
Northern Democrats	85	90
Southern Democrats	54	49
Republicans	26	17

| | Johnson, 1964–68 | |
| | *Nonunanimous* | *Key* |
	Support	*Votes*
Democrats	71	68
Northern Democrats	82	81
Southern Democrats	47	40
Republicans	27	29

| | Carter, 1977–80 | |
| | *Nonunanimous* | *Key* |
	Support	*Votes*
Democrats	63	59
Northern Democrats	68	64
Southern Democrats	51	45
Republicans	31	29

centages of support of all Democrats are also lower for Carter than for Johnson). One may reasonably attribute the differences in support for the two presidents among Democrats to Carter's having supported more conservative policies than Johnson.

In the Senate (table 9.2) the relationships between support for Kennedy and Johnson are similar to those in the House, except that Johnson exceeded his predecessor's support among Southern Democrats on key votes. The results for the comparisons of Johnson and Carter are different, however. Carter maintained his substantial lead over Johnson in support from Southern Democrats, but he also did as well as Johnson among Northern Democrats. Interestingly, Carter obtained less support than Johnson among Republicans.

Despite Carter's relative success, one cannot ignore that Johnson obtained substantially more support than Carter among Northern Democrats in the House on each of the indexes. This support was broad and was not concentrated only among key votes. Because Northern Democrats are always a large bloc in the House, their support is always critical to a Democratic president.

TABLE 9.2   Senate Support for Democratic Presidents (in Percent)

	Kennedy, 1961–63	
	Nonunanimous Support	*Key Votes*
Democrats	65	65
Northern Democrats	75	79
Southern Democrats	44	38
Republicans	33	32

	Johnson, 1964–68	
	Nonunanimous Support	*Key Votes*
Democrats	56	65
Northern Democrats	65	75
Southern Democrats	36	41
Republicans	44	49

	Carter, 1977–80	
	Nonunanimous Support	*Key Votes*
Democrats	63	64
Northern Democrats	66	70
Southern Democrats	54	50
Republicans	38	33

Was this support due to Johnson's greater persuasiveness? Or was it due to less personal factors?

The latter explanation appears best to fit the facts. Kennedy, reputed to be less effective than Johnson with Congress,[26] obtained higher support than Johnson among Northern Democrats. Moreover, Northern Democrats have for reasons that are not clear been moving in the last generation toward less support of presidents, both Democratic and Republican.

Yet other forces were at work. Johnson's average level of public approval over five years was 56 percent, whereas Carter's average over four years was only 47 percent. And Johnson won election by a landslide, whereas Carter barely achieved victory very late on election night.

One must also remember the changes that occurred in Congress between the administrations of Johnson and Carter, which were beyond the president's

26. Halleck, interview by Hess, p. 28; Hale Boggs, interview by Charles T. Morrissey, May 10, 1964, transcript, p. 26, John F. Kennedy Library, Boston.

control. The most visible of these has been the dispersion of power.[27] Committees have been democratized and subcommittees increased in number and in importance in handling legislation. Members of both parties have larger personal, committee, and subcommittee staffs at their disposal, as well as new adjuncts such as the Congressional Budget Office. The number of lobbyists, independent policy analysts, and congressional work groups and caucuses, which are additional sources of expertise, has also exploded. This new freedom and these additional resources, combined with more opportunities to amend legislation and more open hearings and markups, make it easier for members of Congress to inform themselves, challenge the White House (and congressional leadership), and provide alternatives to the president's policies. Further, new representatives and senators have tended not to adopt the norms of apprenticeship, reciprocity, and specialization to the same degree as their predecessors. Instead, they have eagerly taken an active role in all legislation.

Thus the president now has more decision makers to influence. He can no longer rely on dealing with the congressional aristocracy and expect the rest of the members to follow. According to one assistant to Johnson, "In 1965, there were maybe ten or twelve people who you needed to corral in the House and Senate. Without those people, you were in for a tough time. Now, I'd put that figure upwards on one hundred. Believe it, there are so many people who have a shot at derailing a bill that the President has to double his effort for even routine decisions."[28]

An aide to Carter commented on the same point: "Take a good look at comprehensive energy. Look at how many stops it had to make in Congress. There was a great deal of committee interest but more important was the number of subcommittees who took some action. From our standpoint, it was just too complicated. It takes a real effort just to know where the legislation is, when the decisions are going to be made, and what needs to be done. There was a drop in our ability to influence outcomes in that kind of fragmented system."[29] It is worth noting that Ronald Reagan's success in cutting social welfare expenditures in 1981 came only when he was able to bypass the

27. For useful discussions of the dispersion of power see Thomas E. Cavanagh, "The Dispersion of Authority in the House of Representatives," *Political Science Quarterly* 97 (Winter 1982–83): 623–637; Eric L. Davis, "Legislative Reform and the Decline of Presidential Influence on Capitol Hill," *British Journal of Political Science* 9 (October 1979): 465–479; and Barbara Sinclair, "Senate Styles and Senate Decision Making, 1955–1980" (paper presented at the annual meeting at the American Political Science Association, New Orleans, September 1985).

28. Quoted in Light, *The President's Agenda*, p. 211. See also Edwards, *Presidential Influence in Congress*, pp. 194–195.

29. Quoted in Light, *The President's Agenda*, p. 209.

decentralized decision-making process through a single vote on a massive budget proposal offered as an amendment to the House Budget Committee's budget resolution. As Reagan's lobbyist Kenneth Duberstein put it, "For most issues you have to lobby all 435 Congressmen and almost all 100 Senators."[30]

In chapter 5 we saw that an increase in the number of roll calls has increased the visibility of representatives' voting behavior. This has generated more pressure on House members to abandon their party, making it more difficult for the president to gain passage of legislation.

The president's program is now also subject to more cross-cutting demands within Congress as a result of referrals from split and joint committees. This further complicates the president's job. A congressional liaison aide to Carter noted:

> The welfare-reform legislation was most difficult in the House. Disregarding our problems with the bill, we had a lot of trouble coordinating the lobbying effort. We had help from the departments, but on a bill like that the President has to supply the whip. The problem was in finding the horses. That bill moved to four committees in the House alone—Ways and Means, Agriculture, Education and Labor, and a special ad hoc committee on welfare reform. Within at least three of the committees, we had to deal with subcommittees—subcommittees on the budget impact as well as the legislative substance. We just didn't have the manpower. Neither did the departments. Now you tell me, how does the White House influence those kind of decisions in that many committees?[31]

Perhaps the most obvious difference between the Democratic administrations of the 1960s and Jimmy Carter's in the late 1970s is that Carter served during the period of congressional assertiveness that followed Vietnam and Watergate. The diminished deference to the president by individual members of Congress and by the institution as a whole naturally makes presidential influence more problematic. As one Democratic member of Congress said in 1977, "We got such fun out of popping Nixon and Ford. We don't want to give it up and be good boys any more."[32]

Vietnam, Watergate, and a sagging economy have also combined to make the public more skeptical of government policies. The optimism of the race to

30. Quoted in Steven R. Weisman, "No. 1, the President Is Very Result Oriented," *New York Times*, November 12, 1983, p. 10.
31. Quoted in Light, *The President's Agenda*, p. 210. See also p. 209.
32. Quoted in "Shadowboxing," *Newsweek*, June 6, 1977, p. 18.

the moon and the idealism that fueled the war on poverty in the 1960s have been replaced by anxiety over nuclear weapons, energy, and inflation. For a president who desires to establish new programs, the outlook is not promising.

Carter also had the misfortune to preside during a period of substantial inflation and unemployment, whereas Kennedy's and Johnson's years were characterized by stable prices, sustained economic growth, and general prosperity. The prosperity of the 1960s provided the federal government with the funds for new policies, with little political risk. Taxes did not have to be raised nor sacrifices made to help the underprivileged. In the late 1970s resources were more limited, making the passage of new welfare or health programs, for example, more difficult. When resources are scarce, presidents must choose between policies rather than build coalitions for several policies through log-rolling. Instead, they are faced with internal competition for resources and the breakdown of supporting coalitions.

The policies of the 1970s and 1980s seem to lack reliable bases of support. Barbara Sinclair has persuasively demonstrated that coalitions in Congress, especially the Senate, have become more fluid since Johnson's tenure. There are fewer members of Congress on whom a president can rely for support, and new Northern Democrats have been considerably less reliable in their support of party leaders than their predecessors. Moreover, the issues of energy, environmental protection, inflation, consumer protection, and foreign and defense policy have been divisive for Northern Democrats.[33]

In the absence of a party consensus on policy, Carter's White House had to rely on forming discrete coalitions. Yet often the policies it proposed had no natural, organized constituency. The president himself reflected on his experience with Congress:

> I think the main factor that was deleterious to the relationship was the controversial nature of the proposals that I presented to the Congress. We had to face up to some long postponed issues that I felt were in the best interests of our country to address: SALT II. The Middle East, where the Jewish lobby was aroused. Normalization with China, where the Taiwan lobby was aroused. The Panama Canal treaties. . . . Energy legislation, where we aroused the animosity of both consumer groups and the oil industry. The Alaska lands bill, which had been long postponed. The environmental questions, particularly concerning Corps of Engi-

---

33. Barbara Sinclair, "Coping with Uncertainty: Building Coalitions in the House and the Senate," in Thomas E. Mann and Norman J. Ornstein, eds., *The New Congress* (Washington: American Enterprise Institute, 1981), pp. 178–222.

neers projects in individual congressional districts or states. Those kinds
of things were very important to me and . . . to the country. But there
was nothing in any of those issues that I've just described . . . that was
politically beneficial to members of Congress. . . . Quite often it showed
that our country had to face limits, that it had to make compromises, that
it had to protect the environment in spite of opposition from some folks.[34]

An aide to Carter agreed with the president, adding, "We spent weeks and
months trying to organize groups on hospital cost containment, but all the
people that we wanted to feel passionately about it were insulated by insurance from the problem. The other side was able to organize influential people
in the communities, the doctors and so on, the movers and shakers."[35]

In light of the above discussion, it seems reasonable to conclude that at
least most of Carter's relative lack of support among Northern Democrats in
comparison with Johnson's was the result of factors other than differences in
legislative skills between the two chief executives.

Republican Presidents

Comparing the legislative skills of Republican presidents is a difficult
task. Eisenhower was supposedly bungling and ineffective, but this view is
undergoing significant revision.[36] Nixon's efforts were often described as con-
frontational and negative, and so perhaps he would rate as the weakest of the
four Republicans in legislative skills.[37] Gerald Ford was an experienced congressional hand, and his relationships with legislators were cordial. Ronald
Reagan began his term with rave reviews for his handling of Congress, but his
legislative relations soured considerably in the years that followed. About all
that one can safely conclude is that each president was unique in his approach
to Congress and that, based on their legislative skills, one should expect the
lowest support for Nixon.

Table 9.3 gives the average figures for support of Republican presidents
in the House (1974 has been omitted because both Nixon and Ford served in
that year). The patterns across the four presidents are fascinating, but they do
not seem to relate to their legislative skills. Support by Northern Democrats

34. Quoted in Mark Peterson, "Congressional Responses to Presidential Proposals: Impact,
Effort, and Politics" (paper presented at the annual meeting of the Midwest Political Science
Association, Chicago, April 1986), p. 21.

35. Ibid., p. 32.

36. See for example Fred I. Greenstein, *The Hidden-Hand Presidency: Eisenhower as
Leader* (New York: Basic Books, 1982); and John P. Burke, "Eisenhower and the Budget Battle of
1957: Presidential Power Revisited" (unpublished manuscript).

37. Gerald Ford termed Nixon's relations with Congress "terrible." Gerald R. Ford, *A Time
to Heal* (New York: Harper and Row, 1979), p. 156.

TABLE 9.3   House Support for Republican Presidents (in Percent)

	Eisenhower, 1953–60	
	Nonunanimous Support	*Key Votes*
Democrats	42	42
Northern Democrats	49	50
Southern Democrats	33	31
Republicans	64	65

	Nixon, 1969–73	
	Nonunanimous Support	*Key Votes*
Democrats	41	36
Northern Democrats	39	31
Southern Democrats	48	46
Republicans	64	64

	Ford, 1975–76	
	Nonunanimous Support	*Key Votes*
Democrats	35	32
Northern Democrats	29	24
Southern Democrats	48	51
Republicans	68	70

	Reagan, 1981–86	
	Nonunanimous Support	*Key Votes*
Democrats	30	29
Northern Democrats	24	21
Southern Democrats	44	50
Republicans	68	74

steadily diminished for each succeeding president, just as it did for Democratic presidents. Southern Democratic support increased notably but inconsistently after Eisenhower, however. Republican support is nearly identical for Eisenhower and Nixon, presidents with very different approaches to Congress, and is slightly higher for Ford and Reagan.

It is difficult to look across the records of these four Republican presidents and discern patterns of legislative support that are related to their legislative skills. No matter how inclusive or exclusive an index of presidential

TABLE 9.4   Senate Support for Republican Presidents (in Percent)

Eisenhower, 1953–60		
	Nonunanimous Support	*Key Votes*
Democrats	38	37
Northern Democrats	38	35
Southern Democrats	38	39
Republicans	69	71

Nixon, 1969–73		
	Nonunanimous Support	*Key Votes*
Democrats	34	38
Northern Democrats	27	29
Southern Democrats	49	58
Republicans	65	67

Ford, 1975–76		
	Nonuanimous Support	*Key Votes*
Democrats	33	27
Northern Democrats	25	19
Southern Democrats	55	50
Republicans	65	59

Reagan, 1981–86		
	Nonunanimous Support	*Key Votes*
Democrats	32	32
Northern Democrats	27	27
Southern Democrats	47	50
Republicans	76	75

support is employed, one must be impressed by both the broad patterns of support identified above and the limited variance in support among presidents with different legislative styles.

In the Senate (table 9.4) presidents as dissimilar as Nixon and Reagan received similar levels of support from Northern Democrats. Both did worse than Eisenhower but better than the old congressional hand, Gerald Ford. Support among Southern Democratic senators for Republican presidents has increased erratically since Eisenhower. Nixon and Ford, presidents with very different styles and skills, received similar support from Republican senators. They both fared more poorly than Eisenhower, however, whereas Reagan received the highest levels of support from Republicans. Once again, there appears to be no relationship between the support obtained by presidents and their legislative skills.

The foregoing examination of presidents' legislative skills has failed to reveal systematic evidence of their impact on presidential support, even when measures of presidential support that focus on key votes or are not affected by lopsided votes are included. It seems reasonable to assert that legislative skills are not at the core of presidential leadership of Congress, and that they are not resources that can make substantial contributions to presidents attempting to play the role of director. Their utility is at the margins, in exploiting rather than creating opportunities for change.

This conclusion is compatible with that of authors who stress historical context as the prime determinant in the success of presidential attempts to lead Congress.[38] Such analyses are very helpful in explaining the challenges and opportunities different presidents have faced in their leadership efforts and thus in placing legislative skills in perspective. A recurring theme in this book is the importance of the parameters within which efforts at leadership occur. Whether analyzing a particular presidency or a potential source of influence, it is important to understand that the president does not operate in a political or institutional vacuum.

At the same time, conclusions at the macro level about historical context are inherently limited. For example, it is certainly correct to argue that there is a higher probability of success if the president is of the dominant party in Congress and there is consensus on the need for policy change. Yet such a conclusion is virtually a truism and explains very little about the impact of legislative skills or any other source of influence.

Arguments about the significance of historical context do not provide the basis for inferences about the impact of legislative skills or other tools of leadership. It is important to dig beneath the veneer of conclusions at the macro level to explain the role of legislative skills, and to round out the evaluation of presidential legislative skills. To understand the role they play in presidential leadership in Congress, one must focus on presidents' efforts to exercise them.

38. See for example Erwin C. Hargrove and Michael Nelson, *Presidents, Politics, and Policy*, (New York: Alfred A. Knopf, 1984), chap. 3; Stephen Skowronek, "Presidential Leadership in Political Time" in Michael Nelson, ed., *The Presidency and the Political System* (Washington: Congressional Quarterly Press, 1984), pp. 87–132.

CHAPTER TEN

Employing Skills

There is little relationship in the aggregate between the personal legislative skills of presidents and the support they receive in Congress. Yet we have it on good authority that legislative skills can make a difference. The prevailing patterns of voting may mask important variations.[1]

Although legislative skills are not likely to influence Congress broadly, a more complete understanding is needed of their role in presidential leadership. To obtain this one must examine more closely some of the most prominent elements of legislative skills, to see both their advantages and, equally important, the constraints on their use.

There is no lack of observers who criticize presidents for their lack of skill and urge that they be more adroit in their leadership. Implicit in such commentary is the notion that skills are always available for use and that all the president has to do is reach into his inventory and employ the appropriate means of influence. But are things really so straightforward? If so, why do presidents fail to exploit these devices and end up so frequently in stalemate with Congress?

Focusing on the limits of legislative skills will help to explain the absence of an aggregate relationship between skills and support. Because it is obvious that deals, presidential appeals, consultation, and the like should increase the probabilities of support, findings such as those in chapter 9 may seem puzzling. Yet if presidents cannot employ legislative skills as readily as the conventional wisdom suggests, then their lack of broad impact is not surprising.

1. William H. Riker and Donald Niemi, "Stability of Coalitions on Roll Calls in the House of Representatives," *American Political Science Review* 56 (March 1962): 58–65.

Given my earlier findings, one should expect that legislative skills operate within the confines of noteworthy constraints on their use.

Legislative skills come in a variety of forms. Some, such as bargaining, personal appeals, and consultation, are oriented toward what might be termed the tactical level. In other words, the president and his aides employ them to obtain one or a few votes at a time. Other skills, such as setting priorities, exploiting political honeymoons, and structuring votes, may have broader consequence because they affect most or all members of Congress at the same time.

Votes on the Margins

Even if legislative skills do not have a systematic influence on congressional support for the president, it is possible that they have a more restricted impact, albeit still an important one. Instead of focusing on a few votes, as in the index Key Votes, perhaps one should concentrate on a few voters, that is, members of Congress. Legislative skills may be most significant at the margins of coalition building, that is, in gaining the last few votes needed to pass a program. Turning a sizable coalition into a victorious one after broader influences have had their impact can certainly be a critical component of leadership.

The evidence on the importance of legislative skills in marginal votes is mixed. On the one hand, the White House often devotes substantial resources to obtaining votes at the margin of coalitions. Reflecting on the extraordinary economic policies passed by Congress in 1981, David Stockman declared, "I now understand that you probably can't put together a majority coalition unless you are willing to deal with those marginal interests that will give you the votes needed to win. That's where it is fought—on the margins—and unless you deal with those marginal votes, you can't win."[2]

There is reason to be cautious about accepting such a view at face value. For example, Russell Renka examined closely the House votes on major elements of the Great Society. The closest vote (a recommittal motion sponsored by Republicans on Medicare) would have required a swing of twenty-three votes for the White House to have lost. Renka could find no indication in the White House's files that President Johnson had done anything specifically on the issue worth twenty-three votes. Indeed, of the Civil Rights Act of 1964, the Voting Rights Act of 1965, Medicare, and the Elementary and Secondary

2. Quoted in William Greider, "The Education of David Stockman," *Atlantic*, December 1981, p. 52.

TABLE 10.1   Presidential Success on Close Votes[a] (in Percent)

President	House	Senate
Eisenhower	47	49
Kennedy	79	73
Johnson	74	69
Nixon	55	54
Ford	41	66
Carter	76	64
Reagan[b]	63	80

[a]Votes with a winning margin of 10 percent or less
[b]1981–84
SOURCES: Richard Fleisher and Jon Bond, "Presidential Leadership Skill and Success in Congress" (paper presented at the annual meeting of the Southern Political Science Association, Atlanta, November 1986), table 2.

Education Act of 1965, none was even red-flagged by the White House staff for special presidential efforts as it came to the House floor. The president's intervention was not needed.[3]

In an earlier study, I found that in both 1965, when Johnson had a large majority, and 1967, after the Democrats had suffered substantial losses in midterm elections, there were very few marginal victories in either chamber (victories of twenty-five votes or fewer in the House and ten votes or fewer in the Senate). In other words, there were few victories where Johnson's legislative skills could have made the difference between winning and losing. The marginal victories that did occur were generally not on major issues.[4]

Another study examined presidential success on votes decided by a margin of 10 percent or less. If one controls for the status of the president's party in each chamber, one finds little relationship between presidential legislative skills and success (table 10.1);[5] the comparison of Kennedy, Johnson, and Carter is again illuminating.

To understand further the impact of legislative skills, one must turn to more discrete analyses of specific skills, looking for both their potential for increasing presidential support and the ability of presidents to employ them.

3. Russell Renka, "Comparing Presidents Kennedy and Johnson as Legislative Leaders" (paper presented at the annual meeting of the Southern Political Science Association, Savannah, Ga., November 1984), p. 26. See also Carl Albert, interview by Dorothy Pierce McSweeny, July 9, 1969, interview 3, transcript, p. 3, Lyndon Baines Johnson Library, Austin, Tex.

4. George C. Edwards III, *Presidential Influence in Congress*, (San Francisco: W. H. Freeman, 1980), pp. 197–199.

5. Richard Fleisher and Jon Bond, "Presidential Leadership Skill and Success in Congress" (paper presented at the annual meeting of the Southern Political Science Association, Atlanta, November 1986), pp. 29–30.

Bargaining

Bargaining is perhaps the presidential legislative skill that receives the most attention from commentators on the presidency. Richard Neustadt placed bargaining at the core of his model of presidential power. He argued that the president must bargain even with those who agree with him to ensure their support, because most people in government have interests of their own beyond the realm of policy objectives.[6]

Because of the negative aura of bargaining, participants often deny that they have engaged in it. For example, Ronald Reagan claimed that during the fight to sell AWACS planes to Saudi Arabia in 1981, "No deals were made. None were offered. I talked strictly on the merits of the proposal."[7] At the same time, the *Wall Street Journal* published a story entitled "Some Senators Say They Were Promised White House Favors to Vote for Awacs."[8]

Similarly, one of the leading lobbyists for the White House in the 1960s, Henry Hall Wilson, could concluded that "you'd never see anything so crude as a trade,"[9] and another, Mike Manatos, said, "I've never been involved in anything that would even approach a payoff."[10] Yet Clark Clifford, an intimate of Johnson and later secretary of defense, described the White House's inter-action with Congress as follows:

> President Johnson calls in a senator and he says, "Joe," . . . "Does that law partner of yours still want to be a federal judge?" "Oh," he says, "he certainly does." "Well," he says, "you know I've been thinking about that lately and we're going to talk about that. But in the process of talking about that, I want to talk with you about the fact that I think we've got to increase our Social Security program." "Well, Mr. President, I've spoken against that." "Well, I know, Joe. But times have changed. And you think about it awhile. . . . Let a week go by, you call me." Joe calls him in a week and says, "Mr. President, I've been thinking about that and I think there's a lot of merit to your position. And I believe I can change on . . . Social Security. I want to come over and talk to you. And, incidentally, I talked to my partner, and he is just tickled to death." That's the way our

6. Richard E. Neustadt, *Presidential Power: The Politics of Leadership from FDR to Carter* (New York: John Wiley and Sons, 1980), chap. 3.

7. Quoted in "Reagan Reaction to AWACS Vote," *Congressional Quarterly Weekly Report*, October 31, 1981, p. 2136. See also Laurence I. Barrett, *Gambling with History* (New York: Penguin, 1984), pp. 160, 162.

8. Albert R. Hunt, *Wall Street Journal*, October 14, 1981, p. 10.

9. Henry Hall Wilson, interview by Joe B. Frantz, April 11, 1973, transcript, p. 10, Lyndon Baines Johnson Library, Austin, Tex.

10. Mike Manatos, interview by Joe B. Frantz, August 25, 1969, transcript, p. 20, Lyndon Baines Johnson Library, Austin, Tex.

government runs . . . you're constantly trading assets back and forth to
get your program. [11]

There can be no question that many bargains occur and that they take a variety
of forms. [12] Some officials are very explicit about bargaining. Reagan's budget
director David Stockman termed the trading that went into passing Gramm-
Latta II in 1981 "an open vote auction." Regarding the tax cut of 1981, he
recalled that "the last 10 or 20 percent of the votes needed for a majority of
both houses had to be bought, period."[13]

Sometimes bargains consist of trading the backing of the White House on
one policy for that of Congress on another, as when President Reagan agreed
to raise sugar price supports to induce representatives from Louisiana to vote
for his budget cuts in 1981, or when he promised to continue producing A-10
warplanes in exchange for the support of Republicans from Long Island for the
tax increase of 1982. [14] To obtain passage of the tax cut of 1964 and the tax
surcharge of 1968, President Johnson had to agree to limits on expenditures. [15]
President Kennedy was forced to support the Communications Satellite Act of
1962 to please Sen. Robert Kerr, whose aid the president needed on a number
of issues. [16]

More common are bargains involving compromise on one aspect of a
policy or trading support on two provisions of the same policy. To avoid a
congressional veto of the sale of missiles to Saudi Arabia in 1986, President
Reagan deleted the most controversial weapons from his request. Presidents
are quite accustomed to compromising on policies, especially those they want
to see passed and thus require a majority vote. On policies they oppose, the
threat of a veto is a powerful weapon. Because the White House requires only
one-third of the votes plus one in one of the chambers to sustain a veto, it can
be more insistent on behalf of its policy preferences.

11. Quoted in Barbara Kellerman, *The Political Presidency* (New York: Oxford University
Press, 1984), p. 25.

12. See for example Edwards, *Presidential Influence in Congress*, pp. 129–131.

13. David Stockman, *The Triumph of Politics* (New York: Harper and Row, 1986), pp. 208–
209, 214–215, 251, 253, 260–261, 264–265. See also "White House's Lobbying Apparatus . . .
Produces Impressive Tax Vote Victory," *Congressional Quarterly Weekly Report*, August 1,
1981, pp. 1372–1373.

14. Barrett, *Gambling with History*, pp. 160–161, 365; Greider, "The Education of David
Stockman," p. 50; "Stockman, at Nofziger Trial, Recalls Lobby Effort," *New York Times*, February 2, 1988, sec. A, p. 11. For other examples see Greider, pp. 36, 39.

15. Carl Albert, interview by Dorothy Pierce McSweeny, August 13, 1969, interview 4,
transcript, pp. 2–3, Lyndon Johnson Library, Austin, Tex.

16. Mike Mansfield, interview by Seth P. Tillman, June 23, 1964, transcript, pp. 28–29,
John F. Kennedy Library, Boston.

Yet another type of trade involves the "clarification" of policies. President Carter accepted clarifying provisions to gain passage of the treaties governing the Panama Canal. Similarly, during the battle over the sale of AWACS planes to Saudi Arabia in 1981, President Reagan reassured Congress that the planes would be used only for defensive purposes and specified conditions that the Saudis would have to meet to receive them.

In still other instances the president may provide a discrete benefit such as campaign aid or an appointive position for a constituent in exchange for a legislator's support, as when the White House promised campaign appearances by Vice President George Bush to Republican representatives in exchange for their support of the tax increase of 1982.[17] Lyndon Johnson's regular trades with Everett Dirksen are legendary.[18]

Much of the bargaining that occurs is implicit trading on accounts. In effect, members of Congress exchange their support for the president for the administration's responsiveness to their requests for assistance. The White House tries to get members of Congress in its debt by providing favors and sympathetic hearings. Many members try to create favorable impressions in the White House of their support for the president, sometimes writing to the president and reminding him of their vote. For the White House a member of Congress indebted to the president is easier to approach and ask for support. For the member, previous support increases the chances of a request being honored. Thus officeholders at each end of Pennsylvania Avenue seek to be in the favor of those at the other. But although services and favors increase the president's chances of obtaining support, they are usually not exchanged for votes directly.[19]

Instead of offering bargains, the White House tries to create goodwill as a foundation for its future appeals for support. One liaison aide to Reagan called the office of congressional relations "a service organization," while its director, Max Friedersdorf, described as its objective as "[to] establish good, sympathetic relations with all members . . . [so that] when you go back and ask for a vote, you'll have an entree, and they'll give you a fair hearing."[20]

17. Barrett, *Gambling with History*, p. 365.

18. See for example Doris Kearns, *Lyndon Johnson and the American Dream* (New York: Harper and Row, 1976), pp. 182–183; Jack Valenti, *A Very Human President* (New York: W. W. Norton, 1975), pp. 182–183; Russell D. Renka, "Legislative Leadership and Marginal Vote-Gaining Strategies in the Kennedy and Johnson Presidencies" (paper presented at the annual meeting of the Southwestern Political Sciences Association, Houston, April 1978), pp. 28–30.

19. See Edwards, *Presidential Influence in Congress*, pp. 135–141.

20. See Arthur Maass, *Congress and the Common Good* (New York: Basic Books, 1983), pp. 50–53.

One of Friedersdorf's successors in Reagan's administration agreed with
liaison aides of the last three decades in explaining the relationship of implicit
bargaining with Congress: "It's a two way street. Members call us with problems and wanting information, and we have to get back to them as quickly and
as accurately as possible. That's so they depend on us and have confidence in
us, so that when we call them later on for a vote, they are willing to listen."[21]

Despite its record and the prominent attention it receives from observers
of the presidency, bargaining occurs less often and plays a less critical role in
creating presidential coalitions in Congress than the conventional wisdom
indicates.[22] This is especially true when one focuses on trading support on
two or more policies or providing discrete benefits for representatives and
senators.

To begin with, the president does not have to bargain with every member
of Congress to receive his or her support. On controversial issues, on which
bargaining may be useful, a substantial portion of each chamber can be written
off as unalterably opposed. Unless the president is willing to sacrifice the
substance of his policy, which is self-defeating, he will rarely be able to
bargain with his firm opponents.

Equally important, the president almost always starts with a sizable core
of party supporters and may add to this group those of the opposition party
who agree with him on ideological or policy grounds. Others may support him
because of the interests of their constituents or the president's standing with
the public. Thus the president needs to bargain only if this coalition does not
provide him a majority (a two-thirds majority on treaties and overrides of
vetoes), and he need only bargain with enough people to provide him with this
majority.

When the president needs to bargain, he is faced with a number of
significant limitations on his ability to do so. Perhaps the foremost limitation
on bargaining in the 1970s and 1980s was the scarcity of resources. When
budgets are tight, presidents must choose among policies rather than build
coalitions for several through logrolling. For example, they may find it difficult to obtain support from urban interests for a policy to aid rural areas,
in return for rural support for an urban policy, when the budget can support
only one.

President Kennedy included a wide range of educational programs in his
omnibus education bill of 1963, to encourage education groups to work for

21. Quoted in "Reagan's Team on the Hill Getting Members' Praise for Hard Work, Experience," *Congressional Quarterly Weekly Report*," May 21, 1981, p. 749.
22. M. B. Oglesby, quoted in Gerald M. Boyd, "The Presidential Line to and from Capitol
Hill," *New York Times*, February 3, 1985, sec. E, p. 2.

each other's programs.[23] In 1964 President Johnson conceived the idea of trading the food stamps program for his farm bill. He called members supporting each and asked them to support the other.[24] Both Kennedy's and Johnson's strategies worked, but they could exploit these strategies only because slack resources were available to fund the programs.

In addition, even in the best of times there are limits to the number of appointive positions, public works projects, and other discrete benefits the White House can offer to members of Congress, and much of what the president offers in bargaining is ultimately in the hands of the bureaucracy or other members of Congress. Consequently, he must often bargain within the executive branch or Congress before he can bargain with a particular member of Congress whose vote he needs. This saps the president's time, energy, and bargaining resources. In addition, once credit is built up between a department (which has done a favor) and a member of Congress, it may be drawn on by the department without the president's approval.

There is a special burden in bargaining with members of the opposition party. All bargains are not equal. Rewarding one's usual opponents for short-term support is much costlier than rewarding supporters, because the former may not only alienate supporters who did not receive benefits but also give opponents greater strength in the future. On the other hand, rewarding supporters may make them more effective in advancing the president's policies, which multiplies the positive effect of bargains. Thus presidents are constrained in bargaining with the opposition. According to Barefoot Sanders, head of the White House's Office of Congressional Relations during part of Johnson's administration, "there's very little you can do for Republicans in a Democratic administration."[25]

Sometimes what members of Congress want is not the president's to give. A representative told one high official at the White House that he would vote to sustain an important presidential veto "if, and only if, we would get a CAB route into his town." The official responded, "Congressman, that is impossible. We can't touch regulatory agencies." The member voted against the president.[26]

Even if presidents can make bargains, they may choose not to. Raising sugar price supports and spending scarce funds on A-10 planes that the Pen-

23. James L. Sundquist, *Politics and Policy* (Washington: Brookings Institution, 1968), pp. 206, 210.

24. Jack Bell, *The Johnson Treatment* (New York: Harper and Row, 1965), p. 189.

25. Barefoot Sanders, interview by Joe B. Frantz, March 24, 1969, tape 2, transcript, p. 6, Lyndon Baines Johnson Library, Austin, Tex. See also tape 3, p. 36.

26: Stephen J. Wayne, *The Legislative Presidency* (New York: Harper and Row, 1978), p. 160.

tagon planned to phase out was certainly inconsistent with Ronald Reagan's policy goals. Such deals have costs for presidents, who are generally willing to tolerate only so much. President Reagan's adamancy against compromise on his military budget was a central feature of his administration's legislative relations.[27] In 1961 Congressman D. B. Saund of California was angered by President Kennedy's closing of a veterans' hospital in his district, and in retaliation he opposed an important provision of the president's foreign aid bill. Nevertheless, Kennedy refused to reopen the inadequate and unsafe hospital in return for Saund's support on foreign aid (the congressman's opposition was ultimately successful).[28]

The president may find bargaining incompatible with his temperament or orientation toward policy making. Jimmy Carter did not believe in developing measures on the strength of bargains.[29] According to one aide in Carter's White House, when asked to negotiate with a member of Congress, the president might reply, "I don't know why I should spend my time kissing that fellow's ass when he is playing politics and what I want to do is right. Why should I have to compromise when he is using only a political view? I don't understand."[30] Although the president would eventually talk to the member, his reluctance to deal was clear.

The president may even inhibit others from concluding compromises. When President Reagan left Washington to attend an economic summit conference abroad, the Senate proceeded to pass a budget for the next fiscal year, a reorganization of the joint chiefs of staff, and a gun control bill, and the Finance Committee unanimously reported out a major tax reform bill. Some observers felt that the absence of the president, whom they saw as a partisan, polarizing figure more concerned with ideological assertions than practical compromises, allowed the natural forces of conciliation on Capitol Hill to assert themselves.[31]

There is also no guarantee that a tendered bargain will be accepted. The members may not desire what the president offers, or they may be able to obtain what they want on their own. This is of course particularly true of the

27. See for example Barrett, *Gambling with History*, pp. 152–154; "Congress Struggles to Quit, but Does Not Finish," *Congressional Quarterly Weekly Report*, October 16, 1984, pp. 2415–2416.

28. Lawrence F. O'Brien, *No Final Victories* (New York: Ballantine, 1974), p. 122.

29. Erwin C. Hargove and Michael Nelson, *Presidents, Politics, and Policy* (New York: Alfred A. Knopf, 1984), p. 119.

30. Quoted in Mark Peterson, "The President's Legislative Program: More than Meets the "Aye"? (paper presented at the annual meeting of the Midwest Political Science Association, Chicago, April 1984), p. 23.

31. See Steven V. Roberts, "Congress Activity and Reagan Absence," *New York Times*, May 10, 1986, p. 8.

most powerful members, whose support the president may need the most. In 1982 congressional leaders and officials from the White House, including the president, invested weeks in intense negotiations over the budget. Yet when the air cleared, agreement was absent.[32]

Sometimes members of Congress do not want to trade at all. This may be due either to constraints such as the opinions of constituents or to personal views. In 1961 Congressman Jim Delaney cast the vote responsible for holding the federal aid-to-education bill in the House Rules Committee. He wanted to include aid to parochial schools, which President Kennedy opposed. The president desperately needed his vote, but Delaney was not interested in bargaining on other subjects. As Kennedy's legislative liaison chief Lawrence O'Brien exclaimed, "He didn't want a thing. I wish he had."[33]

The very nature of bargaining also limits its utility. If many direct bargains are struck, word will rapidly spread, everyone will want to trade, and efforts at persuasion will fail, while at the same time the cost of winning on a vote will rise. Thus most of the bargains that are reached are implicit.[34]

The lack of respectability surrounding bargaining also encourages implicitness. This has drawbacks, however. The terms of an implicit bargain are likely to be less clear than those of an explicit one, increasing the likelihood of misunderstanding and subsequent ill will when members of Congress wish to reap their rewards for supporting the president.[35] Ronald Reagan enraged some members of Congress in 1982 when he first agreed to cuts in his proposed defense budget in order to obtain support for a tax increase, and then proclaimed that he was not bound by the second and third years of the cuts after the tax bill had passed.[36]

As a result of the limitations on bargaining, the White House initiates relatively few bargains. Most of the pressure for bargaining actually comes from the Hill. When the White House calls and asks for support, representatives and senators frequently raise a question regarding some request that they have made.[37] In the words of an aide to Eisenhower, "Every time we

32. For an account of these negotiations see Barrett, *Gambling with History*, chap. 20.

33. O'Brien, *No Final Victories*, pp. 129–130, 136–137; Theodore C. Sorensen, *Kennedy* (New York: Bantam, 1966), pp. 404–405.

34. Lyndon B. Johnson, *The Vantage Point*, (New York: Popular Library, 1971), p. 457; Kearns, *Lyndon Johnson and the American Dream*, p. 236; "Turning Screws: Winning Votes in Congress," *Congressional Quarterly Weekly Report*, April 24, 1976, pp. 947, 949; Nigel Bowles, *The White House and Capitol Hill* (New York: Oxford University Press, 1987), p. 79.

35. Stanley Kelley, Jr., "Patronage and Presidential Legislative Leadership," in Aaron Wildavsky, ed., *The Presidency* (Boston: Little, Brown, 1969), p. 273.

36. Steven R. Weisman, "Reaganomics and the President's Men," *New York Times Magazine*, November 21, 1982, p. 109; see also pp. 90, 92.

37. "Turning Screws," pp. 947, 949, 954. See also Barbara Sinclair, *Majority Leadership in the U.S. House* (Baltimore: Johns Hopkins University Press, 1983), p. 156.

make a special appeal to a Congressman to change his position, he eventually comes back with a request for a favor ranging in importance from one of the President's packages of matches to a judgeship or cabinet appointment for a worthy constituent."[38]

Sometimes members of Congress go to great lengths to create bargaining resources for themselves. Congressman Harold Rogers, a long-time supporter of the MX missile, was absent from the vote of the House Appropriations Committee on the president's request to purchase twenty-one additional missiles. He missed the vote not because of a change of heart about the weapon, but to gain leverage with which to influence the tobacco support program, a policy of great concern to his constituents. Because the MX was important to the president and the vote was close, the White House wasted no time in arranging a meeting to hear the congressman's complaint.[39]

Reagan's budget director David Stockman was quite candid about the concessions that members of Congress demanded in return for their support for the tax cut of 1981, including special breaks for holders of oil leases, real estate tax shelters, and generous loopholes that virtually eliminated the corporate income tax. "The hogs were really feeding" he said. "The greed level, the level of opportunism, just got out of control."[40] For obvious reasons, the White House does not want to encourage this tendency among members of Congress.

Appeals

The president's personal efforts at persuading members of Congress receive much attention from those who write about the president's legislative skills. These appeals take several forms, including telephone calls and private meetings in the Oval Office. Their common characteristic is that the president personally lobbies a member of Congress intimately, seeking support or at least lack of opposition on a vote.

Appeals to fellow partisans can be useful, but the president operates under rather severe constraints in employing his persuasive skills to lobbying one-on-one (see chapter 5). These constraints include the following: appeals often fail; members of Congress often exploit appeals in attempts to obtain quid pro quos; the uniqueness of appeals must be maintained to preserve their usefulness; some presidents dislike and therefore avoid making personal ap-

---

38. Quoted in Gary W. Reichard, *The Reaffirmation of Republicanism* (Knoxville: University of Tennessee Press, 1975), p. 173.

39. Jonathan Fuerbringer, "Pressures and Rewards Face House Members on MX Vote," *New York Times*, March 26, 1985, sec. A, p. 1.

40. Quoted in Greider, "The Education of David Stockman," p. 51.

peals; making appeals is time-consuming for the president. As a result, one-on-one lobbying by the president is the exception rather than the rule. The White House conserves appeals for obtaining the last few votes on issues of special significance to it.

There is an additional constraint on using personal appeals from the president: the White House is hesitant to employ the president when defeat is likely.[41] To put the president on the line in a very personal way and then lose entails substantial costs for the chief executive, undermining his professional reputation within Washington and his standing with the general public. Appeals are inherently risky, especially to the members of the opposition party (which is why they are rarely made), and the president wants to avoid incurring embarrassing political damage that reflects poorly on his leadership qualities.

An excellent example of this concern for the risks of making personal appeals to members of Congress from the opposition party occurred on one of the most important votes of Ronald Reagan's administration. According to David Stockman, two days before the vote on the second and final budget resolution in 1981, known as Gramm-Latta II, President Reagan invited to the White House all sixty-three of the Southern Democrats who had supported him on the first budget resolution. Fewer than forty even showed up, and defeat appeared certain. The president was not taking an active role in one-on-one lobbying and even left town before the vote was to take place. Then the House Rules Committee refused to propose a rule allowing a single vote of yea or nay on the budget resolution. This move aroused the Republicans' partisan energies, and victory seemed within reach. The critical budget vote actually occurred on the procedural matter of the rule. Only at this point did the president place his calls (from Los Angeles) to individual Democratic representatives.[42]

In this case the president called sixteen "Boll Weevils" and eleven supported him on the vote on the rule.[43] Although it will never be known whether Reagan's telephone calls were the determining factor in the decisions of these representatives, and although the president's persuasiveness must not be arbitrarily dismissed, one should be cautious of accepting the results of the vote on Gramm-Latta II as clear evidence of the impact of presidential appeals. Some of the eleven who supported him might not have done so in the absence of his calls, but the president made personal appeals only to those

---

41. See Mark Peterson, "Congressional Response to Presidential Proposals: Impact, Effort, and Politics" (paper presented at the annual meeting of the Midwest Political Science Association, Chicago, April 1986), p. 20.

42. Stockman, *The Triumph of Politics*, pp. 217–218.

43. Kellerman, *The Political Presidency*, p. 243.

whom his aides identified as swing votes: congressman who were fiscally conservative and inclined to support budget cuts but who remained undecided. In addition, five of the sixteen still voted against the president. The point is not that presidential appeals cannot influence votes, but that the president changed at most a few votes at the end of coalition building. Appeals are at the margins, not the core.

Equally important, 1981 was the high point of presidential appeals in Reagan's administration. The president enjoyed favorable conditions for making appeals in his first year in office. Things were not so favorable in the following years for a variety of reasons, and the president did not press as hard or as often. There was no point to his doing so when politics as usual prevailed and the president's chances of victory dimmed. Appeals are a skill that cannot be used often.

Reagan's hesitancy to intervene personally in the legislative process puzzled some observers who found in him a curious blend of political pragmatism and ideological rigidity, passionate aggressiveness and studied passivity. Part of the explanation of these seeming contradictions is straightforward. Because the White House sensed a lack of responsiveness in Congress to the president's proposals, the president became a more passive participant in the legislative process and fell back on his ideological themes.

If one were interested in comparing presidents on the basis of their personal skills at persuasion, one would want to focus on those few issues on which the president personally lobbied members of Congress, although the task of isolating the impact of efforts to persuade is likely to remain formidable, and one would learn relatively little from such a study. It would be misleading to devote undue attention to these votes, given the relative rarity of personal appeals by presidents, both in the number of issues and the number of members contacted, and given that personal lobbying is only one of a president's many legislative skills, which in turn represent only a portion of the presidential influences on congressional voting. Further, because personal appeals are likely to be made only when there is a reasonable chance of winning and only to those who are potentially open to persuasion, one must be cautious in drawing conclusions about the relative significance of appeals in affecting congressional voting.

In addition, what appears to be the successful use of personal appeals may actually represent the effectiveness of another skill. For example, in 1985 the House initially rejected a tax reform bill that President Reagan had very much wanted passed. After the vote the president called many Republicans (who had overwhelmingly opposed the bill), asking for their support. He even made an unusual trip to Capitol Hill to address his party cohorts. In the end the bill passed, with the help of fifty-four Republicans who changed from opposition to support. Yet the president's personal appeals probably had less influence on Republicans than his assurances that he would veto any tax bill that reached his desk without a number of changes they desired, and the change of heart of the House minority leader, Robert Michel, who decided to support the president. By defeating the bill on the first vote, Republicans created bargaining advantages for themselves, which they used to extract explicit promises from Reagan.[44]

Consultation

Consultation is another aspect of a president's legislative skills that observers often consider crucial to good relations with Congress, and failure to consult is taken as a sign of a lack of leadership skill. For example, Jimmy Carter was criticized by many for his failure to consult with Congress and congressional leaders on his legislative proposals.[45]

There are several advantages to consultation. Members of Congress appreciate advance warning of presidential proposals, especially those that affect their constituencies directly. No official wants to be blindsided, especially not an elected one. Politicians want to be prepared to take credit or avoid blame. In addition, consultation can provide the White House with early commitments of support if members of Congress have had a role in formulating a bill. If members oppose the president's legislation, this is also useful to know. By anticipating congressional objections, it may be possible to preempt them. At the very least, members of Congress will feel that they have had an opportunity to voice their objections.

Despite these advantages, presidential consultation with Congress plays a considerably less prominent role in presidential-congressional relations than one might expect. Often consultation is nothing more than a public relations effort that follows the White House's initiation of a bill rather than precedes it. It is not common for members of Congress to be intimately involved with the president's staff in writing legislation, especially if they belong to the opposition party. According to an aide to Ronald Reagan, "As a general rule, when there was consultation, it was pro forma, purely ceremonial. . . . [Senior White House aides] would listen to what people had to say and then completely disregard it."[46] The White House rarely alters major proposals in

44. "House Reverses Self, Passes Major Tax Overhaul," *Congressional Quarterly Weekly Report*, December 21, 1985, pp. 2705–2711; Elizabeth Drew, "A Reporter in Washington," *New Yorker*, January 6, 1986, pp. 80–81.

45. See Edwards, *Presidential Influence in Congress*, pp. 174–175; Sinclair, *Majority Leadership in the U.S. House*, p. 118.

46. Quoted in Peterson, "The President's Legislative Program," p. 13.

anticipation of congressional reactions, nor does it generally include as bargaining chips provisions that it does not desire and that it can trade away in negotiations with members of Congress. Consultation with Congress does not normally have a significant impact on a president's proposals.[47]

Lyndon Johnson was the modern president most given to consultation,[48] and his use of consultation is instructive.[49] Much of it was in the form of touching base with congressional leaders on the general outlines of legislation and providing advance warning of impending proposals. This may have generated goodwill and help in gauging levels of support, but typically it resulted only in fine-tuning his proposals, not in altering their central provisions. This was especially true of his core programs that constituted the Great Society and that involved education, health, and civil rights. According to Polsby, no members of Congress were consulted or briefed before the legislation beginning the War on Poverty was introduced in Congress in 1964, and few members understood it.[50] Johnson did not fear fighting for what he wanted. Equally important, Johnson was operating within a broad consensus on policy, especially before 1967. It is easier to consult with and accommodate members of Congress in a context of consensus than in the more typical contemporary environment of polarization.

Evidence that presidents generally do not engage in significant consultation with members of Congress does not in itself constitute a compelling argument that they should not do so to increase their legislative support. Yet when patterns of presidential behavior extend across several administrations, one must consider the possibility that there are good reasons why presidents do not consult with Congress more seriously, why they typically drop proposals after they have announced them and found that they met with resistance in Congress.

There are actually a good many reasons why consultation is a less useful skill than it may appear on the surface.[51] If presidents have firm ideas on policy, they are unlikely to want to consult with Congress to make compromises that satisfy congressional desires. According to the *National Journal*, President Reagan had extensive contacts with members of Congress early in

47. Ibid., pp. 11–20; Anna Kasten Nelson, "John Foster Dulles and the Bipartisan Congress," *Presidential Studies Quarterly* 17 (Spring 1987): 43–64.

48. See Edwards, *Presidential Influence in Congress*, pp. 119–120. See also Manatos, interview by Frantz, transcript, p. 47; Sanders, interview by Frantz, tape 2, transcript, p. 30.

49. See Peterson, "The President's Legislative Program," pp. 21–24.

50. Nelson W. Polsby, *Political Innovation in America* (New Haven and London: Yale University Press, 1984), p. 141.

51. See Peterson, "The President's Legislative Program," pp. 811.

52. Dick Kirschten, "Reagan: 'No More Business as Usual,'" *National Journal*, February 21, 1981, p. 300.

his term. Yet "in the main, his purpose [was] to acquaint them with his resolve," not to elicit congressional input that could lead to substantial modifications of his budget and tax proposals.[52] In addition, many presidential proposals are designed by the White House to assuage constituency groups or fulfill campaign promises, and the president operates under tight constraints in modifying these bills in response to consultation with Congress.

The White House is also concerned with the nature of Congress, which it often views as parochial, sievelike, and prone to transforming important matters of state into pork-barrel issues. Officials in the executive branch see some presidential proposals as too sensitive or jurisdictionally complex to allow for consultation with members of Congress. Speaking of the much criticized energy proposal of 1977, a senior aide to Carter explained, "If we tried to work things out with . . . [Congress] ahead of time, we would not have gotten anything out up there, given the fractured and fragmented nature of Congress."[53]

Time is an ever-present factor in operations of the White House, and it influences consultation with Congress as well. If there are severe deadlines on the production of a presidential initiative, as in the case of the energy proposal of 1977, consultation may not be possible. In addition, an aggressive president such as Lyndon Johnson sends a large number of bills to Congress, restricting the time officials can devote to consulting on any one of them.

Setting Priorities

An important aspect of a president's legislative strategy can be the establishment of priorities among legislative proposals. The goal of this effort is to set Congress's agenda. The danger is that if the president is not able to focus Congress's attention on the programs that are a high priority, they will become lost in the complex and overloaded legislative process. As an aide to Gerald Ford remarked, "Congress needs time to digest what the President sends; time to come up with independent analysis; time to schedule hearings and markups. Unless the President gives some indication of what's truly important, Congress will simply put the proposals in a queue."[54]

Setting priorities is also important because presidents and their staff can lobby effectively for only a few bills at a time. The president's political capital is inevitably limited, and it is sensible to focus it on the issues he cares about most. Otherwise this precious resource might be wasted, as in 1977 when

53. Quoted in Peterson, "The President's Legislative Program," p. 10.

54. Quoted in Paul C. Light, *The President's Agenda: Domestic Policy Choice from Kennedy to Carter* (Baltimore: Johns Hopkins University Press, 1982), p. 156.

Jimmy Carter "spent his political capital to a deficit on pork barrel projects," which were not among his priorities.[55]

Jimmy Carter has been widely criticized by the press and scholars for having failed to set legislative priorities, especially in light of the scale, diversity, complexity, and controversial nature of his initial legislative program. Carter actually proposed about the same percentage of new and large programs as Kennedy and Johnson and fewer new programs than Johnson. Yet Carter's critics argue that his failure to rank his legislative proposals made his legislative program seem larger than it was.[56] This problem was aggravated because so many aspects of his program, including energy, tax and welfare reform, health insurance, and the financing of social security, fell within the jurisdiction of the House Ways and Means Committee and the Senate Finance Committee. Without guidance on priorities, the proposals clogged the pipeline and stretched Carter's prestige too thin. As the president's chief of congressional liaison put it, "We overloaded the circuits and blew a fuse."[57]

There are, however, fundamental obstacles to focusing congressional attention on a few items of high priority. In 1981 Ronald Reagan focused attention on his priorities by asking for relatively little, but in the first year of his second term the congressional agenda was crowded by the budget, tax reform, the MX missile, farm credit, sanctions against South Africa, aid to Nicaraguan rebels, and much more. Max Friedersdorf, the head of Reagan's legislative liaison team in both 1981 and 1985, explained: "In '81, during the whole course of the year, we only had three major votes." These votes took place at wide intervals. By May 1985, however, the White House had already "had five or six votes. The circuits have been overloaded."[58]

Several forces are at work here. First, the White House can put off dealing with the full spectrum of national issues for several months at the beginning of a new president's term, but it cannot do so for four years: eventually it must make decisions. By the second year the agenda is full and more policies are in the pipeline, as the administration attempts to satisfy its constituencies and responds to unanticipated or simply overlooked problems.

Moreover, the president himself will inevitably be a distraction from his own priorities. There are so many demands on the president to speak, appear, and attend meetings that it is impossible to organize his schedule for very long

55. Jack Watson, interview with author, West Point, New York, October 19, 1985.
56. See Light, *The President's Agenda*, pp. 119–126, 156–157. See also Laurence E. Lynn, Jr. and Donald deF. Whitman, *The President as Policymaker* (Philadelphia: Temple University Press, 1981), p. 271.
57. Quoted in James P. Pfiffner, *The Strategic Presidency* (Chicago: Dorsey, 1988), p. 145.
58. Quoted in Bernard Weinraub, "Back in the Legislative Strategist's Saddle Again," *New York Times*, May 28, 1985, sec. A, p. 10.

around his major goals, especially if he has been in office for long. An example from Jimmy Carter's administration illustrates this point:

> At the beginning of a two-week period in June, 1979 the President (Carter) met with a congressional delegation to try to rally its support for an expected close vote on the implementation of the Panama Canal Treaty. . . . In the course of it, Carter told two congressmen that he would "whip his (Senator Kennedy's) ass" if the latter tried to run against him. This statement became a big story on the evening news. . . . (Two days later) the President introduced his proposals for national health insurance. Before any campaign could be launched to back his legislation, the President left for Vienna to sign the SALT agreements. When he returned he addressed Congress and the nation on the subject of SALT. . . . The President's next appearance on the news took place the following day, when he spoke at a ceremony after the completion of a solar panel for the White House hot-water system. There he urged the nation to give its attention to this important alternative to oil. Three days later he left for a world economic conference.[59]

Similarly, President Reagan wanted to focus attention on tax reform in 1985. Yet during a short trip to Alabama he had to react to a Senate vote that day on his request for aid to the rebels in Nicaragua and to the Supreme Court's decision on a school prayer case that had arisen in Alabama. As one presidential aide put it, "You can't go to Alabama and not mention the school prayer decision, and if you go to Alabama and mention the school prayer decision, don't think you are going to get covered on tax reform."[60]

In 1986 the president was again pushing for aid to the contras, but his efforts were overtaken by other events. According to the White House's communications director, Patrick J. Buchanan, "the Philippines intruded and dominated for two weeks, making it difficult for us to get the contra aid campaign off the ground." In addition, the president had to give a nationally televised speech on behalf of his defense budget, and the explosion of the space shuttle Challenger also distracted attention from the president's priorities. As one White House aide put it, "The hardest thing to do is not to get into a reactive mode and have your schedule dictated to you by events, rather than dictating events and having a schedule reflective of your priorities."[61]

59. Michael Baruch Grossman and Martha Joynt Kumar, *Portraying the President* (Baltimore: Johns Hopkins University Press, 1981), pp. 99–100; see also p. 314.

60. Quoted in Gerald M. Boyd, "Rethinking a Tax Plan Strategy," *New York Times*, June 12, 1985, sec. A, p. 14.

61. Quoted in Dick Kirschten, "For Reagan Communication Team . . . It's Strictly One Week at a Time," *National Journal*, March 8, 1986, p. 594.

Second, Congress is quite capable of setting its own agenda. The changes in Congress discussed earlier—changes in its aggressiveness, in its institutional capabilities, and in the freedom of individuals and groups to act—have not only made it more difficult for the president to persuade Congress but also to focus its attention. The public expects Congress to take the initiative,[62] and members of Congress have strong electoral incentives to respond. Thus when President Carter sent his large legislative program to Congress, it had to compete for space on the agenda with congressional initiatives. As a presidential aide put it, "Congress was scheduled up before most of the items arrived."[63]

This aggressive role of Congress is not unusual. The major legislative actions of the Ninety-ninth Congress (1985–86) included the reauthorization of the Clean Water Act, the Safe Drinking Water Act, and the "Superfund" for cleaning up hazardous waste, sanctions against South Africa, reorganization of the Pentagon, a measure to combat drug abuse, a major revision of immigration law, the Gramm-Rudman-Hollings bill to reduce the deficit, revisions of the law on gun control, the first authorization for water projects in a decade, an extension of daylight savings time, and extended protection against age discrimination. On none of this legislation did the White House take the lead. Instead, it reacted to congressional initiatives. Even the historic Tax Reform Act of 1986 was as much a product of long-term congressional momentum and committee leadership as it was of presidential agenda-setting. In 1987 President Reagan found Congress already working on his two primary domestic policy initiatives for his last two years in office, catastrophic health insurance and welfare reform.

Finally, presidents may not want to set priorities and concentrate attention on a few items. Lyndon Johnson is often viewed as having been careful to set priorities for Congress, but in reality there was less to his setting of priorities than one might expect. In his memoirs Johnson writes, "One of the President's most important jobs is to help Congress concentrate on the *five or six dozen bills* that make up his legislative program [italics added]."[64] Wilbur Cohen recalls Johnson gathering his administration's legislative liaison people together about ten days after his inauguration in 1965 and telling them he wanted all his legislative proposals passed during that legislative session.[65]

62. See for example Adam Clymer, "Majority in Poll Expect Congress to Cut Spending," *New York Times*, November 17, 1985, sec. 1, p. 1.

63. Quoted in Light, *The President's Agenda*, p. 54. See also Robert Shogan, *Promises to Keep* (New York: Thomas Y. Crowell, 1977), p. 205.

64. Johnson, *The Vantage Point*, p. 448.

65. "Discussion," in William S. Livingston, Lawrence C. Dodd, and Richard L. Schott, eds., *The Presidency and the Congress* (Austin, Tex.: 1979), pp. 300–301.

Lawrence O'Brien, the head of the Office of Congressional Relations, remembers, "Certainly we didn't worry about overburdening our friends in Congress" in 1965.[66] According to Johnson's chief Senate lobbyist, Mike Manatos, and his legislative liaison aide Claude Desautels, the president had a master list of sixty to eighty bills that included priorities, but he carefully followed and pushed each piece of legislation on the list.[67] This was not setting a few legislative priorities and then focusing congressional and public attention on them. Instead, Johnson was more concerned with moving legislation through Congress rapidly to exploit the favorable political environment.[68]

Setting priorities is considerably easier for a president with a short legislative agenda, such as Ronald Reagan, than it is for one with a more ambitious agenda. It is also an advantage if the opposition party is in disarray and lacks alternatives to the president's agenda, a situation enjoyed by the Republicans in 1981 as the Democrats reeled from Reagan's electoral victory and their loss of the Senate.

Moving Fast

Being ready to send legislation to the Hill early in the first year of a new president's term to exploit the honeymoon atmosphere that typically characterizes this period is related to the setting of priorities. Lyndon Johnson explained, "You've got to give it all in you can that first year . . . You've got just one year when they treat you right and before they start worrying about themselves."[69] It is also to the advantage of presidents if they are ready to replace enacted requests with additional items of their legislative program.[70] In other words, it is best to keep Congress concentrating on the president's proposals.

First-year proposals have a considerably better chance of passing Congress than do those sent to the Hill later in an administration. Kennedy, Johnson, Reagan, and to some extent Carter took advantage of this opportunity, whereas Eisenhower and Nixon did not. Further, most presidents are not ready with a second wave of proposals. The exception, as one might expect, was Lyndon Johnson.[71]

66. O'Brien, *No Final Victories*, p. 183.

67. Manatos, interview by Frantz, transcript, pp. 21–22, 50–51; Bowles, *The White House and Capitol Hill*, p. 35.

68. See William E. Leuchtenburg, *In the Shadow of FDR* (Ithaca, N.Y.: Cornell University Press, 1983), p. 146.

69. Quoted in Harry McPherson, *A Political Education* (Boston: Little, Brown, 1972), p. 268.

70. Light, *The President's Agenda*, pp. 58–59.

71. Ibid., pp. 44–49, 58–59.

Although the prospects of passage are enhanced if legislation moves quickly, there are good reasons why many presidents are not able to ensure that it does. For example, Jimmy Carter's proposals for energy, welfare reform, and the containment of hospital costs were complex and controversial policies that took a long time to draft and to clear relevant offices in the White House. He could not turn to a well-established party program as Kennedy and Johnson could. As one aide to Carter put it, "We did not come into office with a handful of already developed programs. If anything, we had a set of ideas that took more than their share of time. There was no set of experts working on hospital cost containment when we came in, and energy was a mess. We had to start the programs all over from scratch. We were the ones who had to canvass the executive branch for ideas. We were also the ones that had to look for some potential solutions."[72]

There is of course an alternative to the methodical, time-consuming drafting of legislation. The president might choose simply to propose a policy without thorough analysis to exploit the favorable political climate of his honeymoon. This appears to have been the strategy of Reagan's White House regarding the budget cuts passed by Congress in 1981. The departments (including cabinet members) and their expertise were kept at a distance during decision making. According to the budget director, David Stockman, "None of us really understands what's going on with all these numbers."[73] Lyndon Johnson's legislation to establish the War on Poverty in 1964 is often faulted for having been understood by virtually no one.[74]

Although the strategy of "move it or lose it" may increase the probability of a bill's the passage and not affront the sensibilities of some one with Ronald Reagan's lack of concern for details, it is not difficult to understand why someone with the temperament of Jimmy Carter may eschew such a process. Although taking time to draft proposals does not guarantee that they will be well conceived, it seems unlikely that rapid drafting of legislation is in the best interests of the nation.

Structuring Choice

Unlike bargaining, appeals, and consultation, and like setting priorities and moving fast, structuring the choices facing Congress can influence many votes

72. Quoted in ibid., p. 218; see also pp. 49–51, 55–56.

73. Quoted in Greider, "The Education of David Stockman," p. 38; see also pp. 40, 43, 45, 54.

74. See for example Daniel P. Moynihan, *Maximum Feasible Misunderstanding* (New York: Free Press, 1969), p. 87; John C. Donovan, *The Politics of Poverty*, 2d ed. (Indianapolis: Bobbs-Merrill, 1973), p. 40; James L. Sundquist, ed., *On Fighting Poverty* (New York: Basic Books, 1969), p. 29.

at the same time. Framing issues in ways that favor the president's programs may set the terms of the debate on his proposals and thus the premises on which members of Congress cast their votes. Because mandates (discussed in chapter 8) are infrequent, however, presidents must typically rely on framing issues one at a time.

The White House is generally quite interested in influencing the terms of debate on issues. As one leading adviser to Reagan put it, "I've always believed that 80 percent of any legislative or political matter is how you frame the debate."[75] Usually this involves emphasizing features of a policy other than its immediate substantive merits and making these other features more prominent in the decisional calculus of members of Congress.

The key vote on Reagan's budget cuts in 1981 was on the rule determining whether there would be a single vote of yea or nay in the House. Once the vote was taken, the White House could frame the issue as a vote for or against the popular president,[76] and the broad nature of the reconciliation bill shifted the debate from the losses of individual programs to the benefits of the package as a whole. Although Reagan could not win an important individual vote on cutting a social welfare program, by structuring the choice facing Congress, he needed only to win one vote and could avoid much of the potential criticism for specific reductions in spending.

In 1985 Reagan asked Congress to appropriate funds for twenty-one additional MX missiles. He had been unable to win the money he had sought in 1984 when the debate focused on the utility of the missiles as strategic weapons. He succeeded the next year, however, after the terms of the debate changed to focus on the impact of building the missiles on the arms control negotiations with the Soviet Union that had recently begun in Geneva. Senators and representatives who lacked confidence in the contribution of the MX to national security were still reluctant to deny American negotiators the bargaining chips they said they required. According to a senior official at the Pentagon, "By the end, we gave up on technical briefings on the missile. . . . It was all based on the unspoken bargaining chip. Without Geneva, we would have died right there.[77]

The program that the president proposed had not changed. The MX was the same missile with essentially the same capabilities in 1985 as in 1984. What had changed were the premises on which members of Congress based

75. Quoted in Gerald M. Boyd, "'General Contractor' of the White House Staff," *New York Times*, March 4, 1986, sec. A, p. 22.

76. See Stockman, *The Triumph of Politics*, p. 174.

77. Quoted in "MX Debate: It's Not Over," *New York Times*, March 30, 1985, pp. 1, 8. See also "Senate Hands Reagan Victory on MX Missile," *Congressional Quarterly Weekly Report*, March 23, 1985, pp. 515–523.

their votes. The burden of proof had shifted from the administration ("MX is a useful weapon") to its opponents ("canceling the MX will not hurt the arms control negotiations"). Structuring of choices is what made the difference, not conversion.

It is important to distinguish the structuring of choices from the setting of the agenda. Changes in the agenda may occur without changes in public policy. Agenda-setting is only one stage in the policy-making process and by itself does not determine the outcomes of the process. In structuring of choices the same issues remain on the agenda, as in the case of the MX, but the questions asked about them change.

Portraying policies in terms of criteria on which there is a consensus and playing down divisive issues is often at the core of efforts to structure choices for Congress. Federal aid to education had been a divisive issue for years before President Johnson proposed the Elementary and Secondary Education Act in 1965. To blunt opposition, he successfully changed the focus of debate from teachers' salaries and classroom shortages to fighting poverty, and from the separation of church and state to aiding children. This change in the premises of congressional decision making eased the path for the bill.[78]

Similarly, Richard Nixon articulated general revenue sharing as a program that made government more efficient and distributed benefits widely. He deemphasized the allocational aspect of the policy, which redistributed federal funds from traditional Democratic constituencies to projects favored by Republicans' middle class constituents.[79] Dwight Eisenhower employed the uncontroversial symbol of national defense during the Cold War, even when it came to naming legislation, to obtain support for aiding education (the National Defense Education Act) and building highways (the Interstate and Defense Highway Act).

Because of the diverse perspectives of members of Congress, presidents often portray the same issue in different terms for different audiences. On a tax question Lyndon Johnson might emphasize budget balancing with Republicans and personal loyalty with Democrats.[80] Likewise, in appealing to Republican senators on the issue of AWACS in 1981, Ronald Reagan stressed party and personal loyalty and the need for Republicans to maintain unity to govern. Equally important, he emphasized the president's need for credibility in the conduct of foreign affairs. "Vote against me," he said privately on several occasions, "and you will cut me off at the knees." To Democrats the

78. See for example Carl Albert, interview by McSweeny, interview 3, transcript, pp. 8–9.

79. See for example Richard P. Nathan et. al., *Revenue Sharing: The Second Round* (Washington: Brookings Institution, 1977).

80. Bell, *The Johnson Treatment*, pp. 93–94; Johnson, *The Vantage Point*, p. 85.

president invoked the bipartisan tradition in American foreign policy.[81] On votes on overriding vetoes presidents appeal to their party cohorts not to undermine their party leader and to the opposition party on more substantive grounds.

Although the structuring of choices can be a useful tool for the president, there is no guarantee that he will succeed. Although there are occasions on which a president can exploit an external event such as arms control negotiations to structure legislators' choices on a single issue, he cannot rely on his environment to be so accommodating. In addition, the White House must advocate the passage of many proposals at roughly the same time, further complicating its strategic position. Finally, opponents of the president's policies are unlikely to defer to his attempts to structure choices on the issues (see chapter 8).

As in making appeals, one can go to the well only so often. In 1986 there was another battle over the sale of arms to Saudi Arabia. During it the president argued that a defeat on this highly visible foreign policy issue would undermine his international credibility and destroy his role as a mediator in the Middle East. Despite all his efforts, the president was able to garner only thirty-four votes in the Senate, then controlled by Republicans.[82]

Attempts to structure decisions may actually hurt the president's cause if they are too heavy-handed and thus create a backlash. In 1986 Ronald Reagan was engaged in his perennial fight to provide aid to the contras in Nicaragua. The president equated opposition to his aid program with support for the Sandinistas. More graphically, the White House's communications director, Patrick J. Buchanan, wrote an editorial in the *Washington Post* that characterized the issue in stark terms: "With the contra vote, the Democratic Party will reveal whether it stands with Ronald Reagan and the resistance or [Nicaraguan President] Daniel Ortega and the communists." These overt efforts to structure the decision for Congress were not successful. Instead, they irritated members of Congress and provoked charges that the White House was engaged in red baiting.[83]

81. Quoted in Barrett, *Gambling with History*, pp. 275–276. See also Albert R. Hunt, "Out of the Fire," *Wall Street Journal*, October 29, 1981, pp. 1, 10; "Senate Supports Reagan an AWACS Sale," *Congressional Quarterly Weekly Report*, October 31, 1981, pp. 2098–3000; Richard F. Fenno, Jr., "Observation, Context, and Sequence in the Study of Politics," *American Political Science Review* 80 (March 1986): 12.

82. Steven V. Roberts, "Senate Upholds Arms for Saudis, Backing Reagan," *New York Times*, June 6, 1986, sec. A, pp. 1, 10. The thirty-four votes did sustain the president's veto, however.

83. "Reagan Loses Ground on 'Contra' Aid Program," *Congressional Quarterly Weekly Report*, March 8, 1986, pp. 535–536.

Lack of Skill

The reverse side of the question of how much legislative skills can help the president's program is that of how much poor skills can hurt. Certainly the press often reports presidential blunders and attributes significance to them. Yet even if the White House bungles the handling of an issue, does it follow that members of Congress will vote against other presidential programs out of irritation about the earlier behavior? There is no evidence to support such an assertion, and it strains credibility to think that very many members of Congress would override their own views and the pressures of party and constituency and oppose the president out of pique. As an aide to Nixon argued, "The mistakes you make will follow you, but they aren't that important in the long run. . . . We made some mistakes on welfare reform, but I doubt that they affected the revenue sharing bills."[84]

An assistant to Carter also cautions against attributing too much influence to poor personal legislative relations: "When we came in, I don't think there was any question that we were viewed as country bumpkins. I don't doubt that it affected Congress. But in comparison to what? Was that as important as the close election? Was that as critical as the drop in popularity? Or Bert Lance?"[85]

On the other hand, the White House can certainly irritate members of Congress, and this is not necessarily cost-free. If the president mishandles an issue, he may alienate some potential supporters, swing votes that could go either way. Ronald Reagan riled House Republicans with his handling of tax reform in 1985, and found himself literally pleading for support after an initial and highly embarrassing defeat resulted from their abandoning him.

Bungling an issue may also provoke a more general estrangement. Jimmy Carter's efforts to cut water projects in 1977 irritated Congress for years.[86] Although it may not be possible to pinpoint the consequences of this disaffection, it is not unreasonable to argue that at least some members of Congress were less willing to grant him the benefit of the doubt for a while on issues on which they were undecided.

Equally important, the absence of skills can undermine efforts to exploit opportunities for the passage of legislation or hinder even the recognition of these opportunities. Because presidents are not in strong positions to create opportunities for legislative success, exploiting those that already exist becomes especially significant.[87] Indeed, it may be the most important skill of all.

84. Quoted in Light, *The President's Agenda*, p. 29.
85. Quoted in ibid., p. 29.
86. Sinclair, *Majority Leadership*, p. 119.
87. See Peterson, "Congressional Response to Presidential Proposals," pp. 29–30.

Interviews with the former Speaker of the House Carl Albert are instructive on this point. He argued that Johnson's tenaciousness and intensity in
pushing legislation were his great talents. Although pressed by the inter-
viewer for specifics on Johnson's legislative skills, Albert responded only that
the president just kept pushing.[88] Russell Renka reached a similar conclusion.
After studying Johnson's legislative relations in great detail, he found no
special legislative touch possessed by the president. Nevertheless, Johnson
moved more legislation through Congress than other contemporary presidents.[89] He understood the opportunity the Eighty-ninth Congress presented to him, and he seized it.

Presidential legislative skills are not closely related to presidential support in Congress; on close examination a president's legislative skills reveal
themselves to be limited in their potential for obtaining support from senators
and representatives. In essence, a president's legislative skills operate in an
environment largely beyond the president's control. In most instances presidents exercise them at the margins of coalition building, not at the core. This is
consistent with Paul Light's finding that "according to the White House staffs,
the President's political power is only marginally related to internal resources
and bargaining skills."[90]

Despite these findings, one should not conclude that presidents should
ignore their legislative skills or that they never matter. Certainly presidents
have successfully intervened with a bargain or amenity, occasionally winning
a crucial vote because of such an effort. Strategic decisions such as setting
priorities and proposing legislation shortly after inauguration day increase the
probability of obtaining congressional support. The important point is that
these skills should be placed in their proper perspective. They do not appear
to be predominant in determining presidential support in Congress on most
roll calls, despite commonly held assumptions to the contrary. Presidential
legislative skills are more useful in exploiting discrete opportunities than in
creating broad possibilities for policy change.

Even when the environment is favorable for the White House, there are
usually severe limits on the exercise of skills. Ronald Reagan's administration,

88. Carl Albert, interview by McSweeny, interview 3, transcript, pp. 7, 11; interview 4,
transcript, pp. 22, 25; Carl Albert, interview by Dorothy Pierce McSweeny, April 28, 1969,
interview 1, transcript, pp. 22–23, Lyndon Baines Johnson Library, Austin, Tex.; Carl Albert,
interview by Dorothy Pierce McSweeny, June 10, 1969, interview 2, transcript, p. 14, Lyndon
Baines Johnson Library, Austin, Tex.
89. Renka, "Comparing Presidents Kennedy and Johnson as Legislative Leaders," p. 18,
table 4. See Light, *The President's Agenda*, p. 57, on the size of Johnson's legislative program.
90. Paul C. Light, "The President's Agenda: Notes on the Timing of Domestic Choice,"
Presidential Studies Quarterly 11 (Winter 1981): 70.

for example, could press hard for its budget and tax policies in 1981, but otherwise had a very limited agenda. When the issue of the sale of AWACS planes to Saudi Arabia arose, the White House initially handled it clumsily and had to come from behind to win a victory that should never have been in doubt. It was simply preoccupied with other matters and could not devote its attention and skills to the next item on the agenda.

These conclusions have broad implications for the way presidential leadership is viewed. Although what are seen as failures of presidential leadership are often attributed to inadequacies in the president's leadership skills, there are much broader and more important forces at work. It seems appropriate to adjust one's expectations of presidential leadership accordingly and acknowledge that presidential legislative skills are rarely at the core of policy making in the American political system.

Assuming that presidents typically operate at the margins of coalition building and that their legislative skills are essentially limited to exploiting rather than creating opportunities for leadership, more effort should be devoted to examining other influences on Congress, such as party leadership and public opinion, and less on personal skills. This personalization of politics can distract one's attention from factors that play a larger role in explaining presidential success in Congress and greatly oversimplify one's understanding of executive-legislative relations.

CHAPTER ELEVEN

Presidential Leadership

It is time to draw some general conclusions about presidential leadership. In this final chapter I reexamine my approach to studying leadership, outline conditions under which presidential leadership of Congress is likely to be successful, and place my findings about the importance of exploiting opportunities for leadership in the perspective of the American political system.

The Utility of Strategic Position

The concept of strategic position has played a prominent role in my analysis of presidential leadership of Congress. By focusing first on the potential of presidential leadership under varying circumstances, one obtains a useful perspective from which to examine and explain the impact of the president's efforts. Often outcomes that are popularly attributed to presidential leadership (positively or negatively) are actually products of other, more powerful forces structuring the environment of executive-legislative relations. These typically leave presidential leadership little room within which to maneuver.

A brief review of parts of the strategic environments of President Carter and President Reagan illustrates summarily the advantage of this approach. Each of these chief executives entered office facing conditions that were in only minor ways a result of his own making. Yet their strategic positions largely determined their relative chances of successfully obtaining their goals in Congress. Moreover, their strategic positions limited the potential of presidential leadership to working at the margins of coalition building.

Perceptions of Victory

Jimmy Carter and Ronald Reagan began their tenures in the White House with some important features of the political landscape in common.

Each won election with 50 to 51 percent of the popular vote, and each brought a change in the party controlling the presidency by defeating an incumbent president.

There the similarities ended. The general view of Carter's victory was one of an opportunity almost lost, the emphasis on the closeness of his election. The Democrats gained only one seat in the House and none in the Senate. In neither the press nor the Congress was there a perception of presidential coattails. Democrats felt they owed Carter nothing and Republicans were unimpressed with the apparent lack of public support for the newly elected chief executive.

Ronald Reagan, in contrast, had much better fortune. The press emphasized the one-sidedness of his victory despite his bare majority in the popular vote. There was an extraordinary misperception of a mandate and of a turn toward conservatism. These images were reinforced by the impressive Republican gains of twelve seats in the Senate, giving the GOP a majority for the first time since 1954, and thirty-four seats in the House. Perceptions of coattails were understandably strong. Congressional Republicans were grateful for what they viewed as the new president's contribution to their election, and Democrats were intimidated by the widespread perception of a major shift in public opinion.

Because of the perceptions of the meaning of his election, Ronald Reagan's victory changed at least for a while the terms of debate over public policy in the United States and the premises of congressional decision making. It placed a stigma on big government and exalted large defense efforts. This change in the political environment gave the president a considerable advantage in obtaining support for his policies.

Relations with Party

Carter and Reagan had common themes in their basic orientations toward public policy. Both advocated fiscal restraint, bureaucratic efficiency, traditional moral values, economic deregulation, and increased defense expenditures. Although Reagan's views were more extreme than Carter's, the central thrusts of many of their policies were similar. Both presidents desired to transcend group bargaining, avoid compromise, and attack fundamental problems with comprehensive, long-range policies.

These policies gave the presidents very different relations with their respective parties. Carter was not the natural leader of the Democratic party. His views ran against the tide of his party and its historic practices, rhetoric, and ideology. Liberals were often critical of the president, and their most visible leader, Edward Kennedy, engaged in a costly challenge to Carter's renomination in 1980.

This divisiveness in the party was exacerbated somewhat by the shift in status of Democratic party and committee leaders in Congress as a result of Carter's election. For the first time since the congressional reforms of the early 1970s, Democratic leaders had to share power with the White House. The moribund nature of the national party organization that the president inherited further diminished his chances for effective party leadership.

Ronald Reagan's prospects for productive relations with his party were much brighter. His policies were quite in step with the overwhelming majority of his party's members in both Congress and the public. Thus Republicans displayed an extremely high cohesion, especially on the economic policy proposals that were Reagan's highest priority in 1981.

In addition, the shift in status of Republican party and committee leaders was one very likely to breed party unity. They were delighted if not astonished to be wielding majority power, and eager to follow their party leader in the White House. This was especially true of the extraordinarily large number of junior Republican senators, but all were eager to show they could govern. The rejuvenated national party apparatus, which was collecting enormous sums of money, further enhanced the president's party leadership.

Public Support

Presidents require public support to lead Congress, and both Carter and Reagan had their ups and downs in the polls. Carter began his term in typical fashion, high in the polls early in his first year, and then, but for a brief respite resulting from Egyptian-Israeli accords signed at Camp David in September 1978, drifting steadily downward until the American embassy in Tehran was seized in November 1979. Because the administration was not ready at the very beginning of 1977 with legislation that it considered a high priority, it was not able to take advantage of its honeymoon period, and the trend in the president's approval was downward when he most needed the resource of public support.

Ronald Reagan started his tenure rather low in the polls, but his fortunes quickly changed. Within minutes of his taking office, the American hostages were released by their Iranian captors. The new president benefited from his predecessor's negotiations and basked in the upsurge of emotion that greeted the hostages' return. Public morale received another boost from the success of the space shuttle Columbia. Finally, although it seems perverse to argue that an assassination attempt can be to the president's advantage, Reagan's approval ratings increased by eight percentage points after the attempt on his life on March 30, 1981.

It is true that the public relations skills of Reagan's administration were impressive, but they could not by themselves create or sustain goodwill. The president was below 50 percent in the polls after only ten months in office and would not obtain the approval of more than half the public again until 1983, despite his staff's efforts at promoting a favorable image. The fundamental conditions of public support in the president's legislatively crucial first year were established outside the White House, but the support was there when he most needed it.

Agendas and Strategies

The size of Carter's and Reagan's legislative agendas differed greatly. As a result the two presidents faced quite different opportunities for the employment of legislative strategies. Jimmy Carter had a very large agenda, one that required positive action by Congress. Consequently, he found it difficult to set priorities for the legislature. Because he could not turn to a well-established party program, he was not able to move rapidly to exploit the favorable conditions of his honeymoon period. Instead, he was involved in the time-consuming drafting of complex programs.

Ronald Reagan, on the other hand, advanced the smallest policy agenda of any modern president, and much of it was negative (that is, dedicated to reducing government activities). Asking for little lessened the burden of setting priorities, and it was easier to move rapidly in introducing legislation focused on cutting back or eliminating programs and having an ideological orientation that simplified the task of policy analysis.

Strategic Position in Perspective

The point of this brief survey of parts of the strategic positions of Carter and Reagan is not to suggest that what presidents do does not matter. Nor is it to deny that Carter's administration sometimes shot itself in the foot (often when the foot was in its mouth) or that Reagan's White House was skilled in congressional relations, particularly at the beginning of the president's tenure.

Instead, the point is that it is important to depersonalize somewhat the study of presidential leadership and examine it from a broader perspective. In this way there are fewer risks of attributing to various aspects of presidential leadership consequences of factors largely beyond the president's control. Similarly, one is less likely to attribute incorrectly the failure of a president to achieve his goals to his failure to lead properly. Things are rarely so simple.

Most important, an emphasis on strategic position helps bring about an understanding of the president's position in the political system. By asking crucial questions about what it is possible for presidential leadership of Congress to accomplish, one obtains a better sense of what to expect from a chief executive and what is necessary to produce policy change. By examining the parameters of presidential leadership and not assuming that presidents will succeed in influencing Congress if they are just skillful enough in employing their resources, one is better positioned to understand the consequences of leadership efforts.

In addition, such a focus forces an examination of the circumstances in which change does occur. If leadership is typically insufficient by itself to bring about change, if the White House cannot mold its environment, then what conditions provide the president with the potential to facilitate change?

Conditions for Success

In evaluating Richard Nixon's relations with Congress, an assistant to the president concluded, "Any President's basic influence rests on his congressional strength—the actual votes in Congress. With only 190 Republicans in 1968, we were hamstrung. The President's electoral margin can give some extra juice. With only 44 percent of the vote in the '68 election, we were in serious trouble. Finally, the President's public approval can help—that was one area where we were strong. But one out of three just wasn't enough."[1]

Similarly, an aide to President Carter reflected on his administration's dealings with Congress: "When Eisenhower was on top of the polls, he couldn't move. Even though he was one of our most popular Presidents, he just didn't have enough strength in Congress. Public opinion couldn't create what the electorate hadn't given him—party control of the House and Senate. In our case, we had the congressional seats. We had the potential support. But, where Eisenhower had the public approval, we had nothing. Our public ratings started to drop fairly quickly, and Congress started to back off. We had the seats, but we didn't have the public approval."[2]

These White House officials support the view that the conditions for successful presidential leadership of Congress are interdependent. Strength in only one resource is seldom enough to sustain leadership efforts. Congressional party cohorts and public support are the principal underpinnings of presidential leadership of Congress. Whereas the party composition of Congress is relatively stable, public approval of the president may be quite volatile. When both are in the president's favor, he may accomplish a great deal, but in the absence of such fortuitous circumstances, stalemate is the most likely relationship with Congress. Party loyalty is not sufficiently strong to

1. Quoted in Paul C. Light, *The President's Agenda: Domestic Policy Choice from Kennedy to Carter* (Baltimore: Johns Hopkins University Press, 1982), p. 31.
2. Quoted in ibid., p. 28.

overcome public skepticism of the president, and members of the opposition party will only move so far in the president's direction in response to public support for the White House.

The interdependence of resources extends beyond the need for a sizable party base in Congress and public support. For example, public support makes the use of legislative skills more effective. A president high in the polls or who is viewed as having a mandate will find members of Congress more responsive to his personal appeals for support. When he is lower in the polls, he is less likely to even seek votes in such a manner.[3] Similarly, only if the president has strong public approval is it sensible to employ the strategies of moving rapidly to exploit this resource, or structuring congressional decisions in terms of support for a popular president or opposition to him. Using the reconciliation process to produce large cuts in federal spending through a single vote of yea or nay could succeed only under the conditions of public support and party cohesion that were prevalent in 1981. Further, in that year the president could gain leverage by promising Republicans to send them letters of thanks and promising Democrats to abstain from personal campaign appearances on behalf of their opponents, but such offers were much less effective as his public support dropped in the following year.

A president who already has strong public approval is also likely to find it easier to move the public to support specific policies, and efforts to mobilize the public are likely to be most effective when the party and White House organize private sector interests that will communicate with Congress. In turn, constituent groups are most enthusiastic about applying pressure on behalf of the White House when the president is high in the polls.

A favorable environment makes some potential resources less effective and others more so. If a president is skilled at bargaining but enjoys a large majority of supporters in Congress, he will have less need to engage in exchanges. Similarly, legislative skills will have less utility if the president emphasizes mobilizing the public to move Congress rather than dealing more directly with legislators. Thus resources such as legislative skills have more relevance in some situations than in others.

Certain discrete conditions enhance the utility of leadership and increase the probability that a president will obtain support in Congress. If members of his party in the House and Senate have personal loyalties and emotional commitments to the president, feel that they have a stake in the administration's success and do not wish to embarrass it, distrust the opposition, and do not want to avoid identification with their own party, then there is likely to be

---

3. "Democrats Showed Renewed Strength in 1983," *Congressional Quarterly Weekly Report*, December 31, 1983, pp. 2781–2782.

greater party unity behind the chief executive. Likewise, if members of the president's party in Congress view him as the natural leader of the party, if there is substantial intraparty consensus on policy, and if there are not strong factions within the party, party cohesion is likely to be greater than if these conditions do not exist.

The president's prospects for obtaining support in Congress are enhanced for a president whose party has just regained majority status in a chamber of the legislature, has not had to change from a minority in opposition to a governing minority, has not just become a minority, and has not just had to share power with the White House after having been the majority party under a president from the opposition party. The White House is in a better position to pass legislation when the congressional leaders of the president's party are loyal and effective, the president and his staff enjoy harmonious relations with them, and the leaders have power within their institution.

The president is more likely to meet with success if he has the appropriate resources, willingness, and organization to provide amenities and services to members of his party (and occasionally to members of the opposition), if he can deny resources that members of Congress desire without creating antagonism, and if the White House can orchestrate pressures on members of Congress from outside Washington. The prospects will brighten for a president to whom the opposition party is potentially a fertile ground for seeking support, and who can restrain his partisanship and appeal to the opposition while not estranging his own party by these efforts.

The likelihood that the president will obtain congressional support for his policies increases considerably if the president stands high in the polls and members of Congress either are concerned with how voters evaluate their support of the White House or use presidential approval ratings as indicators of public opinion. Support will also become more likely if the president's appeals for support are effectively made, the public is receptive to these requests, and the public communicates its support of the president to Congress.

In other circumstances the president may benefit from perceptions of a mandate and find it easier to structure congressional decision making. These circumstances include the appearance at the president's election of long coattails, a tendency by the press to indulge in hyperbole when analyzing his victory, the orientation of the president's campaign around issues, a consistency of policies with the opinions of the country in general and his party in particular, the accession of the president by defeat of an incumbent by a surprisingly large margin, thus providing a sense of a new direction in policy, and success by the White House in influencing perceptions of the meaning of the election.

Bargaining can be to the advantage of a president who serves in a period of slack resources in which bargaining and logrolling are possible if he rather than Congress or the bureaucracy controls these resources, and if he is temperamentally and ideologically suited to bargaining. He has a chance to gain additional support if members of Congress want what the president has to offer and are willing to bargain with him, if the president can create an atmosphere conducive to compromise and does not have to bargain with the opposition party (thus strengthening it with his resources), and if implied bargains do not produce friction over unkept promises.

A president with the temperament and time to make personal appeals to legislators is likely to increase his support. For the appeals to be effective he must not make them too often, members of Congress must not exploit them for quid pro quos, the investment of his prestige must not be too risky, and representatives and senators must be responsive to his appeals. The president may improve his chances of success if he has time to consult with Congress over his proposals and the flexibility to make changes in them without violating his own principles and the promises he has made to others. At the same time, members of Congress must view his proposals from a broad, national perspective and not leak them prematurely or try to turn them into pork-barrel issues.

The president can improve the chances that his program will receive the attention of Congress by proposing a legislative agenda that allows him to set priorities and avoid clogging the congressional pipeline, and by not distracting attention from his own agenda with his statements and actions on the full range of issues with which he must deal. He will also be helped by a Congress that does not take the initiative in proposing policies, an opposition party in disarray that lacks policy alternatives, and an environment that does not force issues upon him.

The White House will find its prospects of success are enhanced if it has proposals ready to send to Congress shortly after the inauguration, either because of a well-established party program or because it is not overly concerned with careful draftsmanship. Finally, the president will be in a better position to structure congressional decisions if his environment allows him to portray an issue in uncontroversial terms, if he can concentrate attention on one issue at a time, if potential opponents accept his portrayal of the issue, and if he does not have to try this tactic too often and does not create a backlash.

Clearly, the conditions for successful presidential leadership of Congress are contingent, and the president's strategic position uncertain. If circumstances are not serendipitous, the potential for leadership is diminished. In such a context it becomes all the more necessary for the president to take advantage of whatever opportunities do appear.

Exploiting Opportunities

Presidents must largely play with the hands that the public deals them through its electoral decisions (both presidential and congressional) and its evaluations of the chief executive's handling of his job. They are rarely in a position to augment substantially their resources. They operate at the margins as facilitators rather than as directors of change.

When the various streams of resources do converge, they create opportunities for leadership. Because a president's resource base is fragile, he must take advantage of the opportunities in his environment to facilitate change. The essential presidential skill in leading Congress is in recognizing and exploiting conditions for change, not in creating them.

This can best be seen in the cases of presidents most often viewed as directors rather than mere facilitators of change. It is actually those presidents most successful with Congress who have best understood their own limitations and taken full advantage of their good fortune in having resources to exploit. When these resources diminished, they fell back to the more typical stalemate that usually characterizes presidential-congressional relations.

When Congress first met in special session in March 1933 after Franklin D. Roosevelt's inauguration, it rapidly passed at the new president's request bills to control the resumption of banking, repeal Prohibition, and effect government economies. This is all FDR originally planned for Congress to do; he expected to reassemble the legislature when permanent and more constructive legislation was ready.[4] Yet the president found a situation ripe for change. James MacGregor Burns described it as follows:

> A dozen days after the inauguration a move of adulation for Roosevelt was sweeping the country. Over ten thousand telegrams swamped the White House in a single week. Newspaper editorials were paeans of praise. . . .
> A flush of hope swept the nation. Gold was flowing back to financial institutions; banks were reopening without crowds of depositors clamoring for their money; employment and production seemed to be turning upward.
> "I will do anything you ask," a congressman from Iowa wrote the President. "You are my leader."[5]

Roosevelt decided to exploit this favorable environment and strike repeatedly with hastily drawn legislation. This period of intense activity came to be known as the Hundred Days.

4. James MacGregor Burns, *Roosevelt: The Lion and the Fox* (New York: Harcourt, Brace and World, 1956), pp. 166–168.
5. Ibid., p. 168.

Lyndon Johnson also knew that his personal leadership could not sustain congressional support for his policies. He had to exploit the opportunities provided by the assassination of President Kennedy and the election of 1964. He told his aide Jack Valenti early in his presidency, "I keep hitting hard because I know this honeymoon won't last. Every day I lose a little more political capital. That's why we have to keep at it, never letting up. One day soon . . . the critics and the snipers will move in and we will be at stalemate. We have to get all we can now, before the roof comes down."[6] Thus in February 1965, after his landslide victory, Johnson assembled the congressional liaison officials from the various departments and told them that his victory at the polls "might be more of a loophole than a mandate," and that because his popularity could decrease rapidly they would have to use it to their advantage while it lasted.[7]

Johnson followed his own advice. At the end of an extraordinarily productive session of Congress in 1965, he tried to push through Congress a bill providing for home rule in the District of Columbia, a feat that several presidents had attempted unsuccessfully. When asked by an aide why he was working seven days a week on the bill when the same liberal majority would be returning in January, he replied that he knew the odds were greatly against his success and that it was the only chance he would have. Despite the returning liberal majority, "they'll all be thinking about their reelections. I'll have made mistakes, my polls will be down, and they'll be trying to put some distance between themselves and me. They won't want to go into the fall with their opponents calling 'em Lyndon Johnson's rubber stamp."[8]

The administration of Ronald Reagan realized from the beginning that it had an opportunity to effect major changes in public policy, but that it had to concentrate its focus and move quickly before the environment became less favorable. The president and his staff moved rapidly in 1981 to exploit the perceptions of a mandate and the dramatic elevation of Republicans to majority status in the Senate. Within a week of the president's having been shot, Michael Deaver convened a meeting of other high-ranking aides at the White House to determine how best to take advantage of the new political capital the assassination attempt had created.

6. Quoted in Jack Valenti, *A Very Human President* (New York: W. W. Norton, 1975), p. 144. See also Doris Kearns, *Lyndon Johnson and the American Dream* (New York: Harper and Row, 1976), pp. 216–217; Eric F. Goldman, *The Tragedy of Lyndon Johnson* (New York: Dell, 1974), pp. 306–307; Harry McPherson, *A Political Education* (Boston: Little, Brown, 1972), pp. 268, 428.

7. Lyndon B. Johnson, *The Vantage Point* (New York: Popular Library, 1971), p. 323. See also Goldman, *The Tragedy of Lyndon Johnson*, pp. 306–307.

8. Quoted in McPherson, *A Political Education*, pp. 267–268.

Commentators often refer to President Reagan as "the great communicator," but his ability to move the public toward his positions on policies was limited. When his views matched the public mood of 1980–81, he did his best to use this congruence to his advantage. Defense was certainly the area of public policy for which the president most desired increased government activity and expenditures. He immediately requested substantial increases for the Pentagon and was unwilling to compromise on this issue. This was a wise move, because the president was successful in obtaining large appropriations increases for defense only in his first two years. Only in 1981 did a majority of the public feel that the country spent too little on defense. By the recession year of 1982, a plurality felt it was spending too much.[9] Once the public's support was lost, Congress was no longer responsive to the president's leadership.

Thus even presidents who appeared to dominate Congress were actually facilitators rather than directors of change. They quite explicitly took advantage of opportunities in their environments and, working at the margins, successfully guided legislation through Congress. They were especially attentive to the state of public opinion in determining their legislative strategies. As the most volatile resource for leadership, public opinion is the factor most likely to determine whether or not an opportunity for change exists. By itself it cannot sustain presidential leadership of Congress, but it is the variable that has the most potential to turn a typical situation into one favorable for change, and, being mercurial, requires expeditious action to take advantage of it.

The facilitating skill required to exploit such opportunities is not to be underrated. Public opinion about matters of politics and policy is often amorphous. It lacks articulation and structure. It requires leadership to tap into it effectively, give it direction, and use it to bring about policy change. The president must sense the nature of the opportunity at hand, clearly associate himself and his policies with favorable public opinion in the minds of political elites, and approach Congress when conditions are most favorable for passing legislation.

Not everyone who occupies the Oval Office will be adept at facilitating change, and some opportunities for passing legislation will be lost by presidents who are not. The facilitator is not an unskilled leader; he is a leader who constantly depends on his environment for creating favorable strategic positions from which he can exercise leadership at the margins to turn opportunities into accomplishments.

9. See for example Robert H. Swansbrough, "Rhetoric and Reality: The Foreign Policy Beliefs and Political Styles of Presidents Carter and Reagan" (paper presented at the annual meeting of the Southern Political Science Association, Atlanta, November 1986), table 1.

That presidents are confined to the role of facilitator is not necessarily cause for concern. The nature of the American system is such that they can be little else. Although there is a certain appeal to explaining major change in terms of personalities, the political system is too complicated, power too decentralized, and interests too diverse for one person, no matter how extraordinary, to dominate.

Sidney Hook expected few event-making leaders in democracies. His principal example of an event-maker in the twentieth century was Lenin.[10] Similarly, Burns concludes, "It is significant that the enduring New Deal emerged not out of Roosevelt's 'hundred days' of 1933, when he gave a brilliant demonstration of executive leadership, but out of the 'second hundred days' of 1935, which emerged out of decades of foment, political action, and legislative as well as executive policy-making."[11]

It follows that we should adjust our expectations of presidential leadership accordingly. American chief executives by themselves will not bring about major changes in public policy. As Neustadt has written, "If the President envisages substantial innovations, whether conservative or liberal, then almost everything in modern history cries caution to such hopes unless accompanied by crises with potential for consensus."[12]

Some may find the role of facilitator unsatisfactory, especially if they desire significant changes in public policy. For those who do, understanding presidential leadership of Congress provides two broad, essential lessons. First, the solution is not just in identifying a great leader. To change the nature of presidential leadership requires changing the system. Second, an understanding of the context of presidential leadership of Congress forces a recognition that providing the environment for the role of director will require alterations in American political culture as well as institutional redesigning.

Such changes are highly unlikely. The United States will be living with facilitators in the White House for the foreseeable future. The president is not the ruler of the American state but a vital centralizing force, providing direction and energy for the nation's policy making. Understanding his relations with Congress remains indispensable to comprehending American politics and policy making.

10. Sidney Hook, *The Hero in History* (Boston: Beacon, 1943), p. 236, chap. 10.

11. James MacGregor Burns, *Leadership* (New York: Harper and Row, 1978), p. 396.

12. Richard E. Neustadt, *Presidential Power: The Politics of Leadership from FDR to Carter* (New York: John Wiley and Sons, 1980), p. 238.

Index

DATE DUE